Inconsequence

INCONSEQUENCE

*Lesbian Representation and
the Logic of Sexual Sequence*

ANNAMARIE JAGOSE

Cornell University Press

ITHACA AND LONDON

Copyright © 2002 by Cornell University

All rights reserved. Except for brief quotations in a review, this book, or parts thereof, must not be reproduced in any form without permission in writing from the publisher. For information, address Cornell University Press, Sage House, 512 East State Street, Ithaca, New York 14850.

First published 2002 by Cornell University Press

Printed in the United States of America
First printing, Cornell Paperbacks, 2002

    Library of Congress Cataloging-in-Publication Data

Jagose, Annamarie.
  Inconsequence : lesbian representation and the logic of sexual sequence/ Annamarie Jagose.
     p. cm.
  Includes bibliographical references and index.
  ISBN 0-8014-4001-7 (cloth : alk. paper)— ISBN 0-8014-8798-6 (pbk. : alk. paper)
  1. English fiction—History and criticism. 2. Lesbians in literature.
3. Homosexuality and literature—Great Britain—History. I. Title.
  PR830.L46 J34 2002
  823.009'353—dc21
                       2001007981

Cornell University Press strives to use environmentally responsible suppliers and materials to the fullest extent possible in the publishing of its books. Such materials include vegetable-based, low-VOC inks and acid-free papers that are recycled, totally chlorine-free, or partly composed of nonwood fibers. For further information, visit our website at www.cornellpress.cornell.edu.

Cloth printing   10 9 8 7 6 5 4 3 2 1
Paperback printing   10 9 8 7 6 5 4 3 2 1

What is most monstrous is sequence.

—E. L. Doctorow, *The Book of Daniel*

Contents

Preface	ix
Acknowledgments	xvii
1. First Things First *Some Second Thoughts on Lesbianism*	1
2. Remembering Miss Wade Little Dorrit *and the Historicizing of Female Perversity*	37
3. Unmarriageable *The Housing of Sexual Cultures in* The Bostonians	57
4. Remembering and Forgetting *The Memorialization of Homosexuality in* Mrs. Dalloway	77
5. First Wife, Second Wife *Sexual Perversion and the Problem of Precedence in* Rebecca	101
6. Wild Life Photography *Pulp Sexology and the Camera*	122
Notes	147
Bibliography	191
Index	205

Preface

in•con•se•quence *n*: **1**: Want of logical sequence; the character of an inference that does not follow from the premises, or of an argument involving such an inference; inconclusiveness, illogicalness. **2**: Want of sequence or natural connexion of ideas, actions, or events; irrelevance; disconnexion, inconsecutiveness; an instance of this, an irrelevant action or circumstance. **3**: As a quality of persons, their thought, or action. **4**: The being of no consequence or importance.

—Oxford English Dictionary

In this book I argue that a sequential logic organizes modern categories of sexual identification. That is, both the reification and the hierarchical valuation of heterosexuality and homosexuality are achieved as if through nothing more than the uninvested narrative mechanisms of numerical order or chronological progression. As second is to first, so the cultural weighting of heterosexuality as first-order and homosexuality as second-order is secured through the self-licensing logic of sequence. These cultural narrativizations of sexual sequence produce the very hierarchies they are taken to describe. In this book I argue that the mechanisms of sexual hierarchisation produce the lesbian as the figure most comprehensively worked over by sequence, secondary and inconsequential in all senses. Widely assumed to have no natural order of her own, to derive her substance from more primary forms of sexual organization, the cultural profile of the lesbian depends on her derivative secondary character. I argue that the enforcement of sexual sequence is a requirement of the cultural imperative to naturalize heterosexuality as the original or pre-eminent modality of sexuality itself.

Yet rather than resist the second-order nature of lesbianism, this book focuses on the sequential switch points of first and second to argue that the logic of sexual sequence disavows the secondary and derived nature of all sexualities, the foundational grammars of which are deferral and displacement. Taking the lesbian as my exemplar, I argue that sexual identity, retrospectively assembled from the behaviors and affects it touts as its natural expression, is always imitative and belated.

Accordingly, I have no investment in an authentic lesbian identity but wish to think productively about the belatedness or derivation of lesbianism that is inextricable from its cultural formation.[1] Of course, the representation of female homosexuality as derivative has been widely and properly critiqued as the synchronized effect of both a homophobic project that renders homosexuality as an imitative form of heterosexuality and a misogynist project that casts femininity as other than a self-authorizing masculinity that assumes for itself the credentials of the generic and the normative. Despite the forcefulness of this critique, it does not follow that lesbian criticism must articulate a resistant discourse of lesbianism uninflected by sexuality's other formations. Rather than fix lesbianism as a sexuality that signifies only in its own terms—that is, rather than assume, in the name of female homosexuality, a version of the very cultural fantasy that produces lesbianism as a second-order sexuality—I argue that it might be more useful to explore how the cultural production of lesbianism as a perverse turn of some other sexual organization that can consequently lay an easier claim to authenticity might be read as a defense, a disavowal of precisely that derivativeness which, far from being the definitional bent of female homosexuality, is the heart of sexuality itself.[2]

This strategy resists the more common formulation of lesbian studies that posits the derivativeness of lesbianism as a problem to be solved, the effect of a homophobic culture's reluctance to recognize the lesbian in her own terms. Rather than take visibility as the term central to the politicized concerns of lesbian representation, my examination of lesbianism and cultural legitimacy in relation to sequence foregrounds the derivative logics that inevitably structure the categories of sexual identity. My prioritizing of sequence over visibility, then, is not merely the substitution of one trope for another. Rather, as I argue in some detail in Chapter 1, the focus on sequence enables a recasting of the terms that structure the deadlocked and perhaps irresolvable debate in lesbian studies about the visibility or invisibility of its foundational identity category.

Because sequence most frequently functions as its own imprimatur, it is worth identifying the mechanisms and ideological effects of the logic of sexual sequence. Here, I address two major sequential paradigms. The first is the chronological—which is also always the hierarchical—organization of first and second that presents the lesbian as an imitative form of some more primary sexual organization. The second is the retrospective narration of relations between present and past that presents the lesbian as anachronistic and belated. These paradigms correspond—and not coincidentally—to two major projects in contemporary lesbian scholarship: the critique of lesbianism's representation as a second-order sexuality and the reparative project of constructing lesbian history. While this book contributes to both of these projects, it also critiques certain grounding assumptions—such as the reification of visibility or the belief that history can function as a corrective to invisibility—that frequently structure their formulation in lesbian theory.

Chapter 1 brokers the force of sequence, particularly its capacity to question knowledges common to both hegemonic discourse and lesbian theory. Through readings of major theorists, I contest the efficacy of assuming visibility as the standard measure for sexual legitimacy. Here I argue that lesbian studies' long-standing focus on visibility and its promise to counter cultural figurations of the lesbian in terms derived from her sexual others draws on the same logics that it contests; thus it obscures the derived nature of all sexual subjectivities, the various ways in which sexuality—both in its taxonomic reification and its psychosocial individualization—is culturally produced as a sequential fiction. I next critique the practice of invoking the historical archive as a solution to the contemporary problem of lesbian invisibility. I do so by examining the figure of "history"—its energizing of the very tropes of before and after that, differently worked, enable the production of lesbianism as derivative.

In the third section of Chapter 1, I read the early-nineteenth-century diaries of Anne Lister against their scholarly reception, identifying the ways in which retrospection can function as a further regulatory effect of the logics of sequence and cautioning against misperceiving retrospection as the critical solution to lesbian derivation. Given how crucial the consolidation of sexual taxonomies in the late nineteenth/early twentieth century was for the emergence of the modern lesbian identity, the fourth section offers close readings of two key texts: Havelock Ellis's *Sexual Inversion* and Sigmund Freud's "The Psychogenesis of a Case of Homosexuality in a Woman." Here I investigate Ellis's and Freud's influential considerations of sexual organization that took female homosexuality as their earliest subject only to construct it as a secondary, back formation. I demonstrate the strategic flexibility of the logic of sexual sequence, the way in which even an apparent reversal of its terms confirms rather than contradicts its representation of sexual hierarchies. I argue that female homosexuality is by definition articulated through tropes of derivation, secondariness, and belatedness and analyze the regulatory capacity of sequence, particularly the ways in which its organization of first and second naturalizes chronology as hierarchy.

In the rest of the book, I maintain my argument through strategic readings of canonic Anglo-American novels from the mid-nineteenth to the mid-twentieth century. This relatively tight historical time frame takes as its pivotal moment the codification of sexual taxonomies, the rise of the individuating system of sexuality. Nudged into a new canon formation, the names of Charles Dickens, Henry James, Virginia Woolf, and Daphne du Maurier are here put to the service of a cultural narrative other than the one they are more frequently presumed to demonstrate—the before and after of sexology, the before and after of the lesbian's historic emergence.[3] I divide these readings into two sections. In the first, I look at Dickens's *Little Dorrit* and James's *The Bostonians*, critiquing the sequential logic that secures the naturalizing force of retrospection and suggesting instead ways of attending to the historical evidence of sexual desire between women that do not simply indenture it to some narrative of modern lesbian identity. In the second section, I look at Woolf's *Mrs. Dalloway* and du Maurier's *Rebecca* to explicate the persistent and at times insidious workings of sequence that constitute the first-order/second-order ranking of sexual hierarchies.

My reading of Dickens's 1857 novel, *Little Dorrit*, foregrounds the risks for any history of sexuality in naturalizing sequence as an interpretative mode. In Chapter 2, I analyze the proleptic representation of modern sexual knowledges through the perverse figure of Miss Wade, demonstrating the critical deformations that necessarily inhabit readings organized by the retroactive force of recognition. I argue that while Miss Wade is frequently taken for a lesbian by contemporary critics, this is no more than an exemplification of the facility with which modern sexual categories recuperate history for a retrospective implantation of the alleged naturalness of their own hierarchical economies. Considering Miss Wade in relation to the discursively contested field of Victorian femininity and its anxious structuring across the oppositional figures of the virtuous woman and the prostitute, I demonstrate the critical importance of a reading sensitive to the difference between female perversity and lesbianism, where the former does not simply function as the prehistory or antecedent of the latter term that retrospectively claims to make sense of it.

If Miss Wade predates the modern sexual system and its definitive hetero/homosexual bifurcation, James's "morbid" Olive Chancellor marks the beginning of its uneasy emergence. Published nearly thirty years after *Little Dorrit*, *The Bostonians* is ambivalently animated by sexology's expansionist ambitions. In Chapter 3, I take the uneven fin de siècle consolidation of categories of sexual identity as my generative context. Forgoing the retrospective clarification of "lesbianism" and its attendant vocabularies, I demonstrate in this chapter the productivity of a reading that works instead with the terms the novel insistently provides—particularly its central focus on marriage. Analyzing the volatile intersection of the mid-1880s discourses of the Boston marriage and sexology, I revisit the long-standing and unresolved critical debate about the novel's ambivalent distribution of narrative sympathy between its protagonists, Olive Chancellor and Basil Ransom. I argue that the narrative voice's ambivalence can be traced less to the psychological interiorities of fictional character per se than to the contest between two emergent sexual cultures that, in *The Bostonians*, take character as their alibi. Arguing that the endlessly symmetrical differences of James's two protagonists index the rise of a much larger system of oppositional difference—the system of modern sexuality as we have come to know it—I read James's narrative as crucially marked by the cultural pressures of the counterweighted emergence of not simply heterosexuality and homosexuality but also male and female homosexuality.

While in James's novel the relationship between heterosexuality and homosexuality is one of grim contest, in Woolf's *Mrs. Dalloway* the contest is already rigged—the logic of sexual sequence aligning the latter with the past, the former with the future. Despite *Mrs. Dalloway*'s formal experimentation with linear sequence, in Chapter 4 I argue that the modernist techniques of representation for which Woolf's novel is renowned are precisely the textual strategies that secure the by now familiar cultural narratives of sexual succession assumed to govern the relationship between categories of sexual identity. *Mrs. Dalloway*'s temporal logics, everywhere evident in the novel's reliance on its central trope of memory, force a chronological distinction between homosexuality and heterosexuality. Drawing on Freudian refinements to sexological models of homosexuality, this chapter pulls Woolf and Freud into an unlikely solidarity, noting that, in the work of both, homosexuality is figured as a problem of memory.

Dickens, James, Woolf, du Maurier: If the latter name strikes a rather bathetic note, it serves as a useful reminder that Chapter 5 shifts to a more popular cultural focus, reading not simply du Maurier's gothic romance but also Alfred Hitchcock's Hollywood adaptation and Susan Hill's novelistic sequel, *Mrs. de Winter*. Arguing that the expected logic of sexual sequence is frustrated in du Maurier's novel—as we might perhaps anticipate in a work that is a hybrid of the backward-looking gothic and the forward-looking romance—I contend in this chapter that *Rebecca*'s final refusal to distinguish chronologically between female heterosexuality and female homosexuality is the disavowed inspiration for its disciplinary remakes. The ideological work of sexual sequence refused in du Maurier's novel can nevertheless be productively traced across the subsequent series of texts that variously attempt to recuperate the first and second, before and after logic so compromised at their point of narrative origin. Caught up in the very sequential relations they seek to reauthorize, the interrelated *Rebecca* texts attest to the anxieties of precedence that attend the cultural representation of female homosexuality.

In the concluding Chapter 6, I revisit the debates about the relationship between lesbianism and visibility that prompted this book's writing. Via the different but nevertheless recognizable inflections of 1950s pulp sexology, my consideration of photography as an ambivalent technology of power makes literal Chapter 1's focus on sexological framings of lesbian visibility. In Chapter 6, I read a photographic essay of a lesbian sex encounter from a post-Kinsey popular sexology text, Frank Caprio's *Female Homosexuality: A Psychodynamic Study of Lesbianism*. I analyze the sixteen images of the photo-narrative and the ways in which their literal sequencing of lesbian sex functions as a supplement to the text's avowed pedagogic project of rendering lesbianism visible. This reading of Caprio functions as the book's theoretical coda, reframing lesbian invisibility as the most prominent symptom of culture's insistence on narrativizing sexuality as sequence.

Before and after: In a book that considers sequence as a regulatory technology, these terms—despite their naturalization in narrative[4]—can never be innocent. Consequently, while primarily focusing on the dynamics of sexual sequence, I attempt in this book to maintain a productive suspicion toward all those knowledges buttressed by nothing more than the licensing force of sequence, of which perhaps this Preface—like many another, written last yet appearing first—might stand as salutary reminder. Noting that the doubled freight of "inconsequence" can be read in the cultural insistence that the irrelevance and lack of importance ascribed to lesbianism is crucially connected to its perceived lack of natural or logical order, I argue that the theoretical preoccupation with lesbian invisibility might be productively reframed by a consideration of the extent to which the hierarchical relations between categories of sexual identity—including those that govern the terms of cultural legibility—are naturalized through the regulatory force of sequence. I diagnose the structuring deadlock of lesbian representation, whereby the lesbian's visibility is always compromised by being figured in terms of her others, as a crucial defense against the unpalatable knowledge that sexuality itself is constituted as a field of meaning by terms that are always and necessarily relational. That is, the prominence and persistence of the problem of lesbian representation is the solution to what might otherwise be equally recognizable as the problem of sexual representation more generally. Moreover, I argue that it is worth bringing analytic pressure to bear on the self-licensing logics of sexual sequence, as the cultural insistence on narrating sexuality as sequence is the mechanism that potentially undoes the first-order/second-order status of categories of sexual identification that it more prominently works to secure. The persistent characterization of lesbianism as a derivative or somehow belated sexual formation is less an identification of some quintessentially lesbian character than an effect of the requirement that lesbianism assume, as its own, the cultural burden of sexuality and identity per se. Far from a capitulation to homophobic valuations of sexual taxonomies, this book's refusal to disavow the secondary status of lesbianism, the way in which its coming to representation persistently rehearses its derivativeness, is a strategic attempt to recognize the secondariness and derivation that indispensably animate the reification of all sexual identities.

ANNAMARIE JAGOSE

Acknowledgments

Various grants bodies and research institutions have made the writing of this book possible. My most substantial thanks are to the Australian Research Council for a Large Grant (1998–2000) that enabled me to conduct archival research in Europe and the United States and, what is perhaps even more important, afforded me the necessary time and space for writing. I am grateful, also, to the Council of the Australian Academy of the Humanities for an Australian Academy of the Humanities Travel Fellowship (1997) and to the Faculty of Arts, University of Melbourne, for a Projects Grant (1997). In 1996–97, I was a visiting scholar at the English Department, Victoria University of Wellington; in 1997, a research associate at the Institute for Research on Gender, University of Auckland; and in 1999, a visiting fellow at the English Department, University of Auckland. I thank each of these institutions for their generous support.

I conducted archival research in post-Kinsey popular sexology using the Barbara Grier and Donna McBride Collection at the James C. Hormel Gay and Lesbian Center, San Francisco Public Library; the Homodok Archive, Amsterdam; and the Willis Collection, Baillieu Library, University of Melbourne. I am grateful to the librarians and archivists who enabled my access to these collections.

Earlier versions of two chapters have appeared elsewhere, and I thank publishers for permission to reprint them here: "Remembering Miss Wade: *Little Dorrit* and the Historicising of Female Perversity," *GLQ: A Journal of Lesbian and Gay Studies* 4, no. 3 (June 1998): 423–51, and "First Wife, Second Wife: Sexual Perversion and the Problem of Precedence in *Re-*

becca," in *Intimacy*, ed. Lauren Berlant (Chicago: University of Chicago Press, 2000), 352–77.

I have been exceedingly fortunate in having the support of a number of individuals whose willingness to engage with this project at various stages has made my task easier. First, I thank Terry Castle, whose thoughtful commentary on the earliest writing toward this project—the first draft of my chapter on *Little Dorrit*—proved critically important to the formulation of my final argument. David Halperin has been more than generous in engaging with my work over the years, particularly in giving me access to his writings (unpublished or in-progress) on the history of homosexuality; these writings pushed my project forward in ways I could not have done myself. One of David's generosities was to introduce me to Valerie Traub. In the closing stages of my writing of this book, Valerie sent me draft versions of the introduction and conclusion to her forthcoming *The Renaissance of Lesbianism in Early Modern England*, and I only hope it pleases her half as much as it pleases me to see the galvanizing effect her work had on my thinking about lesbian visibility and lesbian history. I thank Lauren Berlant, Sharon Marcus, and Martha Vicinus for their transformative readings of early drafts of several chapters and two anonymous readers at Cornell University Press for their productive feedback and critique.

Closer to home, I thank my colleagues in the Department of English with Cultural Studies at the University of Melbourne. Foremost are my thanks to Ken Ruthven—thanks that far exceed anything this book could hope to represent. Since my arrival in the department in 1992 until his retirement in 1999, Ken nurtured my career in countless ways, offering every practical assistance and professional encouragement as lightly as if it were nothing more than the discharge of his professional obligation to me. Ken has actively facilitated the production of this book from its inception as a funding application to its final draft. My gratitude to him outlives his tenure in the department, and he remains for me the exemplar of a professional mentor. As insightful critics of my ongoing work or as colleagues in the everyday business of collaborative teaching, I also thank Marion Campbell, Chris Healy, Brett Farmer, Clara Tuite, and Audrey Yue for a support in which, for me, the registers of friendship and instruction are so pleasantly entangled that I can think myself only enjoying the former while being improved by the latter.

Finally: I hope that a book concerned with the ideological force of sequence might render newly articulate my platitudinous recourse to the logics of precedence, enabling me to say, as if for the first time, *last but not least*, I thank Lee Wallace for her productive interventions in every chapter and, more than that, for living alongside me—even when at some distance—as this book was being written.

Inconsequence

ONE

First Things First

Some Second Thoughts on Lesbianism

VISIBILITY

This book started out as a thinking through of the theoretical issues raised by the persistently difficult question of lesbian representation. If, in the end, its critical investments have turned out otherwise—that is, to hang instead on the oppositions of first and second, origin and derivation, terms organized by what I call the logics of sexual sequence—this speaks to the weirdly centrifugal effects of the very impasse that the book's ongoing development as a writing project seemed to defer: namely, the problem of lesbian representation. What is the problem of lesbian representation? Or, to ask that question differently, why is the problem of lesbianism so frequently a problem of representation? It is now a commonplace, rehearsed in homophobic and antihomophobic discourses alike, that the cultural lot of lesbianism is invisibility. Terry Castle has theorized the traumatized relationship between lesbianism and visibility in her justly influential *The Apparitional Lesbian* through the evocative figure of the ghost: "The lesbian remains a kind of 'ghost effect' in the cinema world of modern life: elusive, vaporous, difficult to spot—even when she is there, in plain view, mortal and magnificent, at the center of the screen."[1] An ectoplasmic trace, a chimerical imagining, at least since the discursive emergence of female homosexuality in late-nineteenth and early-twentieth-century sexology, figurations of sexual desire between women have been energized by their compromising of Western culture's conflation of vision and knowledge.[2]

Tracing the ways in which lesbianism has been figured as a problem of representation—perhaps more properly, a problem of representability—I first unravel some of the cultural investments and effects constituted in the ambivalent relationship between the lesbian and the field of vision. Frequently enough, the diagnostic recognition of lesbian invisibility is critically countered by attempts to negotiate for lesbianism a more straightforward relation to vision, as if the problems of lesbian invisibility might be short-circuited by the reversal of that paradigm. For example, Castle's persuasive documentation of the trope of lesbian apparitionality is counterbalanced by a determination to restore the lesbian to visibility: "My primary goal in this book has been to bring the lesbian back into focus, as it were."[3] Yet insofar as it marks not a withholding but a modality of representation, the familiar figure of the invisible lesbian is animated by a structuring paradox. The persistent rhetorical figuration of lesbianism as unrepresentable, invisible, and impossible brings to representation the very thing that, this figuration claims, remains outside the visual field. Because lesbian invisibility is precisely, if paradoxically, a strategy of representation—even a strategy of visualization—lesbian visibility cannot be imagined as its redress.[4]

Instead, we might ask, What are the structuring mechanisms of lesbian invisibility that produce the lesbian as a negative image, a reversal of the cultural conventions that naturalize (hetero)sexuality as visible? There are at least two answers to this question, the duality of which countermands the ultimate authority of either. Lesbianism is persistently represented as falling outside sexuality's visual field because, on the one hand, femininity cannot register, except as a negativity, within a model of desire imagined always as phallocentric and, on the other, homosexual difference, however much it has come to be a trope of radical alterity for modern culture, is not visibly perceptible.[5] These explanatory paradigms of lesbian invisibility are often understood as working in opposition, the former's rubric of gender pitted against the latter's rubric of sexuality. Consequently, it is sometimes imagined that lesbianism's cultural legibility might be facilitated by its pledging primary allegiance to one modality or other. Attempting to secure for lesbianism a clarity, an outline that might give it some representational heft of its own, the blunt and negative formulations of two recent attempts to define lesbianism attest to the strain of securing lesbian distinction against the crosscutting systems of sex and gender. Castle's recent assertion that "[the lesbian] is not a gay man" resonates with Monique Wittig's famous claim that "the lesbian is not a woman." While the former seems to have a more immediate claim than the latter on what passes for common sense, both are marked by the difficulty that impelled them in the first place—that of specifying lesbianism *in its own terms* without reference to the relational field of its others.[6]

The articulation of the lesbian across the distinct yet interrelated systems of gender and sexuality produces her as a figure whose particularity rests on the fact that she occupies the definitional center of neither femininity nor homosexuality, the two categories whose additive logic is presumed to describe her most fully. Instead, masculinity has persistently been the definitional ambit that enunciates the lesbian as spectacularly visible, lesbianism conventionally becoming legible through female masculinity's perceived clash of codes.[7] Yet masculinity refuses to take the homosexual woman as its proper object, its specification at once its disqualification of lesbianism from the circuits of cultural legitimization. Unable to lay a proprietary claim to the sex/gender categories that nevertheless articulate her, the invisible lesbian is the paradoxical effect of female homosexuality's ascension into cultural definition. Moreover, the lesbian's inability to have authoritative recourse to the categories of her cultural articulation is precisely the mechanism that licenses as authentic the seemingly straightforward but no less relational and arbitrary claims on the founding grammars of gendered and sexual identity of her double, the heterosexual male, and by corollary the already compromised stakes of the heterosexual female and the homosexual male. Of course, this gang of four—the lesbian, the gay man, the straight woman, and the straight man—with its endlessly mutating allegiances and oppositions, does not nearly exhaust the field of gendered or sexual possibility, although its hegemonic stranglehold on what consequently passes for the coordinates of sex/gender potentiality testifies to the persistent dimorphism through which categories of gender and hence sexuality are culturally licensed. As a figure whose entry into culture's field of vision is paradoxically guaranteed by the nimbus of her invisibility, the persistent configuration of the lesbian as an epistemological opacity insists on her symbolically liminal position. This liminality is enforced in relation to both the masculinization of desire and its lightning rod, the phallus, and a sex/gender system everywhere underwritten by the alleged self-evidence of the visual difference that enables heterosexual complementarity. Less an absence than a presence that can't be seen, the lesbian marks the limits of sexuality's cultural visibility, the barest registration of her possibility in the field of the visible not a failure but a strategy of representation in the maintenance of the ideological bulwark of gendered and sexual hierarchy.

Even more than male homosexuality—that love that famously dared not speak its name—female homosexuality has been ambivalently constituted in relation to the logics of vision: It is less the subject of prohibition than of an incredulousness that would deny the space of its possibility.

This distinction doesn't presume to adjudicate between the relative—and not always discrete—representational burdens of male and female homosexuality, to ascertain whether the strictures of cultural inadmissibility are a lighter or heavier load to bear than are those of cultural impossibility. However differently structured, the forbidden and the unthinkable are both effects of productive prohibitions.[8] They are different tropes for securing a reinforced sense of the licit and the allowable. That this discrimination is made by tracking back and forth across the presumed distinction between discourses of sexual acts and discourses of sexual identities is yet another demonstration that modern understandings of sexuality are not wholly discrete from those incoherent fields they might be imagined to supersede. For while the prohibition against male homosexuality takes as its vilified object the imagined subject of a semaphorically stylized sexual act (anal sex), the reductiveness of which nevertheless manages to open out into an abusive nomenclature, as contemptuous as it is capacious,[9] the prohibition against lesbianism—seldom explicitly realized in legislative terms but no less authoritative for all of that—frequently takes the form of a foundational uncertainty or disbelief that is hard put to imagine the existence of the category at all, but nevertheless exercises its epistemological ignorance as a curiosity that cannot be assuaged: "What *do* lesbians do in bed?"[10]

Heterosexuality is the term, perhaps even the dream, that makes sense of those versions of masculinity that must be warned off the too readily imagined offensive practices that signify male homosexuality and those versions of femininity that occupy no imaginable relation to the entirely preposterous abhorrence that alludes to lesbianism. That is, heterosexuality requires a sexually aggressive masculinity and a sexually quiescent femininity to secure the delicately balanced ecosystem of its singular phallic economy, defined in contradistinction to the obscenity of two men and the absurdity of none. This account of heterosexuality, like the supporting fantasies of a homosexuality unspeakable in its male declension, unimaginable in its female, is clearly a fantasmatic rather than an ethnographic one. If this seems a somewhat more self-evident claim for heterosexuality than homosexuality, then this is less the consequence of heterosexuality's alleged transparency—the cover story of its investment in the emotionally committed if not outright marital context of its sex acts, sanctioned in turn by their procreational capacity if not always intention—than the effect of the institutionalization of heterosexuality. It is not simply that heterosexuality seems irreducible to the sex acts that it nevertheless privileges,[11] but also that heterosexuality is naturalized through a range of practices and institutions that don't seem to be about sexuality at all.¹² However distinct their effects—indeed, however much distinction is claimed as their primary effect—the construction and articulation of homosexuality and heterosexuality (that is, of homosexual femininity, homosexual masculinity, heterosexual masculinity, and heterosexual femininity) are not differentiated processes but a counterweighted set of protocols, the historic interarticulation of which produces as a field the sexuality that claims to organize them.

As a means of thinking through the ways in which visibility crucially structures the asymmetrical but interarticulated logics of the sex/gender system, I want to consider the long-standing contestation in feminist and lesbian/gay theory surrounding attempts to negotiate a relationship between the figures of the lesbian and the gay man. Although this move to what risks being read as a lesbian and gay stand-off might seem to let heterosexuality, in both its masculine and feminine declensions, off the hook and consequently to weigh against my earlier contention that the establishment of recognizable sexualities is the effect of a contradictory but tightly worked network of differential relations across the sex/gender system as a whole, I hope it is apparent that my consideration here of the representational conventions that produce the lesbian and the gay man—like any such consideration—necessarily has significant implications for the gendered categories of heterosexuality. There are two well-rehearsed though contradictory models available for thinking about the lesbian and the gay man's morphological relationship to each other. In the first, their identification with different gender categories ensures that the lesbian and the gay man have nothing in common. In this model, male homosexuality is the sublimated structure of the social contract underwritten by the homosocial exchange of women between men—an exchange that cannot figure as a possibility the autonomous female desire whose putative apotheosis is lesbianism.¹³ In the second, their abject relations to masculinity and femininity produce the lesbian and the gay man as similarly, though differently, disenfranchised from the self-legitimating dispensations of gender normativity. In this model, the lesbian, like the gay man, is presented as unnatural, falling outside or between the categories of gender whose oppositional logic licenses heterosexuality.¹⁴ Insofar as these models dramatize the contradiction between the gender-separatist and gender-liminal models identified by Eve Sedgwick as incoherently constituting modern homosexual definition, it is not a matter of finding in favor of one over the other.¹⁵ Rather, remembering that "the most potent effects of modern homo/heterosexual definition tend to spring precisely from the inexplicitness or denial of the gaps between long-coexisting . . . gender-transitive and gender-intransitive understandings of same-sex relations," I want to consider the consequences of the illogical but simultaneous currency of these two models for regimes of sexual visibility.[16]

Rosi Braidotti's gender-separatist take on sexual visibility emphasizes the asymmetric positions of the lesbian and the gay man:

> I do not think the positions of the lesbian and the gay man are reversible or in any way symmetrical, though they both may be equally involved in and committed to the task of redesigning sexuality. The invisibility of the lesbian as other of the other is of a different conceptual and qualitative order.... Whereas the gay man needs to resurrect the shreds of an identity from under the detritus of a triumphant masculine heterosexuality, the lesbian is coming in from the cold. Whereas the gay man needs to deconstruct a representation of the homosexual as the phobic other, the lesbian must move, symbolically, from *unrepresentability* into some sort of representation. The problems may appear analogous, but they are quite different.[17]

For Braidotti, the cultural task of articulating nonnormative sexualities falls differently on the lesbian and the gay man, given the radical asymmetry of the femininity and the masculinity that respectively frame them. For the gay man, the task is to renegotiate a nonphobic relation to the culturally legitimized category of masculinity; for the lesbian, the labor of resignification is exponentially increased, as femininity itself is a category under erasure, the projected fantasy of a masculine imaginary that conceives femininity as its inverse. As "the phobic other," the gay man functions at one remove from the representational legitimizations of masculinity; as the "other of the other," the lesbian experiences her alienation from the gendered codes of sexual visibility as raised to the second power.

Equally attentive to the asymmetry of gender, Lynda Hart's gender-liminal rendering of the differentiated processes by which the lesbian and the gay man become visible as sexual subjects works against Braidotti's identification of the feminine as the proper register for the lesbian, the masculine as the proper register for the gay man:

> When men are excluded from the category of "masculinity," they *fall* into the "degenerate" category of femininity, which is where lesbians, as women, always already were. Gay men become recognisable to the heterosexist spectator as they are "seen" to enter the feminine. In contrast, lesbians are invisible precisely as they are contained within representational apparatuses that depend on Woman as the ground while simultaneously constructing women as the elusive enigma. When lesbians enter the field of visibility as it has been constructed within gender dimorphic parameters, the threat that

they pose to the dominant order is seen as a [*sic*] usurpation of masculine privilege.... Both the male and female homosexual are positioned by the naturalization of heterosexuality in a space that is abject—the nonhuman. But this is a space that is not "other" than masculinity or femininity. On the contrary, as exemplified by gay men who fall into this space and lesbians who are always already there, the abject is *consonant* with the very oppositional hierarchy masculine/feminine.[18]

For Hart, it is the crossing over into femininity that secures visibility for the gay man and the crossing over into masculinity that secures visibility for the lesbian. Yet lesbian masculinity, like gay femininity, is not a space of legitimization but abjection, where that abjection stitches up a legitimacy for the heterosexuality that is naturalized in gender dimorphism.

Despite their obvious differences, Braidotti's and Hart's accounts have much in common: Both draw on a model of sexual indifference in which sexual difference is structured by a single masculine libidinal economy; both represent femininity as unrealized, a symptom of the patriarchal symbolic; both understand sexual visibility as the dynamic effect of the interrelations between categories of gender. More important for my purposes here, despite their near-oppositional representations of the lesbian predicament in relation to the field of vision, both Braidotti and Hart configure lesbian invisibility or lesbian visibility as simply one or other effect of figuring the lesbian in terms of her others—terms that are derivative insofar as, indentured to those others, their conferral of cultural authority and legitimacy cannot extend to her. For Braidotti, lesbianism cannot be a visible sexuality because the representational terms available to the lesbian are not her own; for Hart, lesbianism is secured as a visible sexuality precisely through the lesbian's figuration in terms that are not her own. Far from being the remedy for lesbian invisibility, lesbian visibility is more properly its different inflection. Reading Braidotti and Hart with, rather than against, each other allows a nuanced understanding of the mechanisms of what I earlier described as the problem of lesbian representation. For it demonstrates that the discontinuous but productive modalities of gender separatism and gender liminality render lesbian invisibility and lesbian visibility alike as symptomatic of the derivation and secondariness that mark the emergence of lesbianism as a culturally available category. The synonymous nature of lesbian invisibility and visibility suggests, then, that the politically efficacious task is less to determine under what conditions the lesbian can be seen than to consider the implications of the fact that, invisible or visible, lesbianism depends for its figuration on derivation, and not as a mark of its inadequacy but as the condition of its possibility.

The historic emergence of lesbianism as a category of sexuality draws on the emergent designations of not simply male homosexuality but male and female heterosexuality. As the sexological material discussed at the end of this chapter demonstrates, female homosexuality is secured through the incoherent sampling of modes of sexual morphology emphatically not its own. Disavowed within the discourse of passionlessness that claimed to describe a femininity already indentured to the hierarchical or complementary sexual economy of heterosexuality and, accordingly, figured in terms of a gender inversion that, oppositionally worked, also constitutes male homosexuality, female homosexuality is rendered through a monstrous virility proper to masculine heterosexuality. Unsecured by its own terms (whatever they might be) or even those of femininity, female homosexuality is constituted as a term, a field of possibility, the meanings of which are intimately connected to secondariness and belatedness. I am not suggesting here—as, for example, Randolph Trumbach does—that identity formations based on homosexual desire between women historically lag behind those based on homosexual desire between men.[19] Rather, I am arguing that while identity formations based on homosexual desire between women are frequently represented in some belated or secondary relation to other forms of allegedly precedent sexual organization, this is less an empirical fact concerning the date of their historical emergence than a constituent characterization of the masculinist and heteronormative representational strategies that secure the cultural definition of female homosexuality.[20] The epistemological contradiction of lesbianism is that its specificity is founded less on distinction than on derivation.

History

In this book I am interested in the ways in which the modern category of lesbianism is historicized; that is, I am interested in both the articulation of the conditions of possibility that have governed the emergence of "lesbian" as a meaningful category of identity and the reliance on the historicizing gesture as that which might secure for female homoeroticism a lineage and hence a value all its own. My twofold focus on history is not so much doubled as divided against itself, for while the current and ongoing development of a genealogy of lesbianism promises a more nuanced understanding of the problem of lesbian representability, too often "history" is already figured as its solution. In one sense, this is simply a restatement of the frequently issued post-Foucauldian caution against misrecognizing the historical as always in the service of the present. More important, it suggests that "history," with its apparent promise of recuperation, stands in an overdetermined relationship to the "lesbian," who is persistently figured as unable to secure the grounds of her own representation.

If history has seemed to function, for lesbian studies, as invisibility's indemnification, this might be traced to the specific conditions of the recent consolidation of lesbian historiography—particularly the confluence of the very different traditions of homosexual history marked by the proper names of Michel Foucault and Lillian Faderman.[21] Their different historical formulations of homosexuality aside, both Faderman's model of a largely asexual romantic friendship scuppered by pathologizing medical discourses and Foucault's account of the discursive invention of a generically masculine homosexuality tend to render invisible lesbianism or sexual desire between women, and despite the readily discernible and enabling influence of their work across the field, subsequent developments in lesbian historiography have functioned, in part, as critiques of this tendency.[22]

Faderman's insistence that, before their morbidification in sexology, romantic friendships between women were culturally idealized and not considered sexual even by the romantic friends themselves, coupled with her tendency to minimize the carnal potential of historical relations between women, draws a veil across the representational and embodied histories of sex between women. Terry Castle, for one, is not persuaded. Citing what she describes as Faderman's " 'no lesbians before 1900' hypothesis," Castle mischievously asks, "What did women do who happened to desire one another before the crucial nomenclature appeared? According to the most extreme proponents of the sexological model, they mainly sat around doing needlework, pressing flowers into albums, and writing romantic letters to one another. If they ever got into bed together, it was strictly platonic: a matter of a few cuddles and 'darlings' and a lot of epistemic confusion."[23]

However, because Castle associates Faderman's conviction that pre–twentieth-century women's relations with each other were largely asexual with the constructionist take on sexuality more generally, she misrecognizes the latter as denying the historical existence of sex between women and, consequently, identifies the project of historical recovery as working against the apparitionality that is lesbianism's cultural inheritance: "As more archival research is carried out on the lives of women of the past, I predict that more of these instances of 'premature' lesbian self-awareness will materialize, casting further doubt on the recent invention hypothesis."[24] Lisa Moore also critiques Faderman's idealizing representation of female friendships, emphasizing instead "the conflict between approbatory accounts of the chastity of these relationships and the virulent eighteenth-century discourse about the dangers of female homosexuality in such relationships."[25] Although she sharply distinguishes between historic sexual practices between women and the modern identity formation of lesbianism, Moore characterizes her project as making visible women's carnal relations with each other against the specific interdiction of an intriguingly unidentified group of "feminist historians":

> We have been cautioned by feminist historians not to look for "lesbians" in the eighteenth and nineteenth centuries; curiously, however, this caution against anachronism has most often taken the form of an ahistorical prohibition against reading sex between women in history. In insisting on such a reading—on reading lesbian sex—I do not attempt to find "lesbians" in the eighteenth- and early-nineteenth-century texts examined; rather, these texts demonstrate how powerful a part the category of "sapphism" played in the cultural imagination of the period.[26]

Far from disagreeing with Moore's insistence on the importance of "reading sex between women in history" rather than reading for evidence of lesbianism *avant la lettre*, I am hard-pressed to think of anyone who does. Consequently, her conviction that, in 1997, the caution against historical anachronism in lesbian studies has "most often taken the form of an ahistorical prohibition against reading sex between women in history" is puzzling. Rather, it seems to me that the more frequent caution is the very one that Moore herself makes—that "history" cannot be the guarantor for a project that finds the modern category of "lesbian" anachronistically written across preceding sexual systems of female homoeroticism.[27] Although Moore names no names, the feminist historian who most easily comes to mind as cautioning against an anachronistic focus on genital contact between women is of course Faderman, whose work Moore has just critiqued, and whose obscuring of the historical incidence and significance of sex between women continues to shape lesbian history as invisibility's reparation.

While undeniable, Foucault's influence on lesbian history is, in some sense, less straightforward. Famously indifferent to the regulatory forces of gender, Foucault's discussion of the origin of homosexuality hinges on its specifically male subject:[28]

> As defined by the ancient civil or canonical codes, sodomy was a category of forbidden acts; their perpetrator was nothing more than the juridical sub-

ject of them. The nineteenth-century homosexual became a personage, a past, a case history, and a childhood, in addition to being a type of life, a life form, and a morphology, with an indiscreet anatomy and possibly a mysterious physiology. Nothing that went into his total composition was unaffected by his sexuality. It was everywhere present in him: at the root of all his actions because it was their insidious and indefinitely active principle; written immodestly on his face and body because it was a secret that always gave itself away.... The sodomite had been a temporary aberration; the homosexual was now a species.[29]

Foucault's emphasis on discursive practices—particularly the distinction he makes here between the sodomite and the homosexual—has had a massive influence on gay history, everywhere evidenced in the frequent quotation or paraphrase of this passage.[30] Yet the masculine framing of this historical transfer necessarily raises questions for the genealogy of same-sex desire between women.[31] Emma Donoghue has argued for the importance of a lesbian historiography that imagines itself as other than a second-generation gay historiography. Constructing her research around models other than those juridical or subcultural ones that have proved so productive for delineating the historic formations of same-sex desire between men, Donoghue turns up a wealth of detail regarding same-sex desire between women in Britain during the seventeenth and eighteenth centuries:

> So the evidence turns out to be rich, if we look with an open eye at texts about women rather than hunting for exact equivalents of gay men's sources.... Lesbian historians can exhaust themselves looking for lesbian equivalents to particular aspects of gay history, for example sodomy trials or an early urban bar culture. A study like this one, which looks at lesbians without comparison with gay men, can let us establish our own priorities and ask our own questions.[32]

Similarly, in her account of seventeenth-and eighteenth-century representations of female intimacy, Elizabeth Susan Wahl writes,

> I have ... been conscious of the tendency within critical studies to subsume the figure of the "lesbian" within a universalizing discourse about (male) homosexuality, rendering her doubly "invisible" in some instances, and I have therefore been wary of uncritically adopting theoretical or historical models of male homosexuality or indeed "homosocial" relations to my investigation of female intimacy in both its social and sexual dimensions. The

challenge of trying to understand these earlier models of sexuality in their own terms has been my first concern in this project.[33]

Although they do not mention Foucault explicitly here, both Donoghue's and Wahl's accounts express an anxiety that the influential weight of his work and the subsequent foregrounding in gay history of the sodomitical prehistories of the male homosexual obscures the specificity of a lesbian history. Moreover, insofar as, for Wahl at least, that obscurity is represented as an "invisibility," the implicit project of lesbian history is the rectification of that invisibility.

The refusal to assume that lesbian prehistories will articulate themselves in the same modes and locations as gay-male prehistories is a necessary and valuable one (although, as I argued earlier, there is a need for caution about any absolute refusal of the productive possibilities of thinking about lesbianism as derivative), but what interests me here is the near-axiomatic representation of history as invisibility's redress, the way in which shifts and transformations in historical meaning, acknowledged as crucially inflecting categories of sexual identity, are assumed to have little or no purchase on the cultural codes of sexual legibility which produce invisibility as their effect. While lesbian history is often figured as the solution to the problems of lesbian invisibility, Valerie Traub magisterially demonstrates that the alternating currents of invisibility and visibility that constitute sexual desire between women as a problem of representation derive from a conflict, emergent in the seventeenth century, in the discourses of female erotic embodiment. Traub seeks to explain the early modern discrepancy between the spectacularized figure of the tribade (or female sodomite) and the figure of the femme, taken "either as the invisible, if antithetical complement to a 'masculinized' tribade or as a reflective mirror to her equally insubstantial 'feminine' partner."[34] Acknowledging the high visibility of the tribade and the invisibility of the femme, Traub represents the field of female homoeroticism as cleft in relation to the categories of cultural visibility. The sixteenth- and early-seventeenth-century theatrical presentation of what Traub refers to as " 'femme-femme' love" marks the femme as culturally insignificant: Unlike the tribade, "the 'femme' woman, who challenged neither gender roles nor reproductive imperatives, seems to have been so unworthy of notice that little note was taken of her at all."[35] However, Traub demonstrates that seventeenth-century transformations of the meanings of desire—primarily, those attendant on the dynastic marriage's ideological rearticulation as affective and companionate—converts the formerly chaste figure of the femme into an "object of cultural anxiety" no less than the tribade herself:

> The production of the social necessity for a mutual and exclusive desire in and for marriage rendered chaste female friendships potentially disruptive to the familial basis of social order. Interrupted, redefined, and harnessed into a teleology that demanded an increasingly conscious commitment to heterosexual desire both before and after marriage, same gender female bonds became a focal point of anxiety.[36]

Unlike recuperative lesbian historiography, Traub's project is not to bring the femme to visibility—although that transformation marks her historic career across the seventeenth century—but to determine the shifting contexts of her cultural significance. Traub's historicizing theories about "lesbian" invisibility and her contextual analysis of what makes sexual desire between women significant or not is an important corrective to the more common assumption that the restorative force of history works against invisibility. Visibility, then, cannot be in itself a representational goal: Like invisibility, it is the historical effect of consolidations and transformations in the mutually informing cultural formations of gendered desire. One of the most significant consequences of historicizing prelesbian sexual desire between women remains not the restoring to vision of some lost "lesbian" past but the determination of the inherited incoherencies of our modern sex/gender system that produces the contemporary figure of the lesbian precisely as a problem of visibility.

Retrospection

Given that history cannot function as the key to the solution that the contemporary problem of lesbian invisibility seems to demand, it is worth specifying what might constitute a workable relationship between the modern category of lesbianism, riven as it is with representational contradiction, and earlier depictions of female-female desire.[37] While it is necessary to maintain a distinction between the twentieth-century category of lesbian and its prehistories—indeed, to maintain those prehistories as themselves distinct (the tribade from the mannish woman, for example, or the sapphist from the romantic friend)—I want also to acknowledge that it is my acculturation in and embodied experience of the discourses of lesbianism, and their continuing incoherent implication in those prehistories that they only apparently supersede, that secures my engagement with that past which is not really mine.³⁸ If the mirror cannot be the figure for a lesbian history that gives me back to myself, then neither can the bathysphere—the spherical deep-sea device that maintains a hermetic distinction from the medium that is its object of analysis—be the figure for a lesbian history that is entirely other. Neither the mirror nor the bathysphere, lesbian history might be suggestively figured through their hybrid form, the rounded reflectivity of the disco ball, always turning overhead, its fractured play of light illuminating those sexual stylings, scenes, and conjunctions that we never take as anything less than the proof of our inalienable modernity. Here I want to amplify the twin tensions implicit in this figuration of history—an attentiveness to the historical preconditions of modern sexual categories offset by a modern investment in what "history" might nevertheless be seen to authenticate—through a consideration of the scholarly debate that followed the recent publication of passages from the extraordinary diaries of Anne Lister (1791–1840), a Halifax gentlewoman with a compulsion—no less that of the libertine than the diarist—to record.³⁹

As a publishing event, Helena Whitbread's *I Know My Own Heart: The Diaries of Anne Lister, 1791–1840* so took the form of a wish fulfillment that inevitably it seemed to have the whiff of the hoax about it. Thrown by the contrast between the diary's invocation of the plots of, say, a Jane Austen and a John Cleland, more than a few readers (myself included), questioned the diary's authenticity. Although the tightly cast and geographically circumscribed domestic milieu of Lister's diary, like its gently satirical narrative voice whose mockery of the social investments of others is precisely what enables the maintenance of its own, seemed to register, after Austen, a recognizably decorous female style, the diary's dissonant sexual explicitness generated quite a different effect.⁴⁰ Specifying bodily parts and their narrative conjunction and electrified by the always eroding distinction between the sexually inexperienced and the initiated, Lister's drawing on a conventionally masculine pornographic tradition raised the suspicion that her diary was a literary fake. Alongside her annual accounts, her sharp-eyed estimations of her friends and neighbors, her descriptions of estate business and her program of self-education (Greek, Latin, geometry, the flute), Lister describes her flirtatious courting of young women and her sexual relations with many of them, in passages that, despite—or perhaps because of—their original esoteric coding in a "secret alphabet," maintain as continuous the matter-of-fact and explicitly descriptive tone of the diaries as a whole.⁴¹ Uninterested in marriage and the love of men more generally, Lister describes herself as sexually attuned only to women. Her persistent and cherished hope is to set up an independent household with a woman who would be her sexual partner: "Oh, how my heart longs after a companion & how often I wish for an establishment of my own, but I may then be too old to attach anyone & and my life shall have passed in that dreadful solitude I so ill endure."[42] Lister has cast one of her lovers, Marianna Lawton, in the role of her future life partner, but while she waits for the death of Lawton's husband, she is not slow to audition for the part, or simply dally with, other less favored candidates. Recognizing herself as an oddity in regard to her masculinity and her taste for women—"The people generally remark, as I pass along, how much I am like a man."[43]—Lister reads widely to identify other figurings of same-sex desire between women, often referring to these literary figurations as a means of gauging the sexual predilections and experiences of other women. After a delicate plumbing of a new friend's familiarity with sexual relations between women, and an even more delicate concealment of her own, Lister takes a knowing and literate satisfaction: "Miss Pickford has read the Sixth Satyr of Juvenal. She understands these matters well enough."[44] These and similar extracts describing Lister's sexual ambitions and the only slightly narrower field of her actual sexual relations that articulate, on the one hand, a sexual desire and practice between women and, on the other, an identity formation predicated on those affects and acts, have gone on the high rotation of scholarly citation, the repeated quotation of certain passages seemingly making Lister's diaries, like a schoolgirl's dirty book, fall open at certain pages.

Little known before the publication of Whitbread's editions of her diaries, Anne Lister has become something of a lesbian icon, a historical presence taken to challenge the persistent representation of lesbianism as—variously—invisible, asexual, a late-nineteenth-century sexological construction. Certainly, the identification of Lister as a lesbian is evident from the first in Whitbread's editorial framing of the diaries. In her introduction to *I Know My Own Heart*, she describes the twenty-six-year-old Anne as having "come to terms psychologically and emotionally with her own sexuality," glossing Lister's emphatic statement of her sexual preference—"I love and only love the fairer sex and thus, beloved by them in turn, my heart revolts from any other love than theirs"—as "an explicit statement of lesbian love."[45] Whitbread's identification of Lister as a lesbian has been assumed, in more or less considered ways, by a number of critical discussions of her diaries—a conflation that obscures what might otherwise function as productive differences between Lister's sexual world and that which has latterly come to be known as lesbianism.[46] Yet the frequent scholarly registration of Lister as a lesbian—indeed, the alleged self-evidence of that designation's fit with the terms of her self-description—can only be retrospective, invested more in the definitional terminus of "lesbian" than in the messier prehistories that determine how that term came to signify. Without denying or minimizing the significance of Lister's sexual desire and practice with other women, her masculine self-fashionings, her explanations of the nature of her "oddity," her reading of contemporary and classical literature for accounts of sex between women, and her canny reference to these literary sources as a means of ascertaining other women's sexual knowledge and availability, I suggest that the rich context of the diaries and the sex/gender system they articulate provide an interpretative frame for reading the indisputable articulations of Lister's sexual subjectivity without pressganging them into the modern category of "lesbian."

While the publication of Lister's diaries—particularly their detailed accounts of sex between women and their evolving articulation of an identity predicated on that sexual preference—are of massive interest for lesbian historiography, there is a seemingly slight but significant distinction to be made between Lister's sexual subjectivity and lesbianism, a distinction that follows the distinction between an identity predicated on gender deviance and female-female desire and an identity predicated on sexual object choice.[47] This distinction acknowledges the important archival evidence that Lister had sex exclusively with women and moreover that, on this basis and on the basis of her masculine identification, she understood herself and was sometimes recognized by others as having a distinct erotic preference for women. However, this distinction insists that Lister's erotic preference is not synonymous with lesbianism—a sexual identity that may or may not articulate itself as gender-aberrant but is defined crucially by the gendered equivalence between the subject and her object choice.[48] This is not to suggest that lesbianism has no relation to the still-persistent tropes of sexual inversion. It is clear that the ready appropriation of Lister to the modern category of lesbianism rests in part on the fact that the issues of gender deviance and sexual object choice, far from having been disentangled by the emergence of the category of homosexuality, continue to be predicated on each other in instances that, while not definitional, are neither infrequent nor insignificant.[49] Nevertheless, it is worth trying to put aside the semantic driftnet of "lesbian" long enough to see what floats up in Lister's account of herself; it is worth trying, that is, to catch at her early-nineteenth-century sexual knowledge rather than attempt to detect our own already and presciently in operation.

Of the many things that strike the modern reader of Lister's diaries as surprising, one of the more startling is the extent to which Lister's masculinity and her sexual pursuit of women are widely accepted as little more than a quirk. Despite the fact that her masculine demeanor and her gentlemanly attentiveness to other young women meant she was frequently insulted on the streets by strangers and snubbed at closer quarters by some of her peers, Lister's manner was more often regarded as an acceptable curiosity. As Castle writes, "One of the most striking things about reading Lister's diaries—once one gets over the first shock of their sexual frankness—is the degree of acceptance with which Lister's friends and associates appear to have regarded her, despite her obvious mannishness and eccentricity."[50] While Castle reads this as demonstrating the existence of "a female culture rather more worldly and comprehending than one might expect to find in the dark ages before sexology," I want instead to consider the social acceptance of Lister's eccentricities as evidence of an early-nineteenth-century culture in uneven possession of specific sexual practices that, precisely to the degree that they registered foremost in the field of gender, were not organized as a sexuality until later in the century, in large part through those very discourses of sexology that they only seem to anticipate. As an example of the knowing tolerance of Lister's acquaintances, Castle cites Lister's aunt "who seems to have known exactly what was going on between Lister and M——, for example, and was even aware of her niece's venereal disease."[51] Yet although Lister's aunt is party to her niece's hope that Marianna and she will eventually live together in the ancestral home at Shibden Hall, it is far from clear to what extent she recognizes Lister's relationship with Marianna as sexual.[52] Even the knowledge of Lister's venereal disease, which might seem at least to confirm Lister's sexual activity and to suggest Marianna as its most plausible source, seems in the aunt's calculations to hardly bear down in this direction at all. Having concealed the venereal character of her affliction from her aunt for just over two years, when Lister does finally reveal the nature of her illness, her aunt's equanimity rests on her conviction that a disorder of this sort indicates improprieties of a hygienic rather than a sexual nature: "She guessed I had got it at the Duffins'. Then at Croft.... My aunt took it all quite well. Luckily, thinks the complaint very easily taken by going to the necessary, drinking out of the same glass, etc. & it is lucky enough she does think so."[53] Lucky indeed. While Lister's diaries are often cited as an abundant demonstration of early-nineteenth-century knowledge about sexual relations between women, it is sometimes forgotten that they equally demonstrate the uneven or ambiguous purchase of that knowledge. What Lister's aunt and uncle tolerate—like many of the other indulgent characters that people Lister's diaries—is not necessarily the prospect of sex between women but a gender variance (that raises but by no means confirms the possibility of a same-sex sexual preference) characterized as being at odds with the marriage system even as it is accommodated within the parallel and related economy of female friendship.

Nowhere is the ambivalent nature of female friendship as it pitches between purity and perversion more productively exploited than when Lister, that imperturbable sexual pragmatist, feigns the former in order to cinch the latter. For Lister's cool drawing on the discourses of pure female friendship and her even cooler allusion to the fine discrimination between women's friendship and their sexual connection are not simply strategies of secrecy but also of seduction. In Paris for some months in the mid-1820s, Lister establishes herself in her pension by conducting a number of exploratory flirtations with several of the resident women before settling to the exclusive courtship of the widowed Mrs. Barlow. When Mrs. Barlow provocatively raises the subject of Marie Antoinette, noting that she was accused of "being too fond of women," Lister plays a dead bat:

> I, with perfect mastery of countenance, said I had never heard of it before and could not understand or believe it. Did not see how such a thing could be—what good it would do—but owned I had never heard of the thing. . . . I had before said I could go as far in friendship, love as warmly, as most but could not go beyond a certain degree & did not believe anyone could do it. We agreed it was a scandal invented by the men, who were bad enough for anything.[54]

The comprehensiveness of Lister's refusal of sapphic knowledge is considerable, its excess force expressed as contradiction: She has never heard of such a thing and, having now been told, she cannot comprehend it nor—despite the fact that this presumes comprehension—believe it. Of her partiality for friendship and love she is confident but doubts that a passion in excess of this exists even as a capacity. The audacity of this strategy is not simply that Lister is lying barefaced, or even that she is lying in order to facilitate with Mrs. Barlow precisely the kinds of behavior she claims to know nothing about, but that her falsehood, her insistence on the incomprehensibility of sex between women, enables her to pull into proximity the violently opposed categories of female friendship and sapphism, which she represents not as entirely distinct and incomparable orders, but different only to "a certain degree."[55] Lister is always invoking that single degree of difference between legitimate friendship and sapphic impropriety in order to breach it, assuring Mrs. Barlow that she "went to the utmost extent of friendship but this was enough," that she "should like to have a person always at [her] elbow, to share [her] bedroom & even bed, & to go as far as friendship can go, but this is enough."[56]

Yet while Lister's aunt and even her erstwhile conquests might be gulled by her practiced working of the system of romantic friendship for its capacity to conceal the sexual nature of her interest in women, this dispensation is unavailable to those many young women of Lister's acquaintance—single, married, and widowed alike—who in entry after entry of her diaries tumble before her campaigns of seduction.[57] While the widespread tolerance of Lister's oddities strikes the modern reader as more surprising even than the proclivities they indulge, it is the frequency with which that forbearance shades into an active complicity that beggars belief. Although Lister frequently bemoans the limited opportunities afforded her in the tight confines of Halifax society, the suggestive conversations, the exchange of love letters, the wet-lipped or open-mouthed kisses pressed a moment longer than custom allows, the kissing of breasts, the breaking of a hymen, and the four- and five-orgasm sleepovers she does pull off makes it hard to remember she is feeling the lack of a wider stage of sexual opportunity. Suffering at some distance the democratic distribution of Lister's sexual passions for women, a reproachful Mrs. Barlow writes from Paris "The sex are all angels with you," and so it seems.[58] Similarly anxious, Marianna begs Lister to "be faithful, to consider [herself] as married, & always to act to other women as if [she] was M——'s husband," and while Lister agrees, she is perhaps more literal than Marianna intended insofar as she seems to have taken Marianna's philandering husband, Charles Lawton, as her model.

The near-universal success of Lister's sexual approaches are most scandalously testified to by Marianna's three sisters—Anne, Harriet, and Lou—a weakness for Lister's gallant persuasions seeming to run in the family (although Lister's gallantries take a much wider mark). Because Lister's flirtatious campaigns are counterbalanced by a fierce desire to keep secret her sexual relations with various women (not least from each other), the extent of her involvement with Marianna Lawton's sisters is somewhat unclear.[59] It seems most likely that Lister had sex with Anne in the period before that which the published diaries cover. In 1820, when both were guests at Langton Hall, a Yorkshire country house where Isabella Norcliffe (a sometime lover of Lister's) lived with her family, Lister's romancing of Anne one night in her bedroom implies a shared sexual history:

At first, rather lover-like, reminding her of former days. I believe I could have her again in spite of all she says, if I chose to take the trouble. She will not, because it would be wrong, but owns she loves me & perhaps she has feelings as well as I. She let me kiss her breasts but neither she nor her room seemed very sweet to my nose. I could not help contrasting her with Miss Vallance [another guest from Kent], & felt no real desire to succeed with her. At last she said, "Now you are doing all this & perhaps mean nothing at all." Of course I fought off, bidding her only try me, but I felt a little remorse-struck.

A couple of weeks later, Lister "kissed [Anne], told her I had a pain in my knees—my expression to her for desire—& saw plainly she likes me & would yield again, without much difficulty, to opportunity and importun[ity]."[60] Five years later, during yet another visit to Langton Hall, Lister similarly judged that matters had progressed beyond what might be recuperated as irreproachable friendship with Harriet, Marianna's married sister: "She received my advances well. I saw her feelings were getting a little interested. . . . She kissed me with open lips. I might have taken any liberty I pleased. . . . Whether she can love me or not, she has committed herself. We have both gone too far to retract."[61] Two days later, Lister flirts ferociously with Marianna's sister Lou, musing, "Perhaps I should fall in love with Lou. I never felt anything more like it."[62] Taken aback by the vigor of Harriet's response to her flirtations, Lister finds herself retreating to her bedroom, where she has a glass of cold water and sits "for a few minutes, murmuring to [herself,] 'Well, they are all alike.' " Whether she means women generally or Marianna and her sisters is difficult to say.

After the sexual intrigues and double-crossings, the souveniring of locks of pubic hair, and the almost ubiquitous availability of women for, if not always sex, then sexual dalliance with other women, it comes as something of a relief to the contemporary reader, thrown by the *Carry on Halifax* sexual slapstick of Lister's diaries, to know that Lister herself is sometimes stopped in her tracks by the near-universal susceptibility of young women to her insistent charms. If only because it allows a momentary mirroring in the diaries themselves of the modern reader's unhinging sense of sexual behavior and sexual identity, it might be productive to press on this sense of incredulousness, as it is symptomatic of the discrepancy or slippage between our own sexual knowledge and the early-nineteenth-century sexual knowledge of Lister and her contemporaries. Anna Clark interprets the unexpected frequency of women's amenability to Lister's seductions as evidence of an unrealized capacity for lesbianism: "The fact that Anne seduced so many women reveals how much lesbian potential lurked among the unhappy wives and proud spinsters of middle- and up-per-class Yorkshire."[63] Yet those very seductions speak of a sexual organization that cannot be assimilated into the lesbianism that Clark assumes they anticipate as "potential." Lister's many sexual partners do not understand themselves, any more than she understands them, as sharing with Lister a sexual preference, let alone anything like a sexuality. Without exception, Lister's sexual relations with women are not defined as transacted between subjects of the same gender; they are not even orchestrated under the rubric of a shared sexual subjectivity. The distinctly differentiated understandings of sexual subjectivities described in Lister's diaries, whereby deviance attaches to only one of the two participants in a sexual act, is evidence that sex between women does not itself necessarily constitute identity.[64] The widespread responsiveness of women to Lister's blandishments is clearly systemic (rather than simply indexed to, say, the idiosyncratic charms of Lister herself), but insofar as it articulates less an early-nineteenth-century lesbianism than the indistinctness of the yet-to-be-registered oppositions of homosexuality and heterosexuality, it is inexplicable in terms of our modern system of sexuality.

In drawing attention to the crucial contextual shifts between Lister's sexual world and our own, I mean to emphasize not simply that modern sexuality is recognizable through its production of heterosexuality and homosexuality but that those counterweighted sexual taxonomies are the historically contingent effects of the emergence of sexuality itself as a system of regulatory and normative classification. That is, sexuality is not knitted up by sexual acts or even preferences; nor is it registered most fully when most intimately, privately, or idiosyncratically (although that is certainly one of its most hardwired effects). Even if frequently experienced as the body's articulation of an interiorized desire, sexuality might be more productively—certainly more counterintuitively—thought of as taking the body as its expression. As David Halperin writes, "Sexuality represents a seizure of the body by an historically unique apparatus for producing historically specific forms of subjectivity."[65] It is our seizure by that apparatus—and not only our seizure but our utter obliviousness to that captivating apparatus by which we recognize our desire, in the first place, as "ours"—that causes us to misrecognize Lister as a lesbian, to misrecognize her sexual subjectivity, like ours, as constituted in a universalizing repertoire of desires, acts, and preferences.

Accordingly, Clark reads Lister as a figure whose existence challenges the social constructionist understandings of the history of sexuality dominant in lesbian and gay studies, specifically "the social constructionist paradigm that our sexual identities are shaped, even determined, by discourses rather than by our own desires."[66] Because Clark assumes that an understanding of sexuality as discursively constructed disregards the significance of individual agency in the formation of sexual identity, she emphasizes what she sees as Lister's deliberate and active construction of her lesbian identity.[67] While it enables her argument that Lister "invented her own lesbian identity," Clark's maintenance of an opposition between "discourse" and "agency" in the cultural production of sexuality is problematic insofar as it implies that sexuality is produced in the contest between these two modalities—the former allied with determinism, the latter with voluntarism. Yet the historical and cultural processes whereby subjects are interpellated through sexuality cannot be described by driving a wedge between discourse, on the one hand, and agency on the other. Rather, the processes of sexual subjection, like the processes of subjection more generally, consist, as Judith Butler reminds us, "precisely in this fundamental dependency on a discourse we never chose but that, paradoxically, initiates and sustains our agency."[68] What is radical about the constructionist theory of sexuality is not that discourse counters or prohibits agency but that sexuality is less an expressivity that is vulnerable to repression than an implantation that requires us to take the strategies and effects of sexual discipline as the sites and signs of our most private and cherished sexual selves.

The historiographic work that Lister's diaries have most frequently been assumed to do for lesbianism—whether as a demonstration that women's romantic friendships with each other could be sexually motivated or that the history of lesbianism is a longer one than has been previously supposed—is to counter the invisibility that haunts the relationship between the figure of the lesbian and the field of vision. This narrative is everywhere enabled by the fact that nearly everything about Lister's story—from the cryptic inscription of portions of her diaries in the first place to their transcription circa 1892 by John Lister, who subsequently reconcealed them behind panels at Shibden Hall, to the suppression of their sexual content by scholars in the 1950s to their final publication in 1988 within the contextualizing frame of lesbianism—fortuitously dramatizes a coming to visibility that is frequently understood as the project of lesbian historiography itself.[69] Lister's diaries are an account of a woman making meaningful to herself a sense of gender and a sexual preference across the interference of a cultural static committed to some other frequency. If the diaries have been frequently read as her coming-out story, this is less because Lister was a lesbian than because the genre of the coming-out story is structured by the same disavowed strategies of retrospection that enable that critical misrecognition in the first place.[70] Lister's "lesbianism" is an effect of sequence. It is not simply that the critical reading of Lister as a lesbian annexes her for a later homosexuality, but that the retrospection that recognizes her as lesbian naturalizes the incoherence of the contemporary category, smoothing over the very contradictions—for example, the contradiction between understanding lesbianism as a desiring relation transacted between women and as a masculine identification—that energize lesbian invisibility in what we are still learning to call the twenty-first century.

The drive to recognize or recuperate historical female subjects—particularly, presexological subjects—as lesbian is recognizable as contemporary lesbian theorists' resistant response to the culturally belittling modern formulations of lesbianism as derivative. It is the persistent figuring of lesbianism as a second-order sexuality that contextualizes the urge to retrospectively establish historical origins and lines of continuity, to generate a representational economy that takes the modern lesbian as its authoritative center. Yet if the traumatic everyday effects of the derivative rendering of lesbianism in terms of its others might be seen to underwrite the utopic project of historical recovery, then it does so through a recitation of the same logics that it refuses.[71] Although promising a corrective to the persistent problem of contemporary lesbian invisibility, the retrieval of historical female subjects as lesbians is an operation sustained by the rationale of derivation, wherein the historical subject is rendered in terms that are not her own, in terms of the modern lesbian. Rather than reproducing the first-order/second-order logics that elsewhere maintain the derivative nature of lesbianism, my reading of Lister's sexual subjectivity foregrounds the retrospectivity of her "lesbianism." Not wanting to claim Lister for lesbianism, I nevertheless want to suggest that the retrospective knitting up of her "lesbian" identity through historical reclamation functions less as a remedy for the problems of lesbian derivation than as a productive model for thinking about the derivativeness, culturally displaced onto lesbianism, that structures identity itself. As Lynda Hart writes, "Always produced retroactively, identities are belated. Constructed backwards from their structural effects, identities are rather like (after)effects; that is, they are the effects of effects, not the causes for which they are taken."[72] The cultural reification of sexual identity—particularly the categories of majoritarian identity—displaces the temporal switchbacks intrinsic to identity formation onto a lesbianism imagined as always already derivative. Rather than refusing the derivativeness of lesbianism, I now articulate the widespread disavowal that energizes the logics of sexual sequence and thus produces the lesbian as secondary while maintaining the cultural precedence of her others.

SEQUENCE

In this chapter so far, I have been working to identify the coordinates of a widespread conceptual impasse in contemporary lesbian theory in which the problem of lesbian representability is nearly indistinguishable from its alleged solution. Given that lesbian invisibility is understood as the effect of lesbianism's derivative articulation, its description in terms of its others, the recourse to history for a more authentic lesbian genealogy is complicated by the way in which the retrospective act of historical recovery too frequently naturalizes its own annexation of historical others in terms of—which is to say in the representational interests of—lesbianism's modern formation. That is, what is deemed an illegitimate operation in the negotiation of relations of sexual difference returns as the privileged tactic in the recuperative articulation of historical lesbian similitude. To trace not simply the construction of the female homosexual as derivative but the constitutional implication of her sexual others in the very logics of sexual sequence that purport to distinguish between them, I turn now to sexology's founding definitional project, its production of sexuality as a sequential effect. This last section is organized around the term *sequence*, not because its apparent teleological drive offers a solution to the self-sustaining circuits of the problem of lesbian representation but because its logics both enable the cultural formulation of lesbianism as derivative and provide a template for a potentially resistant theory or politics that would figure the lesbian otherwise.

Given Foucault's and Faderman's influential accounts of the historical advent of homosexuality, with their different but mutual foregroundings of the transformative force of sexology, a significant counterformation in recent lesbian studies has been to refute the sexologists' definitive role in the emergence of the lesbian identity. Some argue that the category of "lesbian" preexisted sexological formations. Terry Castle, for example, holds that, despite the influence customarily ceded to sexology, the pre-sexological discourses of European literary representation circulated a fairly coherent understanding of the lesbian as a sexual type.[73] Focusing on "a variety of [nineteenth-century] professional and popular discourses, including sexual advice manuals, popular fiction, and Darwinian theories of variation," Marylynne Diggs similarly argues that "before the emergence of sexology as a specific professional discourse dedicated to studying sexual variation, there were other discourses of sexual advice, sexual health, and sexual pathology which began to construct and represent lesbian identity."[74] Others assert that the sexological definitions of female homosexuality or lesbianism were not immediately—if ever—taken up in the public domain in any coherent sense. Reading the British parliamentary proceedings of 1920 and 1921 concerning the unsuccessful attempts to criminalize sex between women, Laura Doan argues that, despite the fact that "by 1920, over two decades had passed since the initial publication of most of the influential sexological material on female sexual inversion," parliamentarians remained uncertain about the nature or even existence of lesbianism: "female sexual inversion as a coherent sexological construction did not exist within 1920's legal discourse."[75] Similarly, in discussing the Maud Allan libel trial of 1918, which drew widely if erratically on sexological sources, Lucy Bland argues that the defense's case, like the prosecution's, was ludicrously structured by the fact that "there was no common understanding of what constituted lesbianism."[76]

Far from indifferent to these qualifications of sexological influence, my turn here to sexology—specifically to the work of Havelock Ellis and Sigmund Freud—is animated by its status as disputed origin. The problems of sequence—the vexed relations of continuity and transformation—that energize current debates about the significance of sexological paradigms for the articulation of modern homosexual identities equally structure sexology's framing of sexual categories, its definition and enforcement of sexual registration itself through the regulatory techniques of sequence. Neither simply a coining of late-nineteenth-century sexology nor entirely abandoned with the waning of sexology's cultural authority, the logics of sexual sequence—particularly their hierarchical delineation of forms of sexual variation—are hardened off in the contradictory first principles of sexology's systematic conceptualization of normal and perverse sexual orientation.

Such contradiction can be seen in Havelock Ellis's preface to the first edition of *Sexual Inversion*, which appeared as the inaugural volume in his monumental *Studies in the Psychology of Sex*. Anxious that his treatment of sexual inversion might seem to buck the system of sexual precedence, the logic of which requires the normal sexual instinct to precede its derivative deviation, Ellis is moved to give some account for the appearance in first place of sexuality's heir presumptive: "It was not my intention to publish a study of an abnormal manifestation of the sexual instinct before discussing its normal manifestations. It has happened, however, that this part of my work is ready first, and, since I thus gain a longer period to develop the central part of my subject, I do not regret the change of plan."[77]

Ellis's brief prefatory remarks clear the way for his extensive consideration of sexual inversion with a nod in the direction of the unassailable precedence of the normal sexual organization: It was not his intention, but an unmotivated happenstance, that brings the work on sexual inversion to publication first; moreover, this leaves more time to study the normal sexual instinct, which remains, if not the first, then nevertheless the primary focus of his work. The scandal of inversion that Ellis's preface attempts to alleviate is less a sexual than a sequential one—the improper priority of sexual inversion usurping the rightful place of that normal sexual disposition to which it must always play second fiddle.

The reordering of the constituent volumes in subsequent editions of *Studies in the Psychology of Sex* insists with as much strategic force as the original preface on the secondariness of sexual inversion. In his foreword to the 1935 reissue of *Studies in the Psychology of Sex*, Ellis describes his pleasure when, in his first American edition, *Sexual Inversion* was ousted from its primary position:

> As soon as possible, in 1901, [Mr. Davis, Ellis's American publisher] issued "The Evolution of Modesty," etc. as Volume I and "Sexual Inversion" speedily followed as Volume II. I was pleased to be able to effect this change of order, for, as already mentioned, I had not originally proposed to start the *Studies* with what was inevitably regarded as an abnormal subject, and to put it at the head served to excuse the not uncommon error of describing my *Studies* as "pathological."[78]

Keen for his own work to avoid the pathological taint of inversion, Ellis welcomes the belated opportunity to delay the appearance of *Sexual Inversion* in the sequence of his *Studies in the Psychology of Sex*. Up front, displacing the normal sexual instinct's claims to primacy and originality, sexual inversion puts a hold on Ellis's work that no amount of subsequent material can break—the tenacity of its grip enforced by consecution, the logic of precedence in which to be temporally is also to be qualitatively superior. It is not simply that in appearing first sexual inversion sets an unsuitable tone for Ellis's complete *Studies in the Psychology of Sex*, but that in appearing first it takes the place of the normal sexual instinct.

Ellis restores the natural order of things not only through the literal reordering of the volumes of his work but also through his insistence that it is his abiding interest in normal sexuality that licenses, in the first place, his interest in inversion:

> The original inspiration of my own work, and the guiding motive throughout, was the study of normal sexuality. I have always been careful to show that even the abnormal phenomena throw light on the normal impulse, since they have their origin either in an exaggeration or a diminution of that impulse; while, reversely, we are better able to understand the abnormal when we realise how closely it is related to the normal.[79]

Under the brutish sexual logic of first things first, the implied reciprocal relation between the abnormal and the normal fails, every sexual disposition taking its bearings from the true north of the normal sexual instinct. The abnormal sexual impulse is, more or less—that is, through "exaggeration" or "diminution"—the normal one while, "reversely," the unreversed same thing is true: The abnormal sexual instinct is, more or less, the normal one.

The animating anxiety that is recognizable in all of Ellis's forewords and prefaces to the various editions of *Sexual Inversion*, and that is evident no less in his citing than his flaunting of the laws of sexual sequence that ostensibly determine the proper relationship between the normal and the inverted sexual instincts, less spectacularly but no less insistently structures that work's internal divisions and arguments about the relations between male and female inversion. If the primacy of male inversion and the secondariness of female inversion is suggested by the order of Ellis's chapters—Chapter 4, "Sexual Inversion in Women," deferentially follows the chapter "Sexual Inversion in Men"—this suggestion takes on the force of assertion in Ellis's tendency to conscript female inversion to the elaboration of a sexual organization that remains indicatively male. While Ellis's discussion of sexual inversion in men takes no account of sexual inversion in women, his discussion of the latter frequently takes the former as its reference: "The same kind of aberrations that are found among men in lower races are also seen in women, though they are less frequently recorded"; "As with male homosexuality, there are geographical, or rather, perhaps, racial peculiarities in the distribution of female homosexuality"; "With girls, as with boys, it is in the school, at the evolution of puberty, that homosexuality first shows itself."[80]

Yet just as Ellis's attempts to insist on the priority of the normal sexual organization are made precarious by his initial discussion of the inverted instinct—the ideological claims of first and second becoming increasingly tangled in his attempts to restore to the sexual field a natural order—so here his conceptualization of female inversion as a secondary instantiation of the principles of male inversion soon comes unstuck with the familiar ambush of the secondary appearing in first place. Despite its derivative framing, female inversion, Ellis argues, comes to stand as the founding object for sexology itself, nominating Carl Westphal's 1870 case study of an inverted woman as the publication that "may be said to inaugurate the scientific study of sexual inversion."[81] More interesting than the simple reversal effected by female inversion's originating status is the fact that the breakdown in the precedential ordering of relations between male and female inversion more frequently effects not the female invert's ascension to first place but her embodiment of a more widely worked derivation. That is, although to some extent Ellis's consideration of his masculine subject works against the presumptions of effeminization that, in underwriting both the trope of inversion and consequently the originating nature of heterosexual desire, license the logics of sexual sequence that govern relations between normal and perverse sexual organization, his consideration of his female subject takes derivation and secondariness as her definitive heart. Despite subsuming female inversion to the generic paradigm of male inversion, Ellis nevertheless distinguishes between them by insisting that the derivative and imitative relations to the always-heterosexualized modes of gender, which he largely refutes for her male counterpart, properly define and characterize the female invert.

Ellis divides his case studies of male inversion into two categories—the first twenty-two cases displaying what he calls "simple inversion" and the second seven cases displaying "psycho-sexual hermaphroditism." As he explains the clinical distinction, "the first class include[es] all those individuals who are sexually attracted only to their own sex, the second class those who are attracted to both sexes."[82] Ellis's broadest definition of simple male inversion, then, does not depend on a heterosexualized but a homosexual trajectory of desire. Indeed, his subsequent narration and interpretation of his case histories are not bent in the service of articulating male inversion across a cross-gendered desire but are invested in other taxonomies altogether, demonstrating a far more consistent and systematic interest in whether inversion is best represented as a congenital or an acquired orientation, and determining the extent of the correspondence between anal sex—which Ellis refers to as *paedicatio*—and inversion.[83] If in subsequent discussion of specific cases of male inversion, Ellis notes that one informant is "exclusively passive" and has "sexual organs [that] have never been fully developed," another "has curly hair and moustache, and well-developed sexual organs."[84] Others still—the man who "smokes freely [but] cannot whistle" or the man who "likes boating and skating, though not cricket or football"—roll together the signs of gender into hybrid combinations that challenge interpretation.[85] For every man ("formerly effeminate . . . not now of unmanly appearance") for whom it is true that "big muscular men have little attraction," another "of active, slight, muscular build" may be found who declares his tastes otherwise: "Anything effeminate in a man . . . repels me very decisively."[86] As should be clear even from these brief extracts, the point here is not that gender has no significance for Ellis's accounts of male inversion but that, on any conceptual chart, its oppositional coordinates map a wild series of points that defy any geometrical coherence. Indeed, when it comes to male inversion, Ellis perceives the semiotics of gender not as evidence of but as a demonstration of the inadequacy of the popular conception of homosexual desire as transacted between categories of masculinity and femininity: "It is sometimes supposed that in homosexual relationships one person is always active, physically and emotionally, the other passive. Between men, at all events, this is very frequently not the case, and the invert cannot tell if he feels like a man or like a woman."[87]

As the telltale phrasing of "between men, at all events" implies, the matter is markedly different in Ellis's discussion of female inversion, which is by definition organized around gender inversion: "The chief characteristic of the sexually inverted woman is a certain degree of masculinity."[88] Ellis's conceptual stake in this "certain degree of masculinity," elsewhere referred to as "a more or less distinct trace of masculinity," is everywhere evident in his increasingly fine-tuned ability to detect it even in quite unpromising circumstances.[89] As the ur-signifier of female inversion, masculinity starts to seem like Ellis's one trick, some rabbit-from-the-hat routine in which a disappearing object is produced again and again:

> And when [sexually inverted women] still retain female garments these usually show some traits of masculine simplicity, and there is nearly always a disdain for the petty feminine artifices of the toilet. Even when this is not obvious there are all sorts of instinctive gestures and habits which may suggest to female acquaintances the remark that such a person "ought to have been a man."[90]

Having identified transvestism as a common characteristic of female inversion, Ellis goes on to show that, even in masculinity's absence, other traces of it may be remarked and, in *their* absence, still what remains is yet further evidence of masculinity.

One of the most significant effects of the female invert's breaking from the already-established model of male inversion in the work of Ellis is that she is more comprehensively written into the circuits of sexual sequence that she seems in that shift to evade. For while Ellis—and Freud, too, as we shall see—reconceptualized sexual behavior outside the normalizing frame of sexual sequence, its as-if-irresistible narrative force continued to impel his account of inversion and homosexuality, particularly in its feminine declension. Like the genre fiction that sticks to its story across any plot or cast of characters, Ellis and Freud continued to conscript homosexual bodies and desires to the story of heterosexuality, even while they undermined the grounds for doing so. Predictably enough, for Ellis as for Freud, the sexological reliance on sexual sequence, with its reinforcing modalities of chronology and precedence, is most notable in its production of those related if not synonymous figures of the female invert and the female homosexual whose consequent characterization as derivative is the recognizable cultural inheritance of lesbianism.

The 1920 publication of "The Psychogenesis of a Case of Homosexuality in a Woman" is Freud's most sustained consideration of the subject of female homosexuality. His patient, "a beautiful and clever girl of eighteen, belonging to a family of good standing," had fallen in love with an older and disreputable "society lady," an attachment whose homosexuality, although it did not discomfort the young woman herself, upset her parents to the extent that she was prepared to undergo analysis for their sake. Encouraged both by his patient's willingness to enter analysis and the fact that, her homosexual desires having been physically unsatisfied, her libidinal dispositions remained relatively unfixed, Freud took up the case. He notes, however, that whereas the girl's father was hoping for nothing less than a complete cure, the ambitions of the psychoanalyst must be considerably more modest: "It is not for psychoanalysis to solve the problem of homosexuality. It must rest content with disclosing the psychical mechanisms that resulted in determining the object-choice, and with tracing back the paths from them to the instinctual dispositions."[91] Yet even when he has laid bare the psychic displacements and renunciations through which the origins and developments of his patient's homosexuality are articulated, Freud is not quite persuaded by his own etiological narrative, detecting in the retrospectivity of his account a misordering of cause and effect in which the latter determines the former:

> So long as we trace the development from its final outcome backwards, the chain of events appears continuous, and we feel we have gained an insight which is completely satisfactory or even exhaustive. But if we proceed the reverse way, if we start from the premises inferred from the analysis and try to follow these up to the final result, then we no longer get the impression of an inevitable sequence of events which could not have been otherwise determined. We notice at once that there might have been another result, and

that we might have been just as well able to understand and explain the latter. The synthesis is thus not so satisfactory as the analysis; in other words, from a knowledge of the premises we could not have foretold the nature of the result.[92]

Although Freud's observations about retrospective narration are offered as commentary on the analytic techniques of psychoanalysis generally and although his very next sentence minimizes their disruptive potential for the case history at hand— "It is very easy to account for this disturbing state of affairs"—it is significant that these anxieties of sequence arise in the context of his attempt to plot a chain of events that results in female homosexuality.[93] In large part through its sexological consolidations, homosexuality has registered itself in the cultural imaginary as a problem of sequence—that is, as a problem both of origin and outcome and primacy and secondariness. Despite the fact that the descriptive neologism of "homosexuality" itself predates and overdetermines the subsequent back-formation of "heterosexuality," a point frequently observed by deconstructionist gay theorists, the novelty of the term's sexological coining never usurped for a moment the cultural primacy of the alpha-sexuality, which soon came to be constituted isomorphically as heterosexuality. If, as I argue here, female homosexuality takes up a particularly fraught relationship to sequence and retrospectivity, it is because it is not simply a first-order but a second-order derivation, figured in belated relation not only to heterosexuality but also, and no less significantly, to male homosexuality.

Freud's case history of the "beautiful and clever girl of eighteen" draws on both of these figurations of lesbianism, representing it as mimicking at one remove the libidinal logics of both heterosexuality and male homosexuality. In ascertaining the psychic mechanisms of the young woman's passion for her "society lady," Freud uncovers a regressive chain of substitutions that tell a much more familiar story—that of the heterosexual family romance, sustained by the daughter's Oedipal love for her father and her unconscious desire to bear him a child. In Freud's analysis, the cruel frustration of this desire—her mother's giving birth to her father's son when the young woman was about sixteen—was the catalyst for her threefold repudiation of "her wish for a child, her love of men, and the feminine role in general."[94] Revenging herself on her father, she takes her mother as her love object and, perhaps realizing from her recent disappointment the impossibility of these interfamilial desires, begins immediately to "search for a substitute mother to whom she could become passionately attached."[95]

Freud's analysis posits female homosexuality as a stand-in for, a derivation of, a more abiding female heterosexuality: His young patient is homosexual only insofar as her female lover stands in for her mother where her mother is already standing in for her father. That is, Freud's substitutive logic reads female homosexuality as underwriting not only the very heterosexuality from which it might seem most obviously to deviate but also the seat of its reproduction, the desiring binds of the Oedipal family. Insofar as it reinscribes homosexuality within the grammar of gender, which is already bent to the service of heterosexuality that poses as its natural outcome, Freud's analysis reinforces the sexological knowledges it claims to supersede.[96] Revisiting his earlier critique of sexological understandings of inversion in *Three Essays on the Theory of Sexuality* (1905), Freud argues in his 1920 case history that there is not necessarily any gendered correlation between the physical or mental sexual character of the subject and his or her sexual object choice. "The mystery of homosexuality," he writes, "is therefore by no means so simple as it is commonly depicted in popular expositions— 'a feminine mind, bound therefore to love a man, but unhappily attached to a masculine body; a masculine mind, irresistibly attracted by women, but, alas! imprisoned in a feminine body.' "[97] This strange, and strangely persistent, representation of the female homosexual as "a masculine mind ... imprisoned in a feminine body" that Freud here disparages is recognizably part of an influential sexological understanding of sexual desire that structures that polymorphous field across the oppositionally attracting poles of masculinity and femininity, as if desire—even when it most patently is not (perhaps *especially* then)—were always already heterosexual.[98] That is, the emergence of the category of homosexuality within the discourse of sexology at the close of the nineteenth century—its accession to the status of a sexuality—turns on a crucial specification of gender inversion whereby the underlying grammar of a foundational attraction between genders remains unchallenged, even reinforced.[99] This explanatory model—in which masculine or feminine souls might be displaced somehow into feminine or masculine bodies, in which sexual deviation is understood less as a straying from than a retracing of heterosexuality's beaten track—accounts for same-sex sexual identities while maintaining the primacy of heterosexuality not simply as *the* normative sexual identity but also as a kind of sexual ur-logic.

While sexology posited inversion as the gendered discrepancy between the external body and its internal nature or appetite, the psychoanalytic vocabulary of sexual instinct and sexual object is frequently characterized as working against the cultural sway of this formulation by denaturalizing any connection assumed between instinct and object and hence any notion of a properly gendered sexual desire. In the first of his *Three Essays on the Theory of Sexuality*, Freud argues that the link between instinct and object is arbitrary—one that is, moreover, naturalized by its apparently logical occurrence in heterosexuality:

> Experience of the cases that are considered abnormal has shown us that in them the sexual instinct and the sexual object are merely soldered together—a fact which we have been in danger of overlooking in consequence of the normal picture, where the object appears to form part and parcel of the instinct. We are thus warned to loosen the bond that exists in our thoughts between instinct and object. It seems probable that the sexual instinct is in the first instance independent of its object; nor is its origin likely to be due to its object's attractions.[100]

If, as Freud argues, the instinct is not constitutive of the object, the recourse to notions of a natural sexuality can only be rhetorical, as there no longer holds any normative trajectory between the desiring subject and the object of her desire.

Yet in subsequent discussions of homosexuality, Freud relies on precisely those tropes of inversion that he debunks here, installing heterosexuality as sexuality's template through a dogged insistence on the structuring role of gender in the mutually exclusive play of identification and desire.[101] It is not necessary here to summarize Freud's reliance on a fundamentally heterosexualized, cross-gendered identification and desire in his accounts of homosexuality.[102] It is enough to say that his homosexual case histories, however seemingly free-wheeling or associative their narratives, are informed by a sex-segregated understanding of desire and identification that takes heterosexuality as its precedent.[103] And so, in ways that reinforce rather than sever the lines of continuity between the models of sexology and psychoanalysis, the desire of one woman for another is explicable through a cross-gendered identification that heterosexualizes her same-sex desire: "she changed into a man and took her mother in place of her father as the object of her love."[104] Freud braces his reader for the magnitude of this transformation: "What actually happened was the most extreme case." Although he asserts that "at this point a number of very different things might have happened," there is, for someone inducted into the heterosexual logics of Freud's narratives of homosexual etiology, something grimly unspectacular and perhaps even predictable about his assertion that his young female patient "changed into a man."[105]

Despite the yoking together of the young woman's two changes, which suggests that her switch in gender identification and her shift in object choice are coincident, readers of Freud, familiar with the doubled burden of transformation that falls even to normative femininity, will recognize in that seemingly uninflected "and" the freight of causality: The young woman changed into a man *in order that* she might take her mother as the object of her love.[106] The transformation of Freud's patient into a man is, after all, what licenses her taking another woman as her sexual object; his interpretive swerve is naturalized by the inevitability of the requirement that desire be heterosexual. Yet if she is a man only so that she might love a woman, how is it, then, that she remains a man to love another? For while the young woman's passion for the older woman seems fairly arbitrary—being more properly and importantly the disguised operation of her love for her own mother ("The analysis revealed beyond all shadow of doubt that the lady-love was a substitute for—her mother"), which is, in turn, nothing more than a screen for her love for her father—what cinches the older woman's suitability as an understudy in the house of love is neither her resemblance to the mother nor even to the father but to the young woman's older brother:

> The specially intense bond with her latest love had still another basis which the girl discovered quite easily one day. Her lady's slender figure, severe beauty, and downright manner reminded her of the brother who was a little older than herself. Her latest choice corresponded, therefore, not only to her feminine but also to her masculine ideal; it combined satisfaction of the homosexual tendency with that of the heterosexual one.[107]

When Freud momentarily lets up his ceaseless demonstration that homosexuality is nothing other than a derivative expression of heterosexuality, when homosexuality appears as if under its own colors, it is already transposed into the masculine, being that homosexuality insinuated when one woman, as if she were a man, loves another woman who reminds her of a man.[108] Pressed on one side by his patient's parents, who find repugnant the "feeling she had displayed of recent years for other members of her own sex," and on the other by his patient's unruffled acceptance of her own homosexuality ("she could not conceive of any other way of being in love"), the one thing that Freud is unable to bring to representation is the very female homosexuality that brings his patient to him; he finds there instead a second-order manifestation of some other, more primary sexual organization.

And this occurs despite the fact that Freud's representation of the analytic significance of his case history depends on what he perceives as female homosexuality's more common tendency to be eclipsed by male homosexuality:

> Homosexuality in women, which is certainly not less common than in men, although much less glaring, has not only been neglected by the law, but has also been neglected by psychoanalytic research. The narration of a single case, not too pronounced in type, in which it was possible to trace its origin and development in the mind with complete certainty and almost without a gap may, therefore, have a certain claim to attention.[109]

As ubiquitous as male homosexuality, female homosexuality is somehow less recognizable, less secure in the regimes of visibility that are constituted in part by the discourses of law and psychoanalysis, an illegibility that Freud intends to counter with his "narration of a single case." Yet far from describing lesbianism in terms particular to itself, Freud's attention to the specifics of female homosexuality depends on its derivativeness, as his narration of the case effects the alchemical transformation of female homosexuality into its sexual others. Hypersensitive to the difficulties of converting a homosexual patient to heterosexuality ("Such an achievement—the removal of genital inversion or homosexuality—is in my experience never a simple matter"), Freud secures that conversion at the level of the sex/gender paradigms through which he figures female homosexuality.[110]

It does not take much—or at least not much more than the thoroughgoing skepticism of the sexually disenfranchised—to see that one of the strategic effects of the representation of homosexuality as derivative is to secure the originality and primacy of a heterosexual culture from whose entitlements the former is debarred. A homosexuality unrendered by heterosexual isomorphism marks for Freud, as it did for sexology, a point of impossibility. Yet that impossibility is everywhere written into the structures of its prohibition. A heterosexuality so invested in its originality that it must imagine its other in precisely its own terms is a sexuality already inhabited by its reverse. By this, I mean to bring to mind more than the now-commonplace but by no means redundant reminder that heterosexuality crystallizes as a normative sexuality with the emergence of homosexuality as a demarcated taxonomic field. I mean to suggest also and more emphatically that heterosexuality, in asserting itself as the originating form of sexuality of which all others are secondary derivations, allows in advance the possible unraveling of its ontological superiority by definitively installing the notion of the derivative turn or twist, the detour, at the heart of sexuality itself. And if the secondary derivation that proleptically counters heterosexuality is not simply a generic homosexuality, referencing equally and as easily male and female forms, but an androgenic one, making its allegedly universal case in the masculine, then what can be made of female homosexuality, of lesbianism, that sexuality whose genealogical history is crucially, and not only neglectfully, derivative?

Raising to the second power the derivativeness of male inversion and homosexuality and, in the same stroke, naturalizing the precedence and priority of the normal sexual instinct, the figure of the female invert, like that of the female homosexual, is a tightly worked effect of sequence. Yet if Ellis's female invert and Freud's female homosexual demonstrate the furthest reach of the logics of sexual sequence—the temporal, which is also always the precedential, ordering of categories of sexual identification—then equally their very embodiment of that sequential logic might be better read as symptomatic of the anxiety it was designed to assuage. The recuperative narrative mechanisms that suture to the master narrative of heterosexuality its deviations—no less Freud's transferential relays of female-female desire than Ellis's cross-gendering of inverted women's bodies and their sexual instincts—denaturalize the apparently self-evident priority of heterosexuality itself, particularly the sequential logics that establish it as the last because always the first word on desire.

TWO

Remembering Miss Wade

Little Dorrit *and the Historicizing of Female Perversity*

More than a decade ago, when I was writing my doctoral thesis, I was taken, almost therapeutically, by friends to see *Little Dorrit*, Christine Edzard's 1988 film adaptation of Charles Dickens's novel. It was six hours long and screened in two parts, as if to convey cinematically the heft of the original—a novel that, years later and in another country, I would set for my graduate students who, themselves Victorian, would confess to being stranded part-way through, unable to complete the book because of its lengthiness.[1] The end of the film—like the end of the novel, as it turned out—was so densely packed with dovetailed coincidences and the unlikely vaulting of impediments to personal and narrative satisfaction that none of us sitting in that afternoon cinema could specify precisely the crucial lines of inheritance, of kinship and patronage, that knitted up the families Clennam and Dorrit.[2] In between the literal and inexplicable collapse of the Clennam house and the no less symbolically freighted marriage of Arthur Clennam and Amy Dorrit, I had missed something, a niggling something that sent me back to the novel for what I was still thinking of as clarification.

What I found instead was an entire narrative strand—the story of the compelling Miss Wade—whose neat excision from the cinematic adaptation was no measure of the extent to which it both collaborated with and compromised the heterosexual marriage plot that structures this, as many another, Victorian novel. Long after I had forgotten the fortuitous connections between characters seemingly remote, after I had forgotten even the "specific scenes and details . . . lent an almost emblematic or even visionary significance," which Peter Ackroyd claims haunt the reader of *Little Dorrit*, I remembered Miss Wade, not only her frighteningly intense—and no less intense because opaque—representation of same-sex desire but the unspeakably pathological framework within which such representation is couched and that would very shortly in the history of sexuality be annexed for female homosexuality.[3]

Miss Wade and the Discourses of Victorian Femininity

That Miss Wade has lodged so immovably in my memory is surely the consequence of a series of connections and associations whose investment in the present should not be misrecognized as any purchase on the past. Remembering her has seemed at times a treacherous project, equally though differently weighed about with the blandishments of identification, however disavowed, and the demands of a historically nuanced understanding of the category "lesbian." Yet for me, "the handsome young Englishwoman, travelling quite alone" continues to cast her shadow across subsequent debates about the historicizing of categories of sexual identification, the self-serving capacities of retrospective narration in the domain of sexuality, and the status of "lesbian" in lesbian studies.[4] Taking for granted the now almost-axiomatic understanding in lesbian and gay studies that sexuality is a historically specific construction, Miss Wade functions as an alluring figure for those cultural knowledges of sexual perversion between women from which—less than fifty years later—the modern lesbian identity would emerge. Yet I do not want to suggest—as the syntax of that previous sentence might imply—that through some chronological indelicacy Miss Wade might be made to breach the epistemological distance between then and now. However recognizable she seems in terms of a modern lesbian identity, I want to argue that the weight of that recognition is retrospective (although no less compelling for all that). Despite the way in which a certain kind of historical research takes its measure by the extent to which it finds modern sexual identities always emergent at earlier and earlier dates, I am not interested here in reading Miss Wade as somehow a lesbian *avant la lettre*, or even a protolesbian.[5] Rather, I want to suggest that the force with which she seems recognizable within contemporary tropes of lesbianism follows from a retrospective misordering of cause and effect in which her as-if-nascent lesbianism is read as the origin of the modern category toward which it then seems unerringly to gesture. That is, it is a kind of perspectival error that takes Miss Wade as the imaginary origin of the modern lesbian identity. As counter to that interpretative strategy, I want to argue that the quite specific disorders that Miss Wade effects in the discourses of Victorian femininity function retrospectively as symptoms of what comes to be known as a sexuality, that the subsequent order of female homosexuality finds quite spacious accommodation in the domain of female perversity marked out by such a figure as Miss Wade.

While clearly the discourses that constituted Victorian femininity were far from monolithic or univocal—recent Victorian studies specifying with increasing precision the ambivalence inherent in nineteenth-century paradigms of femininity[6]—there is nevertheless considerable critical consensus on the broad articulation of that field. In the middle decades of the nineteenth century, femininity constituted a discursively contested field; it was a source of both comfort and anxiety in a rapidly changing cultural milieu. Victorian discourses on femininity have been variously shown to shore up the hegemonic interests of masculinity, class, industrial capitalism, nation, and empire.[7] Held in polarized distinction to a masculinity that shaped the commercialized public sphere, the virtuous ideal of Victorian femininity inhabited and enabled domestic life, with marriage and motherhood sounding the depths of its most complete satisfaction: "woman's moral and sexual purity guaranteed the home as a haven and a source of social stability, and, in turn, feminine purity itself was ensured through the shelter and protection of the domestic sanctuary."[8] Securing the masculine identity of her husband and the moral health of not simply her family but the nation, the overinvested figure of the virtuous woman was shadowed by another equally prominent rendering of femininity: the alarming figure of the prostitute.

Even more than the bourgeois wife and mother, the social fact—or, more commonly, the social problem—of the prostitute was exceeded by her iconic dimension. Variously available as "the public symbol of female vice" or "the symbolic nexus of a variety of social and physical contaminants," the prostitute constituted a threat to all those things held in place by the virtuous woman: family, nation, empire.[9] Both the cause and consequence of social disorder, the prostitute was represented in contradictory terms as the dangerous site of corruption and disease and the tragic victim of a heartless society.[10] Bound about by lines of pestilential transmission, the prostitute—very frequently represented as disease itself—contaminated the safe enclosure of the bourgeois family and, beyond that, the more expansive reaches of England.[11] The boundless networks of disease transmission that took the prostitute as their dizzying center were overlaid by those economic ones that equally took the measure of her impropriety. Outside the proper feminine sphere of the home, the prostitute was uneasily viewed as both a commercial agent and a commodity, actively entering economic relations, her sexuality traded in the marketplace.[12] In inhabiting the commercial public sphere, the prostitute countered idealized understandings of not just femininity but also masculinity. Figuring an emphatically undomesticated femininity, the prostitute functioned as a cipher for the anonymity and impermanence of urban spaces, which were more properly articulated by the classically masculine subjectivity of the flaneur, whom she ambivalently doubled: "no figure was more equivocal, yet more crucial to the structured public landscape of the male flaneur, than the woman in public."[13]

The oppositional structures of feminine virtuousness and feminine vice were connected not just by the intolerable prospect of the slide from one to the other, scripted by the regulatory Victorian narrative of fallenness, but equally and perhaps more troublingly by the frequent difficulty in telling them apart.[14] Victorian investigations into prostitution, with their frequent reliance on first-person accounts and their representation of prostitution as a temporary and reversible occupation, did much "to close the gap between fallenness and respectability," putting into circulation "the unsettling possibility that 'bad' and 'good' women were interchangeable."[15] Consequently, the regulatory strategies devised to police prostitution were frequently hamstrung by their inability to distinguish it from the respectability they thus sought to protect:

> In the mid- and late-Victorian period, even as police cleared the streets and theaters of prostitutes to make room for respectable women, these two categories constantly overlapped and intersected at the juncture of commerce and femininity. . . . In the elegant shopping districts around Regent Street, prostitutes, dressed in "meretricious finery," could and did pass as respectable, while virtuous ladies wandering through the streets, "window gazing at their leisure," often found themselves accosted as streetwalkers.[16]

Constructed in opposition to each other yet not always able to maintain that distinction, the virtuous woman and the prostitute are central to the discursive figurations of Victorian femininity.

It is no surprise, then, that places are secured for the virtuous woman and the prostitute within the representational field of *Little Dorrit*. The eponymous Little Dorrit is of course the virtuous woman, her devotion to family economically legible in the eschewing of her first name for the diminutive patronym, as when she asks only to be called " 'Little Dorrit. Never any other name' " (926). The self-denying corrective to her father's inflated sense of his position, her brother's idle wastefulness, and her sister's heartless desire to marry well, Little Dorrit is the moral center of the domestic household, the frequently unpalatable epitome of Victorian femininity.[17] The prostitute is a less substantial presence in the novel, a walk-on part in the unfolding drama of Little Dorrit's kindness. While "the gratuitousness of the episode, which has no bearing on any event in the novel" has been noted, most critical treatments of the passage in which Little Dorrit chances upon a prostitute naturalize the prostitute's diegetically implausible appearance in terms of the doubling it effects between virtue and vice, between the respectable and the fallen woman.[18]

Like the bourgeois ideal of femininity, Miss Wade, a lady of small but independent means, holds herself clear of cycles of capital production, investing herself instead in the domestic sphere. Like the prostitute, she has a perilous existence outside the sanctuary of family, her exteriority to familial structures ambiguously figuring her as at once a threat to society and its pitiful victim. If no one could mistake Miss Wade for a respectable woman, then no one could mistake her for a prostitute either. It is not simply that she cannot be described through the oppositional terms of virtue or vice but that she falls outside the feminine economy that their continuum implies.[19] *Little Dorrit*'s most definitive account of Miss Wade concerns her attempt to circumvent the patriarchal household and its investment in patronymic reproduction. Short-circuiting the masculine prerogatives of the bourgeois family, Miss Wade sets up home with a young woman, Tattycoram, a still-bristling refugee from a middle-class household that located her ambivalently between daughter and servant. The novel figures this project as a failure, depicting the all-female coordinates of Miss Wade's partnership in terms of a sterile similarity rather than the fecund difference through which the Victorian prioritization of separate spheres licensed heterosexuality not only as normative but also as economically viable. Single and singular, angry and awkward in the amiable company of middle-class families, possessed by something that no one can specify yet everyone can volubly suspect, figured in terms of contagion and disease, more at home in France than England, drawn to women who subsequently risk becoming like her, Miss Wade is represented through a "syntax of desires not readily named," although the grammatical comprehensiveness of this syntax can nevertheless "provide the sites upon which later sexual orders and later sexual identities could batten."[20] While Miss Wade is a minor character in a single Victorian novel, her representation—and the narratological work such a representation necessitates—foregrounds some of the discursive formations available to the cultural production of sexual identifications, not just in relation to the Victorian period but of equal pertinence to contemporary understandings of sexual knowledges.[21] The desire to read Miss Wade in terms of both Victorian attitudes toward femininity and current framings of same-sex desire between women negotiates the discontinuities and continuities between then and now less as a way of structuring those differences through relations of causality than as "a means of understanding the historical antecedents to modern identities."[22]

SUSPICION: AN INTERLUDE

One of the least productive aspects of the recent attention to the historicity of categories of sexual identification has been a scrupulous refusal to allow the possibility of *any* meaningful continuity in the construction of sexualities across historical periods—a scrupulousness that frequently effects yet another licensing of the injunction to say nothing of homosexuality.[23] This intellectual bluff is particularly murderous for the unacknowledged ways in which it latches on to the post–fin de siècle mechanisms that circulate homosexuality as the open secret, as that cultural knowledge which need not be specified in order to be transmitted. Suspicion has long been the force field of homosexuality. This is not only to say that the figure of the homosexual raises the premium on the mechanisms of suspicion but also that homosexuality is, to some extent, an effect of suspicion, disseminated widely in a connotative register that "allow[s] homosexual meaning to be elided even as it is also being elaborated."[24] In modern Western culture, where the privileging of heterosexuality and the devalorizing of homosexuality profoundly and paranoically draw a line between the two, suspicion proceeds from the superimposition of the absolute imperative and the ultimate inability to distinguish categorically between them. The nervous distinction drawn between heterosexuality and homosexuality is easily vaulted by the very suspicion that necessitated its installation in the first place.

Published in 1857, *Little Dorrit* precedes that cultural moment when heterosexuality and homosexuality less parcel out than constitute the field of sexuality between them—that late-nineteenth-century moment when sexuality becomes crucially constructed around an opposition, however incoherently consolidated. Yet the mid-Victorian discourses of female sexuality that structure *Little Dorrit* might be said to specify the symptoms of feminine deviance on which a later moment articulates itself, to provide the template for, without being able to anticipate, the content of the structuring knowledges of what will come to be known as homosexuality. Caught up in the pathologizing discourses of disease and contagion, fashioned after but other than the prostitute and defined in sharp distinction to a domesticated bourgeois femininity that takes Little Dorrit as its evolutionary pinnacle, Miss Wade's perversity is nevertheless most recognizable in the workings of suspicion that—figuring her as diseased, pathological, illegitimate, angry, immodest, indecent, and an impediment to the bourgeois household and its lines of reproduction—encircle her more and more closely.

"To suspect me of the plague is to give me the plague"

The first mention of Miss Wade places her with her traveling companions, fresh from quarantine. About to reenter England, a group of travelers "from the East" (19), strangers to one another, are held in quarantine in Marseilles. Of all the travelers who make up the impounded party of about thirty, it is that bluff family man, Mr. Meagles, who has been most disquieted by his confinement. The same Mr. Meagles, who, as we shall see, comes closest to—that is, who is most oblique about—articulating Miss Wade's same-sex preferences, provides a succinct account of the insidious workings of suspicion: " 'I am like a sane man shut up in a madhouse; I can't stand the suspicion of the thing. I came here as well as ever I was in my life; but *to suspect me of the plague is to give me the plague*' " (20; my emphasis). If Mr. Meagles takes his own quarantine with bad grace, he cannot countenance the quarantining of his daughter: " 'Now, I ask you,' said Mr. Meagles in the blandest confidence. . . . 'DID you ever hear of such damned nonsense as putting Pet in quarantine?' " (20–21).

If *no* quarantine seems most suitable for Pet, a double quarantine is hardly sufficient for Miss Wade. Even at the site of decontamination, a further cordon sanitaire has been drawn around her, whether by herself or the remaining company "nobody, herself excepted perhaps, could have quite decided which" (26–27). This indeterminate placement of Miss Wade is repeated throughout the novel, not only in terms of her ambivalent hovering between retreat and exile—"And yet it would have been as difficult as ever to say, positively, whether she avoided the rest, or was avoided" (28)—but also in terms of her activity and passivity, her butch and femme, sadism and masochism.[25] Such equivocation about Miss Wade's identity provides the definitional ambit for a female homosexuality whose history will soon cement it in metonymic relation to ambiguity, uncertainty, and indeterminacy.

Much *Little Dorrit* criticism annexes the quarantine setting to the larger theme most routinely observed in the novel—that of the prison. Still, the quarantine is not only—strictly speaking, not even—a prison. In addition to the prison's themes of incarceration and detainment, it puts into prominent circulation notions of contagion and containment. This potent framing of same-sex desire within the medical discourses of disease and contamination rather than the juridical discourses of crime and punishment also has resonance for a later figuration of female homosexuality. The setting of the quarantine, albeit at the moment when "the travellers were at liberty to depart whithersoever they would" (26), at the moment when Miss Wade "walks," not only raises anxieties about the uncontainability of a specific sexual perversion but equally points up the multidirectional, although entirely unpredictable, trajectories of suspicion itself. For when, as Mr. Meagles observes, to suspect someone of having the plague is tantamount to giving it to them, the extreme contagiousness of not the plague but suspicion itself is demonstrated. And the motility of that suspicion, never quite detachable from the thing it suspects, puts everyone in dangerous proximity to the knowledge that to suspect someone of having "the plague" is to come very close to having it oneself.

The repeated bemusement over the status of Miss Wade's detachment figures the source of her isolation as something that ought to be known but is not. Whether that avoidance comes from Miss Wade or the rest of the party is "as difficult as ever to say." What is clear is that the quarantined travelers are cleaved into two disproportionate groups—Miss Wade versus the rest—where that cleavage is structured by disavowal, something that ought to be known but is not. And what is that fearful knowledge against which this group disavowal defends itself? Certainly nothing as simple as Miss Wade's affectional preference, but rather the precise nature of her containment. For what is simultaneously known and not known is not Miss Wade's sexual perversity—of which there cannot be the slightest doubt, or, rather, as Mr. Meagles's analysis of suspicion allows, which comes into existence precisely at the moment of the slightest doubt. What is known and not known is the specific agency by which Miss Wade, "the solitary young lady" (28), is held apart—that is, distinguished—from the rest of the wholesome group.

Just as "nobody, herself excepted perhaps, could have quite decided" whether Miss Wade's remoteness was chosen or imposed, there seems also to be some doubt as to what Tattycoram's shift from the household of the Meagles to that of Miss Wade might be attributed to. Tattycoram, a foundling the Meagles took in as a maid for Pet, runs away from the house one night and goes to live with Miss Wade. In Mr. Meagles's morose account to Clennam, the volition is all Tattycoram's: " 'Wouldn't count five-and-twenty, sir; couldn't be got to do it; stopped at eight and took herself off. . . . A team of horses couldn't draw her back now; the bolts and bars of the old Bastille couldn't keep her'" (359). Despite Mr. Meagles's conviction that it is "the chafing and firing of that girl" (360) that has impelled her from his house, critical opinion is less sure, either holding the Meagles family responsible for the departure of "their servant Tattycoram, whom they drive to the arms of Miss Wade through their patronising" or drawing attention to the will of "Miss Wade, who seduces Tattycoram from the Meagles."[26]

It is less a matter of adjudicating between these contradictory positions than noting that in all of them—barring Mr. Meagles's own—Tattycoram passes between houses without any personal motivation; she is repelled or attracted by the actions of others. This unmotivated passage of Tattycoram emphasizes her character less than her function. As a kind of movable barrier between the Meagles and Miss Wade, she resembles that cordon sanitaire whose thin width marks the easily vaulted distinction between contaminated and uncontaminated. Despite Mr. Meagles's avowed tendency to contract infection at the slightest suspicion of his having done so, it is not he who risks contamination here. Rather, it is his daughter, Pet—"a fair girl with rich brown hair hanging free in natural ringlets. A lovely girl, with a frank face, and wonderful eyes; so large, so soft, so bright, set to such perfection in her kind good head" (20)—whose appearance seemed somehow for her proud father to guarantee her place beyond contamination. That Tattycoram marks the limits of Miss Wade's contagious reach is nowhere better demonstrated than at a dinner held at the house of the Meagles before her departure:

> "And Miss Wade," said Mr Meagles, after they had recalled a number of fellow-travellers. "Has anybody seen Miss Wade?"
>
> "I have," said Tattycoram.
>
> She had brought a little mantle which her young mistress had sent for, and was bending over her, putting it on, when she lifted up her dark eyes, and made this unexpected answer. . . .
>
> "Oh, Tatty!" murmured her mistress, "take your hands away. I feel as if some one else was touching me!" (221–22)

What repulses Pet is not Tattycoram's touch per se but its function as a point of contact between her and some ulterior contamination.

It comes as no surprise to the reader already inducted into *Little Dorrit*'s network of suspicion that of all the characters in the novel, of all the "men and women already on their road, who have their business to do . . . and who will do it" (30), it is Tattycoram whose movements will facilitate Miss Wade's, Tattycoram who will be as Miss Wade's glove puppet. She is, after all, too like Miss Wade to provide any satisfactory bulwark against her advances. Mr. Meagles, imagining that such a resemblance can be overcome, is prepared "to give the poor passionate girl another chance" (363). Attempting to persuade Tattycoram to return home with him, he searches with Clennam for Miss Wade's house. Even Miss Wade's address seems to circulate via the insinuating workings of suspicion. Mr. Meagles does not know precisely where she lives, although he has a vague idea, which he explains to Clennam: " 'There is one of those odd impressions in my house, which do mysteriously get into houses sometimes, which nobody seems to have picked up in a distinct form from anybody, and yet which everybody seems to have got hold of loosely from somebody and let go again, that she lives, or was living, thereabouts. . . . The very name of the street may have been floating in the air, for, as I tell you, none of my people can say where they got it from' " (363). With an alarming ability to penetrate the privacy of the domestic sphere, no verifiable origin yet eminently transmissible, never literally specified yet securely known, Miss Wade's address, like her same-sex desires, circulates within an economy of suspicion. Although in his showdown with Miss Wade, Mr. Meagles reminds her that "you were a mystery to all of us, and had nothing in common with any of us" (367), the overwhelming similarities between Miss Wade and Tattycoram have already been established, perhaps nowhere more strenuously than in Marseilles, where Miss Wade observes Tattycoram in the throes of a tantrum, standing "with her hand upon her own bosom, looking at the girl, as one afflicted with a diseased part might curiously watch the dissection and exposition of an analogous case" (33).

At the moment when Mr. Meagles confesses to being confounded by the prospect of Miss Wade and Tattycoram—"What can you two be together?" (369)—his very question gives substance to some allegedly unimaginable social order, a counter to the idealized forms of femininity and the narratives of family life they guarantee.[27] The doubt and uncertainty that Mr. Meagles professes to have in relation to Miss Wade—"I don't know what you are" (369)—seems unable to find any foothold in the passage. The effect of Mr. Meagles's conditional and circumlocutory accusation of perversity is certainly not one of obfuscation: "If it should happen that you are a woman, who, from whatever cause, has a perverted delight in making a sister-woman as wretched as she is (I am old enough to have heard of such), I warn her against you, and I warn you against yourself" (369 and 371). Once again, Mr. Meagles's framing of Miss Wade, his simultaneous claims to knowledge—"(I am old enough to have heard of such)"—and his disclaimer—"I don't know what you are"—have the strength of disavowal. The defense against knowledge that disavowal affords is only partial, because—just as Miss Wade's composure suggests "(as a veil will suggest the form it covers), the unquenchable passion of her own nature" (367)—the framing of what is allegedly not known is already and fundamentally shaped by what is. Narratively speaking, "I don't know what you are" is not a moment of deferral but one of disclosure, even—given the eloquence argued here for an economy of suspicion—one of confirmation.

TWENTIETH-CENTURY MISS WADE

Much twentieth-century *Little Dorrit* criticism might be read as a knowing mobilization of homosexuality's connotative economy. Its determination to stand clear from the very knowledge it continues to circulate is the match of Mr. Meagles's, although its effects are more specific given that they are played out in charged proximity to the culturally available category of homosexuality. Taking up the novel's terms in a contemporary frame, a large body of twentieth-century *Little Dorrit* criticism fixes Miss Wade within an inferential network of lesbian signification. It is hard to sustain *as criticism* the observation that the key tropes used to describe Miss Wade in secondary texts map faithfully on to those used in the novel itself unless the notion of disavowal is given its full force, unless some account is taken of the sheer volume of those critical assessments whose sometimes extensive descriptions of Miss Wade have nothing to say of her sexuality yet are able to maintain her within those tropes of alterity, disease, and neurosis that constitute the widely recognizable although avowedly unnamable profile of lesbianism.[28]

Homosexuality's open-secret structure means there can be no direct rebuttal of homophobia's practice of neither confirming nor denying—which certainly does not allay, but raises to the second power, the suspicion of homosexuality. Not saying what the text itself does not say—usually the mark of scholastic integrity—can be read, in a field structured by homophobia's double bind, as collusive neglect. Attempts to go by the book are outflanked when everywhere the charge of homosexuality is already "proved" not by hard fact but by suspicion and suggestion, where the naming of the thing itself might provoke incredulity but the *not* naming of it is confirmation beyond the shadow of a doubt, where, in fact, "the shadow of a doubt" is the precise mechanism of homosexuality's ratification.

In an article that attributes Miss Wade's "vague impression that [she] was not like other people" (753) to her illegitimacy, Randolph Splitter characterizes her as subject to "paranoid jealousy" and "passionate attachments," pathologizing her account of herself by referring to it as "a case history."²⁹ It is worth repeating that here I am not accusing Splitter of misreading the text—*Little Dorrit* equally characterizes Miss Wade's difference as stemming from her illegitimacy—but of being complicit in a reading marked above all by proficiency. Taking his cue from the novel, Splitter, while avowedly offering a portrait of illegitimacy, constructs one that is more recognizably lesbian. In describing the relationship between Miss Wade and Tattycoram, Splitter writes, "Miss Wade inflames Tattycoram's resentment and also, in effect, 'seduces' her, becoming the mother she would like to have had to the child she once was."³⁰ His qualifying "in effect," along with his sequestering of "seduces" in quotation marks, manages to reference sexual thrall while ostensibly describing something else. Lesbian seduction is mentioned but only as a metaphor, as a figure for some other, more real relation that, whatever it might be, is emphatically not lesbian seduction. Splitter's justification of his seduction metaphor, while returning to the purportedly safe ground of the mother-daughter relationship, has recourse to the very model of intergenerational, familial cross-hatched trajectories of desire and identification by which psychoanalysis makes a narrative of lesbianism, recalling Luce Irigaray's description of the double flip—"this extra turn, this extra twist"—required of the little girl who, in Freud's account, must change both "her erotogenic zone and her object" precisely in order *not* to be a lesbian.³¹

Patricia Cahill argues that Miss Wade is the "logical conclusion" of Dickens's representations of the "dark lady" because, where Dickens's earlier dark ladies "rose to heroism," Miss Wade is to be found "battering her head against a wall of bitterness and insanity."³² This "conclusion," while "logical" enough, is not Dickens's but Cahill's. Although Miss Wade is hardly certified as such in *Little Dorrit*, Cahill describes her as "a madwoman," baldly insisting that her "situation is hopeless, for she is insane."³³ It is not so much that Cahill misreads *Little Dorrit* but that, in intuitively annexing the representation of Miss Wade as mad to the tropes of disease, alterity, and perversity already in circulation in the novel, she reveals what she never claims to know—that Miss Wade is a lesbian. For this confident elaboration of Miss Wade's characterization is only explicable when it is understood that the lesbian marks a point of tropic coagulation where madness has the same currency as disease or a perverse singularity.

When twentieth-century criticism does finally broach the subject of Miss Wade's sexuality, the surprise is less a consequence of the revelation itself than the fact that anyone feels the need to abandon the eloquent convenience of lesbianism's periphrastic stand-ins. Mary Murphy initially draws a parallel between Rosa Dartle of *David Copperfield* and Miss Wade on the strength of their both having been "wounded by males" and being consequently "frustrated."³⁴ However, Miss Wade soon distinguishes herself from Rosa, a certain pathos and pathology marking her out from the latter's "tragic proportions": "Miss Wade, on the other hand, appears to be a woman pathologically traumatised early in her life who, while evoking some sympathy, remains a rather pathetic victim of her own imagination."³⁵ Furthermore, Miss Wade's "sexual union" with Henry Gowan is marked by a "perverse sophistication," in marked contrast, as we might expect, to "the naturalness of Rosa's response to James."³⁶ Miss Wade's "desire" is "abnormal"; her "passion" is "distorted"; she has not only a "perverse nature" but a "psychological illness"; she is "repressed," "unnatural," and—finally—possessed of a "latent homosexuality."³⁷

Given the caution with which even suggestions of "latent" homosexuality are made, it seems disingenuous for Edward Heatley to assert that "the question as to whether Miss Wade is lesbian is a subject of endless fascination."³⁸ However, having claimed to find infinite charm in the subject of Miss Wade's sexuality, his next sentence avoids—or, as might be expected by now, refigures—the subject of lesbianism entirely: "For the present purpose it will suffice to say that she is a female on a masculine rampage of neurotic intensity."³⁹ For as long as the "fascination" with lesbianism is as "endless" as it is unspecified, it will *always* suffice to say it otherwise, as Heatley demonstrates here by importing the trope of masculinity that, while nowhere inflecting the novel's characterization of Miss Wade, meshes convincingly with those tropes by which she is described. From here, it takes only one more backwards step from that purportedly fascinating subject to argue that even a literal lesbian seduction might profitably be figured as something else: "If Miss Wade herself seduces the young females with whom she comes in contact, it is less the seduction of one female by another than the exertion of the mesmeric will by a Dracula-type figure."⁴⁰ Again, Dracula is not the lesbian's substitute but her beard.⁴¹ The sleight-of-hand that allows *vampire* to stand in for *lesbian* does nothing to diminish the hegemony of the latter term, as the trope of vampirism is not only a way of avoiding—but equally another way of saying—lesbian.

This frenzy of saying while not saying, knowing while not knowing, that marks the novel's critical elaborations, establishes Miss Wade's lesbianism as highly communicable; that is, able both *to be put into circulation* via a hermeneutics of suspicion and *to be contracted*. Indeed, the twin fields of representation and transmission, fortuitously brought together in the notion of communicability, already structure the novelistic knowledge of Miss Wade's sexual perversion as disavowal. When the articulation of same-sex desire through an economy of suspicion ensures that the unstable relation of knowledge runs a line between subjects, stressing the barely discernible difference made between "knowing" and "being," disavowal clears one from the accusation that it simultaneously puts into surreptitious circulation.

Reading Dickens's Narrative Strategies

Little Dorrit's narrative structurally maps the doubled workings of disavowal. Miss Wade's embedded narrative, what Hillis Miller calls "the extraordinary chapter of 'The History of a Self-Tormentor,'" demonstrates the ways in which the narration of *Little Dorrit* constitutes that prototypical dynamic of knowing and not knowing around the figure of sexual perversity.[42] The omniscient narration of *Little Dorrit*, like omniscient narration most generally, is a voice without source—that is, a voice not aligned to any specific character—with untrammeled access to the allegedly private interiorities of its characters. Traditionally, the mobility and invisibility of the omniscient narrator, when compared to the corporealized limitations of character, are understood to secure the highest point of authority within the narratological model. Of a higher order than character, omniscience is represented as accessing a body of boundless knowledge: In short, to narrate is to know.

Perhaps unsurprisingly, post-Foucauldian readings of the novel have made connections between narratological and disciplinary structures, reading this coalescence of knowledge and authority as marking points of disciplinary power. Where traditional power made a spectacle of itself, deriving its authority from its visibility, disciplinary power places the burden of visibility on its subjects and demonstrates its own authority by its inaccessibility to the gaze. Reading a connection between omniscience and modern power on the basis of not only their absolute knowledge but also their invisible presence finds power rearticulated "in the very practice of novelistic representation."[43] As D. A. Miller argues,

> Omniscient narration assumes a fully panoptic view of the world it places under surveillance. Nothing worth knowing escapes its notation, and its complete knowledge includes the knowledge that it is always right.... [T]his panoptic vision constitutes its own immunity from being seen in turn. For it intrinsically deprives us of the outside position from which it might be "placed." There is no other perspective on the world than its own, because the world entirely coincides with that perspective. We are always situated inside the narrator's viewpoint, and even to speak of a "narrator" at all is to misunderstand a technique that, never identified with a *person*, institutes a faceless and multilateral regard.[44]

Given the tight fit between omniscience and the nineteenth-century novel, it is not surprising that Miller's description seems already to have *Little Dorrit* in mind. Yet *Little Dorrit* eschews its claims to panopticism with Miss Wade's embedded narrative, "The History of a Self-Tormentor." Miss Wade's story is marked off from the rest of the narration less because it is an embedded narrative than because of the unconvincing diegetic explanation for its embedding. After all, two other chapters—both called "A Letter from Little Dorrit"—are also embedded without similar effect. Returning to the generic structure of the novel's epistolary origin, Little Dorrit's letters to Clennam are diegetically motivated, the long-distance correspondence of one character to another. The document that constitutes Miss Wade's embedded narrative, however, has none of the easy elegance of a letter. Although she does not expect Clennam's visit, going as far as to "manifest . . . great surprise on seeing [him]" (739), she has prepared for him a written account of her early years.[45] These pages have been held in the inner drawer of a locked bureau for presumably just such an occasion as Clennam's unexpected visit. Miss Wade explains what has caused her first to write and now to offer up her account: "For this reason I have for some time inclined to tell you what my life has been—not to propitiate your opinion, for I set no value on it; but, that you may comprehend . . . what I mean by hating. Shall I give you something I have written and put by for your perusal, or shall I hold my hand?" (744). The preposterousness of this "explanation" for Miss Wade's narrative accession is only emphasized by the mediating final words of the omniscient narration: "On the way [to London] he [Clennam] unfolded the sheets of paper, and read in them what is reproduced in the next chapter" (747).

In a letter to John Forster, Dickens also feels impelled to provide an explanation for the narrative structuring of Miss Wade's chapter:

> I don't see the practicability of making the History of a Self-Tormentor, with which I took great pains, a written narrative. But I do see the possibility . . . of making it a chapter by itself, which might enable me to dispense with the necessity of the turned commas. Do you think that would be better? I have no doubt that a great part of Fielding's reason for the introduced story, and Smollett's also, was, that it is sometimes really impossible to present, in a full book, the idea it contains (which yet it may be on all accounts desirable to present), without supposing the reader to be possessed of almost as much romantic allowance as would put him on a level with the writer. In Miss Wade, I had an idea, which I thought a new one, of making the introduced story so fit into surroundings impossible of separation from the main story, as to make the life-blood of the book circulate through both.[46]

Far from being part of the organic whole of the novel, "the life-blood of the book circulat[ing] through both," "The History of a Self-Tormentor" is marked out as singular, without precedent, not impossible to separate from the rest of the novel but eminently detachable. Given his stated intention to graft the embedded or "introduced story" on to the omniscient or "main story," we can conclude with Forster that Dickens had "not exactly succeeded in this."[47]

In the original chapter-by-chapter blocking out of *Little Dorrit*, these notes sketch the outlines of the twentieth chapter of the novel's second book: "*Containing the history of a Self-Tormentor.* Calais at Low Water. Clennam lands from the Packet, to seek information of Rigaud/Blandois from Miss Wade. (Pancks supposed to have found her address by diving among the Patriarch's papers) Calais Lodging. *Miss Wade's Story.* Unconsciously laying bare all her character. Then shew Tattycoram like her, and the two torturing each other. No information. Clennam goes back."[48] This plan is emended by further notes that instruct "change this to two chapters, getting the Self-Tormentor Narrative by itself." These later emendations—"XX Clennam's visit, XXI Narrative"—describe the eventual shape of the published novel.[49] Writing to Forster at the time he was making these changes, Dickens does not see the "practicability" of including the details of Miss Wade's background in the omniscient or "written narrative," although he allows for the "possibility" of its forming an embedded narrative, "a chapter by itself." Two reasons are given for making this narrative distinction. First, Dickens's avowed wish is "to dispense with the necessity of the turned commas," an unexpected inclination in a novel that has been critically recognized as being "marked by unusually great quantities of dialogue."[50] Second, Dickens reasons that to include the necessary information in the omniscient narration would assume too knowing a position for the reader, crediting him with "as much romantic allowance as would put him on a level with the writer." Yet, allowing for a certain disjunction in terminology, Miller offers a corrective for Dickens's anxiety, observing that the reader is necessarily "on a level with the writer" insofar as she is "always situated inside the narrator's viewpoint."

Dickens's admission that "it is sometimes really impossible to present, in a full book, the idea [the introduced story] contains (which yet it may be on all accounts desirable to present)" outlines as more problematic than either the anti-aesthetics of the turned comma or the limits of the reader's knowledge the difficulty of conveying an "idea" whose presentation is at once "impossible" and "desirable." Characterizing the shift from omniscient to embedded narration as a solution to problems of "presentation," "The History of a Self-Tormentor" overcomes the difficulty effected by ideas whose narrative circulation is desirable but about which knowledge is impossible. The diegetic implausibility of Miss Wade's narrative testifies to omniscience's disavowal. Known but not known, quarantined from the rest of the narrative proper, "The History of a Self-Tormentor" is marked not only by the crude necessity of conveying information but also by the cruder necessity of not being seen to convey it.

And so "The History of a Self-Tormentor" is offered up as if without narrative intervention. Framed by the omniscient narration, it is nevertheless of a different order. In speaking herself, Miss Wade seems to appeal to that authority which omniscient narration continually debunks—the private, inaccessible knowledge a character has of herself. Miss Wade, in her interview with Clennam, privileges such a knowledge when she suggests that he does not know her fully; nor can he know "with what care I have studied myself" (744). Moreover, in speaking herself, Miss Wade ensures that no one else—not even "a faceless and multilateral regard"—is marked by that contaminatory knowledge to which *Little Dorrit* frequently alludes but never specifies.

Whatever miseries the self-tormentor subjects herself to, her attempts to erect a retrospective explanatory framework about herself confirms her placement within that conceptual paradigm into which her circumlocution delivers her. Miss Wade's fascination with origins, her projection of a chain of cause and effect, with its schoolgirl crushes and heterosexual disappointment, while explaining nothing in itself, figures that impotent curiosity that we might call "gay": "When I as gay person *go backward* to find or write the story of my sexuality, I am making it up because sexuality has no absolute origin or motivation, though because sexuality is structured like a narrative with crux, climax, and dénouement, we are always hoping to unknot its beginning."[51] Yet it is not that, when given the chance, Miss Wade unknots her beginning, explicitly revealing that knowledge of herself which has been kept in circulation by the ubiquitous protestation that no one knows what she is. Her account of herself, like the novel's account of her, represents her degeneracy by not representing it. That is, she represents it through a coolly displaced documentation of the origins of her same-sex desire, through those very explanations that ostensibly have nothing to say of sexual perversion: illegitimacy, being raised in a girls' boarding school, an unrequited passion for a young fellow pupil, and bad experience with men.[52] Furthermore, Dickens's classification of Miss Wade as a self-tormentor, as a particular class of person rather than someone—anyone—who undertakes a specific action, licenses her narrative. The extradiegetic introduction of the term *self-tormentor* not only effects a pathologization of identity that is soon to be mobilized in the crystallization of homosexuality but also recalls, through the negligible distinction between self-torment and self-abuse, the common metonymy that will structure the negligible difference between autoeroticism and homosexuality.

Whatever Miss Wade says, she is framed from the start, bounded on all sides by an omniscience that pretends to have no knowledge of her. If the reader cannot immediately see that Miss Wade is an unreliable narrator, then a corrective is effected by the higher interpretative authority of not only the chapter's title but also its running titles, which include "Miseries of a Morbid Beast" and "Distorted Vision." If more proof were needed for the way in which the autobiographical or confessional folds back into the interests of those discourses of power from which it strives to distinguish itself, "The History of a Self-Tormentor" would furnish it. Or, given the way in which the embedded narrative, always subordinate to the omniscient, functions for that larger narrative as a fantasy of ignorance, perhaps it would be more accurate to say that here the discourse of novelistic power, striving to distinguish itself from Miss Wade's narrative, never stops violating the allegedly hermetic seal of that narrative for the interests of its own project.

And if here omniscience's project looks uncannily like omniscience's projection, it is because it seeks to verify, *as if from another source*, not simply knowledge of Miss Wade's difference but its own ignorance about precisely what that knowledge might be. Miss Wade's widely promoted difference, guaranteed by her access to knowledge ostensibly beyond everyone else's certain possession, is an effect of the very omniscient narration that purports to have limited knowledge of her. It is not only that there is no difference between the omniscient narrative's account of Miss Wade and her own account of herself but also that there is no difference between Miss Wade's and the omniscient narration insofar as Miss Wade's narration is already a strategy of a larger narrative field. Far from effectively containing Miss Wade's dangerous knowledge, the narrative quarantining of her "History" testifies to the anxiety that an intimate knowledge of her must not contaminate the broad sweep of omniscience.

Omniscience is itself also an effect of narrative organization, rather than an all-knowing consciousness that, always in excess of the narrative, tells a story. In a persuasive retelling of omniscience, Audrey Jaffe argues that its "assertion of knowledge and authority . . . does not necessarily reflect their secure possession," preferring to locate omniscience in the tension between presence and absence, "between a voice that implies presence and the lack of any character to attach it to, between a narratorial configuration that refuses character and the characters it requires to define itself."[53] While not disagreeing with this model, when it comes to sexual knowledge—and specifically a knowledge of same-sex sexual desire—omniscience's "fantasmatics of knowledge" are hollowed out by its commitment to a suddenly more imperative fantasy of ignorance.[54]

My reading of *Little Dorrit* contends that knowledge of Miss Wade's sexual perversity is that which everyone has but nobody owns. When the very possession of knowledge erodes the distinction between the knowing and the known subject, disavowal is the doubled gesture of defense. The simulation of ignorance, far from impeding, facilitates the spread of knowledge while nevertheless protecting the subject who knows with an insulation of incomprehension. The omniscient narration does not stand clear from this transmission of disavowed knowledge that it most prominently assigns to the level of character. Rather, what omniscience claims not to know—like what it claims to know—is a defense against the erosion of the distinction made between character and narrator, where "the latter's insistence on that difference betrays anxiety about *the potential similarity between observer and observed.*"[55]

The economy of suspicion that congeals about Miss Wade, but equally fails to distinguish between her and not only other characters but also the strategies of omniscience themselves, has already struck a line between Miss Wade and the omniscient narration. In the chapter in which Miss Wade is introduced, she frightens Pet with her deterministic observation that "in our course through life we shall meet the people who are coming to meet *us*, from many strange places and by many strange roads . . . and what it is set to us to do to them, and what it is set to them to do to us, will all be done" (30). Many critics cite this passage as evidence of Miss Wade's pathological pessimism. Yet rather than provide quotable evidence of Miss Wade's difference, this passage more ably demonstrates the similarity between her and the omniscient narrative, anticipating—but also confounding the pure origin of—the chapter's omniscient closure: "And thus ever, by day and night, under the sun and under the stars, climbing the dusty hills and toiling along the weary plains, journeying by land and journeying by sea, coming and going so strangely to act and to react on one another, move all we restless travellers through the pilgrimage of life" (33).

Coda

The anxiety that resemblance will install itself as the proper relationship between objects most emphatically represented as incommensurable is not peculiar to the strategies of omniscience. More recognizably, it has come to structure the labile field of homosexual knowledge where the urgency that surrounds the homophobic attribution of homosexuality is not only complicated but intensified for being located in an arena so fraught with reversals that even to possess certain knowledges is to risk being possessed by them.[56] Despite their apparent recognizability to the twentieth-century reader, the strategies of homophobic regulation—like the specifications of lesbian identity—are neither evident nor emergent in *Little Dorrit*. Rather than suture Miss Wade to a modern lesbian identity through some ostensibly evolutionary sequence of cause and effect, this chapter suggests instead that the apparent lesbian legibility of Miss Wade is the effect of a later historical moment that not only produces modern taxonomies of sexuality but also constitutes us as their most thoroughly interpellated subjects. That is, both the specific—if avowedly unspecifiable—disorder Miss Wade constitutes in the discourses of Victorian femininity and the regulatory techniques through which the novel secures her are mobilized subsequently by the late-nineteenth-/early-twentieth-century crystallizations of female homosexuality. Consequently, the glib worldliness with which much twentieth-century critical interpretation of *Little Dorrit* "recognizes" Miss Wade as a lesbian, withholding that specific term from her in order to fasten her to it more securely, might be critiqued as not only homophobic—although that is a solid enough critique for those readings to wear—but also shaped by a retrospection that does not declare itself as such, that misrecognizes the present as some fantastic destination toward which all histories tend.

THREE

Unmarriageable

The Housing of Sexual Cultures in The Bostonians

Critical readings of Henry James's *The Bostonians* demonstrate that the abiding interpretative dilemma raised by the novel concerns the distribution of narrative sympathy: With whom of its two warring protagonists does it side? Although this question seems somewhat crude—the Jamesian techniques that sustain its viability anything but—I want to reroute its attentiveness away from the waveringly unsteady narrative prioritization of counterpoised character positions and toward the equally counterpoised sexual economies that the novel analogously insinuates. The persistence of critical fascination with the discrepant character positions alternately authorized by *The Bostonians* is impelled by the fact that the novel's narrative ambivalence is structured less across character than across a sexual field whose defining coordinates have not yet hardened off under the indisputable logics of first and second. James's representation of the relationship between Olive Chancellor and Verena Tarrant and particularly his representation of the symmetrical oppositions between that relationship and the one between Basil Ransom and Verena, draws its exceptional ambivalence from the late-nineteenth-century signification of the Boston marriage: In 1885, on the cusp of its possible sexualization, when its annulment must be effected with an extraordinary cultural violence, the Boston marriage see-sawed between respectability and perversion. Taking marriage as its organizing trope—both the marriage that signals at once heterosexual license and novelistic closure and the putatively derivative architecture of the Boston marriage—in this chapter I argue that the unsettling narrative ambivalence of *The Bostonians* assumes much of its force from its refusal either to endorse or resist the sequential logics that determine relations between male heterosexuality and female homosexuality.

In the closing pages of *The Bostonians*, the drawn-out struggle of Olive and Basil for Verena is finally resolved in the public location of the "high, dim, dignified Music Hall."[1] Theatrical even in its off-stage spaces, Boston's largest auditorium seems barely big enough to stage the resolution of this triangulated romance that, for all its heart-stopping domestic scale, has never stopped flexing the muscle of its ideological effects. As the Music Hall fills with those who have come to hear Verena speak, Basil "felt as he could imagine a young man to feel who, waiting in a public place, has made up his mind, for reasons of his own, to discharge a pistol at the king or the president" (414). The metaphor of the public assassin, its figurative rendering of Basil's love as a politicized violence, finds its more literal counterpart in Olive's posting at the door of her and Verena's waiting room, against the possibility of Basil's interruptions, "a robust policeman, in his helmet and brass buttons" (416). If the unexpected appearance of a uniformed policeman gives the reader pause—much as it momentarily stops Basil in his tracks—it is less because through that agent the delicately private affairs of love seem to have been sideswiped by the flat-footed intervention of regulatory power than because, from the first, the novel's hitching of its romance to the coordinates of power makes the belated advent of that functionary redundant.

In a book-length study of Henry James, Mark Seltzer argues—after Foucault—for a recognition of "the dissemination of power throughout the most everyday social practices and institutions, including the institution of the novel itself."[2] Arguing for a careful and almost counterintuitive reading of James and the novel more generally, Seltzer demonstrates that the strategies of power, of surveillance and regulation, more commonly considered to operate as the limits of the aesthetic or the literary, can be detected at the very heart of the novel's strategies of representation. So, for example, Seltzer reads *The Golden Bowl*, against that novel's avowed ideological project and the weight of its critical tradition, as crucially hinged by the synonymous nature of love and power: "the name that James gives to the exercising of power in *The Golden Bowl* is love."[3] Yet despite the persuasively disruptive force of Seltzer's model for traditional readings of the Jamesian oeuvre, this interpretative paradigm—Seltzer's insistence that, contrary to their apparent opposition, love is the disguised operation of power—does not discompose the critical heritage of *The Bostonians*, where it has long functioned as the default setting for the most casual, the least thoughtful reading of the novel. The hallmark of *The Bostonians* is the fact that its central romance narrative—Olive and

Basil's affective contest for Verena—never loses its ideological cast, its unsubtle choreography of power. Structured from the first as a contest, the novel insistently activates—but just as insistently refuses to comply with—the coordinates of first and second that underwrite the heterostructuration of the logics of sexual sequence.

Despite its triangulated romance and its quest narrative structure, it is hard to identify *The Bostonians*—let alone identify with it—as a love story. As more than a hundred years of criticism have demonstrated, it is barely a hermeneutic exercise to read the ostensible romance narrative back into those strategies of power that differently license and invest in heterocentric and homocentric ambitions and outcomes.[4] More than the famously ambivalent narrative closure is implicated here, although Basil's strong-armed backstage removal of a tearful Verena from Olive and her waiting public at the Music Hall is an exemplary instance of the way in which the love story of *The Bostonians* registers an ideological contest in flagrant excess of its protagonists. To this extent, it often can seem that the novel's investment in the idiosyncratic detail of its narrative particulars stands as something of a sop in relation to power's narrative juggernaut and its systemic overdetermination of the trajectory of its story, a story we have come to know too well, that hails us as its perfect, even when resistant, readers.[5]

That story is, of course, the story of heterosexual transcendency—a story that, for all of its seemingly infinite variation and persistent fascination, never seems to tire of its own simple plot: A homosexual relationship comes undone in the vicinity of the more attractive or even more plausible possibility of a heterosexual relationship for one of its parties (optional: death for the abandoned party).[6] Accordingly, Verena's inarticulate swerve to Basil in the last book of *The Bostonians*, almost inexplicable in the novel's own terms, registers a logic more comprehensive than its immediate narrative frame.[7] Yet while the inevitability of both Basil's triumph and Olive's painful learning of a lesson she alone seemed not to know might seem to legitimize his worldview at the expense of hers, there has long been readerly and critical uncertainty as to which—if either—of the two characters secures the novel's narrative sympathies.[8]

Much criticism of *The Bostonians* is structured by the cleft of this dilemma, the simple enunciation of which belies the extravagance of its critical elaboration: Does James—or, in accounts more inclined to formalism, his narrator—side with Olive Chancellor or with Basil Ransom?[9] Locked in conflict over the divided affections of Verena Tarrant—a conflict whose escalation from chill civility to a blunter brutality is the most graspable gauge of the narrative's progress—Olive and Basil signal a string of oppositions, also much flagged by criticism—North and South, freedom and slavery, Boston and New York, feminine and masculine, feminism and chauvinism, homocentrism and heterocentrism, "the people who take things hard and the people who take them easy"—the implacable and perfect balance of which starts to suggest that, each other's opposites in every imagined respect, Olive and Basil might equally be each other's measure.[10]

In suggesting here, as others have done before me, that Olive and Basil might be each other's measure I mean to do more than point up the formalist irony of Jamesian characterization that installs similitude within hollowed-out structures of difference.[11] I want to draw attention to the ways in which together, at once each other's opposite and each other's likeness, Olive and Basil take the measure of some almost unimaginably more vast system of calibration beginning at this late-nineteenth-century moment to formalize its ground rules, the regulatory outcome of which we have come latterly to recognize as the monumentally bifurcated field of modern sexuality. In the shifting sexual force fields of the 1880s, the as-if-natural reification of Olive and Basil's symmetrical oppositions becomes indexed to some narrative larger than the novelistic, held hostage by a soon-to-be-hegemonic sexual order. Moreover, because the novel's ambivalent narrative sympathies defer any prioritization of one sexual economy over another, and because the novel's narrative ultimately refuses to organize those sexual economies sequentially, the proper names of Olive and Basil invoke but fall short of securing the sequential logics that choreograph relations between homosexuality and heterosexuality.

The Question of Narrative Sympathy

Always iconic, always demonstrating the logic of some representational order not immediately their own, Olive and Basil, from the very first, are indelibly marked with their narrative fate. Although there can be no surprise when Basil gets the girl in the novel's final paragraph, neither can there be much satisfaction—even for those for whom narrative gratification might take this form—as this scene of heterosexual restitution is undercut by Verena's shrieking for Olive, requiring Basil to wrench her away "by muscular force" (432). If when Basil bundles her on to the street Verena "was glad," then she was also "in tears" (433) and, so far from the heterosexual union marking the point of narrative satisfaction with the resumption of the proper sequence of things, the novel's often-cited last line disparages the alliance, barring Verena from the traditional romance's happy ending: "It is to be feared that with the union, so far from brilliant, into which she was about to enter, these [tears] were not the last she was destined to shed" (433). Taking Verena from Olive but only to demonstrate that Basil will make her unhappy, the narrative refrains from ruling between the two terms that, for its duration, have been conspicuously polarized, maintaining to the very end the ambiguously forked character of its own investments. For although there is something cartoonishly simple and predictable about the plotting and closure of the novel, something that lays an easy claim on us, like a hated tune whose annoyance is mostly felt in the fact that we know it by heart, there are very many things slippery and elusive about its narration, which make us less sure of ourselves in relation to the novel's structures of address. The point of the narrative's origin and the weighting of its sympathy remain unfathomable, despite the occasional intrusions of a narrative voice. Too infrequent to delineate anything as coherent as a narrator, yet frequent enough to raise the suspicion that at the back of the story there is some organizing sensibility or system of values, the observations made in this narrative voice are frequently curtailed under pressure of some obscure compulsion, either internal ("These are mysteries into which I shall not attempt to enter" [397]) or—even more puzzlingly—external ("This interview, which had some curious features, would be worth describing, but I am forbidden to do more than mention the most striking of these" [176]). Unable to determine the narratological hierarchies, the tone of the thing, yet with abundant evidence to defend any number of quite contradictory interpretations, James's reader—interpellated in the opening pages as one "who likes a complete image, who desires to read with the senses as well as the reason" (36)—goes carefully, for fear of being instead like Olive's bubble-headed sister, Adeline, "the dupe of confusions in which the worse was apt to be mistaken for the better" (203).

Working, at times quite strenuously, against the authorizing of single characters or ideological positions—and, at the same time, intensely committed to the elaboration of those characters, those ideological positions as oppositional—the narrative's unevenly satirical tone and its unmarked and shifting focalization of various characters' perspectives makes for a fairly rudderless reading. It is difficult in a limited space to render the effect that the narration builds up across the full length of the novel, but consider the opening passages in which Olive and Basil meet each other for the first time. In the initial circumspect description, there is not much between them—"He was tall and lean, and dressed throughout in black" (36) and "She was habited in a plain dark dress" (40)—although, when the narration takes the measure of their interiorities, they are alike only in the intensity of their opposition. It becomes more than clear to the initiated reader that, should Basil's not-so-secret interior ever be comparably laid out for Olive, his unspoken preference that women be "private and passive"—"That was the way he liked them—not to think too much, not to feel any responsibility for the government of the world" (41)—would twang her highly wrought nerves beyond endurance, despite the considerably more strenuous demand of "the most secret, the most sacred hope of her nature . . . that she might be a martyr and die for something" (43). Nevertheless, if it becomes clear to even the dullest or most cursory reader what kind of characters these are, what remains obscure is the attitude of the narrative technology that frames them. From what might we take our bearings, for instance, in the following passage—"But this pale girl, with her light-green eyes, her pointed features and nervous manner, was visibly morbid; it was as plain as day that she was morbid" (41)—in which the narration's familiar cadences are put aside for, or are asked momentarily to bear, what might be taken for Basil's simpler idiom?[12] And although the narrative voice immediately weighs in to take Basil down— "Poor Ransom announced this fact to himself as if he had made a great discovery; but in reality he had never been so 'Boeotian' as at that moment" (41), pronouncing judgment on him by enclosing in quotation marks a word that only pages earlier he assumed took the measure of his elegant phrasing—this intervention cannot—and perhaps does not even presume to—cancel out the effects of the statement from which it draws back. The frequently sounded double chime of free indirect discourse, in which the voice of one or other character comes to inhabit the apparently less partisan voice of the narrative itself, magnifies the status of certain sentiments, while also and emphatically concealing the source, or even the existence, of their authority.

It is not, of course, as the history of criticism of *The Bostonians* demonstrates, that the reader feels unsure of her preferences in relation to the taxonomies represented by Olive and Basil's opposition but that, faced with a narration whose unreliability is not even reliable, she struggles to certify what perspective the novel authorizes. Across the novel's changing tonal modalities—the broad satire of the first book, the gentler and frequently empathetic comedy of the second, the almost tragic conclusion of the third—the narration continues to have it both ways: It sympathizes here with Olive, there with her rival, Basil; here it dignifies Olive's passionate affection for Verena, if not the full narrative of feminism, and there it dignifies Basil's good-humored resistance to northern culture, if not the unlimited extent of his nostalgia for a less "nervous, hysterical, chattering, canting age" (327). Again and again, the novel's ambivalent narrative sympathies work to foreground a sexual contest that remains unordered by the sequential claims of first and second. Whether the reader favors Olive or Basil, she is blindsided by the same question: What or whose is the sensibility that can—that can afford to—find equally ridiculous and sensitive in turn a feminist as ardently, as delicately tuned to gender injustice as she is to the erotic appeal of her own sex, and an unreconstructed chauvinist whose code of chivalry rests more lightly on himself than any of those ladies it claims to hold in such high esteem?

Symptomatic of the interpretative unease generated by the apparently incoherent distribution of narrative sympathies, the reader, rather than the impeccably credentialed narratee, has come to dominate my account of the novel's narrative strategies. As the critical tradition of *The Bostonians* demonstrates, the weird instability of the narration, its "mystifying and often self-contradictory" character, has frequently encouraged a consideration less of narrator/narratee than author/reader relations.[13] Unable to call definitively on the narrative adjudication between Olive and Basil, criticism of *The Bostonians* has frequently reached beyond the diegesis for a term that might stabilize the novel's double-handed satire. That the term most frequently arrived at is "Henry James," a term at least as divided in terms of gender relations, sexual identifications, feminism, cultural hegemonies, and subcultural resistance as the novel itself, only escalates the critical dilemma it has been wheeled in to resolve. Since the mid-1980s, the representation of James as patrician master committed to upholding cultural authority has been undermined by a series of contestatory representations depicting him as "a conflicted writer who struggled with changing attitudes toward gender, sexuality, class, and ethnicity."[14] Anxiously animated by the historical development of mass culture, homosexual identification, feminism, and the New Woman, this Henry James has often—if differently—been taken as the point from which the blurry lines of sympathy in *The Bostonians* might be brought into focus.

A number of critics have identified James's own ambivalence about gender and sexuality as underwriting the novel's slippery narration.[15] Claire Kahane argues that the tremulousness of the narrative is attributable to James's gender anxiety: "With its unreliable narrator, its shifting identifications, its digressions and contradictions, James's hysterical narrative . . . manifests in symptoms an anxiety about gender that it cannot speak directly. . . . He envisions a kind of impending doom of aphanisis, . . . a loss of desire which, since desire depends on difference, is a consequence of women's 'agitation' for equality."[16] Although the primary terms of Kahane's analysis are *masculinity* and *femininity*—the difference desire requires being here a gendered one—toward the end of her argument there is an implication that James's anxieties about sexuality, no less than his anxieties about gender, are central to a reading of *The Bostonians*. While this line of thought is almost immediately recuperated for the larger feminist argument regarding "the inevitable unhappiness of women who assume the feminine position of silence and passive desire," Kahane momentarily raises the possibility of James making an "extremely disturbing" identification with Olive on the basis of their mutual homo-eroticism: "The character who will never marry, whose most passionate relationships are with her own sex, Olive ultimately figures James's own problematic sexuality most closely."[17] The way in which Kahane's raising of James's cross-gendered sexual identification with Olive drains back into the more predictable terrain of gender opposition demonstrates the difficulty—but no less the desirability—of thinking about homosexuality as a category whose periodic coherence might enable capacitating identifications across the stratifications of gender while remaining sensitive to the still consequentially gendered differentials of value and power that are seemingly vaulted in that moment. More than James's other works that have been recently read as constituting something of a homosexual canon, *The Bostonians*, with its alignment of masculinity with heterosexuality and homosexuality with not simply femininity but feminism, asks for such attention.[18]

In an essay on Willa Cather, Eve Kosofsky Sedgwick, in a brief but characteristically substantial aside, reads James's novel as asking this loaded question:

> We could ask, for instance, about a text like James's *The Bostonians*, whether certain vindictive wrenchings of it out of "shape," warpings in its illusionistic surface of authorial control and address, might not represent less a static parti pris *against* women's desire for women than a dangerously unresolved question *about* it. How far, the novel asks . . . are these two things parallel or comparable: the ventriloquistic, half-contemptuous hot desire of Olive Chancellor for a girl like Verena Tarrant; the ventriloquistic, half-contemptuous hot desire of Henry James for a boy like Basil Ransome [*sic*]?[19]

The weird unevenness of the novel's narration, its resistance to prioritizing either inclination of the hysterical pendulum it swings between its embattled protagonists, invites a consideration of Olive as a skewed point of identification for James—her angular, tightly drawn face superimposed with the imminently jowled face of the older man whose passionate serial friendships with young men in the last decades of his life are biographically taken to index his less buttoned-down (if not quite unbuttoned) relation to homosexuality.[20]

The Bostonians was written in London and published when male homosexuality was emerging as a recognizable cultural category, largely through an intensification of regulatory discourses around it (the novel was first serialized in 1885, the year in which Britain's infamously antihomosexual Criminal Law Amendment Act was passed). The novel's focus on a morbid female sexuality that had as yet less of a coherent grip on the cultural imagination can be read in part as a substitution motivated by the logics of sequence.[21] Similarly, James's setting of *The Bostonians* in the 1870s—the novel's one date divulged in connection with Verena's coming to live with Olive in "the winter of 187–, a season which ushered in the most momentous period of Miss Chancellor's life" (170)—while more commonly annexed to his representation of the Reconstruction period, is equally significant in terms of its projection of 1880s sexual knowledges onto the previous decade, enabling his description of a romantic friendship to carry the whiff of a sexual morbidity that would, in the next decade, carry it off.[22] So when Olive asks Verena, visiting her house for the first time, to be her "friend of friends, beyond everyone, everything, forever and forever" (102), that desire is rendered suspect by the terms of her earlier description—"irregular," "perverse," and "curious"; "something very modern and highly developed in her aspect" (48)—that resonate with the expansionist aspirations of the developing sexological vocabulary. The late-nineteenth-century historical formations of female homosexuality in America—afforded the partial legitimacy of a waning female friendship, teetering on the brink of pathologization, and cut through by the discourses of first-wave feminism—are not, of course, the same as those that fashioned the increasingly fraught but persistent relations of bourgeois male homosexuality. Yet taking up the disconnected discourses of a not fully superceded female homosociality on the one hand and a not fully intelligible female homosexuality on the other, and running the former as interference for the latter, it is more the obliquity than the directness of their engagement with the analogous possibility of male-male sexual desire that enables James, if not to embrace homosexuality, then to hold it at arm's length—that affective distance commonly experienced as the most painful and difficult to maintain.

As interesting and as necessary as it is to reconsider the person of James in relation to homosexuality—and perhaps even more interesting to consider the transgendered authorial workouts of same-sex identification in *The Bostonians*—there is also something to be said for going by the book, for thinking about the narrative's wavering inconsistencies not as symptomatic of some impossible dilemma whose solution resides elsewhere but as the distinguishing marks of a strategy internal to the narrative's representational project. If criticism repeatedly cites as problematic the limitations of the novel's narrative, no one is more insistent on this characterization than the inconstant narrative voice itself, which never stops drawing attention to its bounded jurisdiction: "It is not in my power" (36), "I am but the reporter" (75), "I know not" (85), "I hardly know" (173), "I have not taken space to mention" (173), "I am forbidden" (176), "I shall take no place to describe" (192), "If the opportunity were not denied me here" (196), "I know not exactly" (199), "I shall not attempt" (199), "I need not reproduce it *in extenso*" (200), "I know not" (234), "It would take some time for me to explain to the reader" (251), "I am not sure" (280), "I shall not attempt" (397). Given that the narrative voice has such a comprehensive stake in representing itself as incomplete, blocked in the circuits of authority that it more properly constitutes, "to reach beyond the text" for a solution to the interpretative impasse into which the narrative's alleged lack of power and coherence delivers its reader does not mark a break from the novel's narrative strategies but is the effect of one of its most insistent solicitations.[23]

Rather, the narrative peculiarities that have long structured critical debate as to the basic ideological tenor of *The Bostonians*—the hot denunciations and the more opaque reinforcements of first Olive and then Basil, the narrative voice that intrudes only to assert its own ineffectualness, the stranglehold of satire broken now and then by calls on sentimentality—might be marshaled for the argument not that the narrative sympathies are invested in one particular character, or even distributed, incoherently or democratically, across all of them, but that the narration—pitting Olive and Basil against each other with an even-handed indifference—is relatively uninvested in character as such. Olive and Basil might properly be read as the most reified signs of the novel's fascination with sexual sequence, the ways in which it constantly invokes but only to defer those first-order/second-order logics that produce the relationship between heterosexuality and homosexuality as sequential. More than character, then, the narration of *The Bostonians* follows the contest between two counterweighted sexual cultures whose fraught emergence has been promoted by the late-nineteenth-century erosion of the assumed division between public and private spheres and the attendant ideological contestations over gender and sexuality.[24] In the narrative's meticulous tracking of the interpenetration of private and public across a range of discourses and institutions, what it remains most mesmerized by are its unstable prioritizations of sexual economies—both those half-imagined ones between women afforded, if not quite licensed, by the new order of things and those correctively traditional ones between women and men, the alleged function of which is to buttress the separation of public and private worlds. Much more than the personality clash implied by a character-based reading, the narrative is taken with the sequential distinction between these sexual cultures, while never ceasing to play off against each other the two characters whom the narrative represents as these cultures' most naturalized and riveting effects.

To speak of the sexual cultures that produce Olive and Basil as their emissaries might seem trite in the twenty-first century, when the acculturation of a sexual identity is able to be measured by the extent to which it secures its own legibility across a range of discursive practices, which might include a vernacular, a sumptuary code, a set of commercial locations, or a popular cultural representation. In this rich sense to which we have grown accustomed, neither Olive nor Basil could be said to occupy the contextualizing frame of a sexual culture at all. Indeed, the very representational gestures that sexualize Olive work to singularize her: She is the saddest sexual community of one, her dispositions marking her out as a "type" without the bolstering context of those others whom she might typify. And if Basil's cultural identifications seem to stop at his being a southerner, it is because his unremarkable sexuality hardly seems his own (or, indeed, even sexual), being facilitated everywhere by the culture at large. Yet the notion of sexual cultures is useful here not for its identification of a coherent mesh of practices and identities, the terms of which are universally intelligible, but for its insistence that "a figure is nothing without a setting" (195), its emphasis on culture—its dominant and contested conceptions and institutions—rather than individuated personality or character, as the formative location for sexual identification.

Marriage and Domesticity

Insofar as the proper names of Olive and Basil function to demarcate less those interior, psychological truths that crystallize around character in realist fiction than the oppositional and self-evacuating terms that come to structure a field of sexuality, they put me in mind of the barometrical couple in their insinuatingly Tyrolean cottage which sat high on a shelf in the bedroom of my older sister's and my proximate but not quite shared adolescence. When the forecast was fine, the woman would emerge, blue-skirted, white-bloused, a basketful of flowers on her arm; when rain or stormy weather was predicted, the man would come out, his long raincoat opened over the cunning detail of his costume, his rain hat pulled low to obscure the features of his face. Like Olive and Basil, what united the miniature figures were their endlessly symmetrical differences. Unlike

Olive and Basil, it was precisely this—their perfectly counterpoised relation to the world—that marked out the barometer's figures as a couple, that made sense of their cohabitation, that ran a connection between them—a connection as unequivocal as the thin metal bar on which at each end they stood—which we might as well call heterosexuality, although I hadn't the word then. As I read and reread *The Bostonians*, I think of the domestic arrangements of Mr. and Mrs. Weather as a kind of shorthand for not only the avowed sexual difference of heterosexuality and homosexuality or even the strange licensing of heterosexuality's oppositional logics but also, and perhaps most important, the way in which the interior of the house seems to guarantee that distinction between private and public, the compromising of which secures in the first place the illusion of the home as the seat and safeguard of privacy. Just as I used to peer into the cottage's entirely featureless interior as if it were possible to glimpse some evidence of the private lives of its inhabitants, so now I want to think about marriage and domesticity—their crisscrossing of the distinction between public and private spheres—as the governing tropes for the representation of sexual cultures in *The Bostonians*.

While representationally enshrined in character, sexuality assumes a form in the novel's narration as the effect of a sustained and largely unresolved negotiation of the fraught and shifting thresholds of public and private as they pertain to marriage—the legal marriage of Basil's insistent proposal but also the Boston marriage alluded to in the novel's title. (Marginal to my main argument precisely to the extent that it is marginalized by the novel's narrative—that is to say, incidental yet further complicating, in the name of marriage, the eroticization of private and public—is the complex marriage propounded by the Cayuga community to which Verena's father had once belonged and whose principles of free union, much to Olive's discomfort in their first intimate interview, still secure Verena's casual adherence.)[25] Considering *The Bostonians* through its privileged figure of marriage enables a reading structured less by the retrospectively reified categories of modern sexual identification than by the historically specific, late-nineteenth-century forms that licensed sexuality as culturally visible.[26] Although more prominently figured in relation to privacy, marriage, then as now, organized its subjects in relation both to the private and the public sphere, the family and the state.[27] The novel's fascination with marriage, then, is discernible less as a straightforward consequence of its relationship to privacy and intimacy than because of its ambiguous characterization as both private and public—its inscription, on the one hand, in the discourses of love, consent, and futurity and, on the other, in the discourses of law, public policy, and state sanction. With its twin traversal of the private and public spheres, marriage—both the legal joining of man and wife and the Boston marriage's resistant troping of same-sex intimacy—is the central term in the novel's elaboration of sexual cultures.

So far in this account, the concept of marriage has been put to quite elastic service—the apparent capaciousness of the term seeming to denote as easily the "very close and very beautiful tie" (224) between women as that contracted between women and men. Yet the very terminology of the "Boston marriage" testifies to the exclusivity of the institution of marriage, its supplementary adjective diminishing rather than augmenting its claims to those by-products of happiness, prosperity, and recognition somehow secured by the balder, unadorned form of "marriage." Marriage, then, is less the concept that pulls Olive and Basil into a synonymous relationship than that which distinguishes between them on the basis of their uneven enfranchisements. Unlike many nineteenth-century novels, *The Bostonians* does not hold marriage as the transcendental signifier of its representational system, its attainment marking the end of the necessity to narrate, as, for the novel as a whole, as for Mrs. Tarrant, "the implications of matrimony were for the most part wanting in brightness" (117).[28] The novel's definitive binarism is not that of the married and the unmarried but that of the marriageable and the unmarriageable.[29]

Although Basil and Olive are not married when they first meet—nor, indeed, do either of them marry during the narrative's duration—their respectively unmarried states do not signal an equivalence between them, Basil immediately perceiving that "Miss Chancellor was a signal old maid. That was her quality, her destiny; nothing could be more distinctly written. There are women who are unmarried by accident, and others who are unmarried by option; but Olive Chancellor was unmarried by every implication of her being. She was a spinster as Shelley was a lyric poet, or as the month of August is sultry" (47). Both a mark of her peculiar character ("her quality") and her inevitable fate ("her destiny"), Olive's being unmarried is not a simple declaration of her marital status—married or unmarried—but an indication that she is altogether beyond the institution of marriage, with its organizing of affect and kinship, its authorizations and its dispensations.[30] Unmarried by neither chance ("by accident") nor design ("by option")—these two conditions commonly being understood to explain the circumstances of any event—the narration goes to some lengths to secure that fact which "could [not] be more distinctly written": Olive is a spinster by definition. Against the tolling of the narrative's repeated "unmarried," "unmarried," "unmarried," a harder truth can be heard: Olive is unmarriageable.

Given the cultural logic that assumes that marriage is, for women, the highest imaginable attainment, unmarriageability falls as a forfeit on those whose shortcomings in the tightly competitive field of normative femininity disqualify them from marriage, at once the reward and partial respite of that disciplinary order. Yet Olive's unmarriageability is of a different order: It is not a penalty weighing against her fondest hopes but a structural effect of the regulatory exclusions of marriage. In this respect, although not in all those others to which she lays frequent histrionic claim, Olive is like the slaves whose unseen collectivity underwrites many of the novel's representational gambits—the differentiation of the South from the North, for instance, or the connection between the emancipation and the suffrage movements.[31] Precisely because of the ease with which the novel draws connections between the lot of women and the lot of slaves, there must be some hesitancy about any critical point that makes the same inaugurating gesture. Given the novel's reliance on slavery as a trope—no less Olive's trivializing representation of women as "the whole enslaved sisterhood" (160) than Basil's mocking description of them as "the other slaves" (222)—the slaves have little substance in the narrative: They seldom stand for themselves but figure a gendered injustice whose universalized terms are indifferent to the racial coordinates of their oppression. Yet even as it implies—and mocks the implication—that femininity is a form of enslavement, the novel's metonymies suggest that what the almost entirely imaginary slaves of *The Bostonians* and Olive have in common are not "the lash and manacles" (172) under which she fantasizes herself doubled but their similarly disenfranchised relations to legal marriage.[32]

While the narrative satirizes the outlandish discrepancy between Olive's upholstered situation in the Back Bay and her sense of herself "cramped and chained to receive [the intolerable load of fate]" (191), it turns out that Olive is most slavelike (which is still to say, not very) not when she takes stock of her abuse at the hands of "the brutal, blood-stained, ravening race" of men (64) but at those moments when she imagines herself to be most free and untrammeled, enjoying with Verena "the refreshment of a pretty house, a drawing-room full of flowers, a crackling hearth . . . , an imported tea-service, a Chickering piano, and the *Deutsche Rundschau*" (190). The elaborate domestications Olive throws up as so many lines of defense around the life she has made with Verena imitate the everyday forms of marriage but fail to confer marital legitimacy. Olive's intense investments in her home space are not explicable in terms of the usual narrative of women's domesticity, with its securing of family, propriety, and morality.[33] Rather, her domestic-mindedness is an attempt to obtain, through the affective interior of her home, public legitimization for her literally extramarital affairs. Yet however richly appointed, Olive's house—the very site of domesticity, "the constitutive setting of the novel"—cannot license her relationship with Verena as anything more than happenstance, cannot lend it the recognition or cultural space of marriage.[34] As Olive has always suspected, while the lived experience of marriage is most frequently the domestic, domesticity's day-to-day does not stitch up the immunities and disbursements of marriage. More than a place, or even a space, *The Bostonians* represents the domestic as a strenuous achievement, with domesticity's cultural work, its ambivalent negotiation of public and private spheres, evident in its housing of sexual identities, hegemonic and emergent.

The novel's interest in the domestic—apparent in its detailed descriptions of interiors, both real and imagined; in its insistence on the minutiae of Olive's household and its refusal to divulge Basil's; in its characterization of Olive and Basil's conflict over Verena as the struggle over her domestication—like its interest in marriage, is underwritten by its investment in the contest between those sexual economies represented by Olive and Basil.[35] For Basil, the dream of conjugal domesticity is alluring to the extent that it enables his intervention in the construction of public opinion. His sustaining fantasy of himself as a man of letters, actively contributing to the literary public sphere, requires the securing of a wife and her securing in turn one of those feminized domestic interiors to which he proves so susceptible that, throughout the course of the narrative, he can scarcely stand in a woman's parlor without imagining a married life with that woman.[36] As Basil sits with Olive's sister, Adeline, in her small back drawing room, his apprehension of the domestic interior's codings of femininity and privacy predictably lures him into a marital fantasy that projects him well beyond the lamplight's fall—into the rational-critical debate of the public sphere with the imagined publication of his political opinions:

> The lamp-light was soft, the fire crackled pleasantly, everything that surrounded him betrayed a woman's taste and touch; the place was decorated and cushioned in perfection, delightfully private and personal, the picture of a well-appointed home. . . . At the end of an hour he felt, I will not say almost marriageable, but almost married. Images of leisure played before him, leisure in which he saw himself covering foolscap paper with his views on several subjects, and with favourable illustrations of Southern eloquence. It became tolerably vivid to him that if editors wouldn't print one's lucubrations, it would be a comfort to feel that one was able to publish them at one's own expense. (205)

For Olive, the dream of domesticity takes not simply a different turn but a different vocabulary. She has already, as Basil covetously notes, established herself domestically, and while her fierce hopes for "a union of soul," "a double consent" (101) with Verena might seem fashioned after marriage, she recognizes her desires outside the legitimizing frame of conjugality: "Olive had no views about the marriage-tie except that she should hate it for herself" (105). The fantasies that make her short of breath nevertheless take a specific form: a domestic companionship with another woman, secluded from the world outside, hemmed about with the rituals of taking tea and reading aloud. Generic in their form, Olive soon recognizes these fantasies are animated at their heart by a Verena-shaped hole, as when on the occasion of Verena's first visit to her home "Olive almost panted; and while she spoke the peaceful picture hung before her of still winter evenings under the lamp, with falling snow outside, and tea on a little table, and successful renderings with a chosen companion, of Goethe. . . . Such a vision as this was the highest indulgence she could offer herself; she had it only at considerable intervals" (107).[37]

Although criticism of *The Bostonians* most frequently draws Olive and Basil together on the basis of their singular pursuit of Verena, their respective investments in her are quite at odds in relation to both the domestic space a partnership with her enables and the intimacies it affords. If, for Basil, the most enabling aspect of the conjugal household is its capacity to fashion him as a public man—and his ambitions here do not stop short of the presidency of the United States—for Olive, a significant attraction of public political life is the way it promises to secure a cover story for her homosocial domestic economy.

Arguing that "a basic assumption governing *The Bostonians* is that domesticity exerts a strong pull even over women who have dedicated their lives to taking a public stand against it," Valerie Fulton furnishes in a footnote an example that, by way of its perceived outlandishness, she offers as a limit case that guarantees the universality of her argument: "even Olive Chancellor—her intense opposition to marriage notwithstanding—is tacitly motivated by a longing for domestic happiness."[38] This idea that Olive's desire for domestic happiness is in some pathologically contradictory relation to her aversion to marriage—or, more generally, that the ambitions of domesticity, on the one hand, and feminism, on the other, are irreconcilable—has quite a hold on criticism of *The Bostonians*, if less of a purchase on the novel itself.[39] If Olive seems momentarily to suggest that a home life in which one might "give up everything and draw the curtains to and pass one's life in an artificial atmosphere, with rose-coloured lamps" is only available to those too unwitting or selfish to perceive the necessity for "the struggle" (169), the name under which Olive's domesticity nevertheless continues to be secured is not, of course, marriage but feminism:

> Miss Chancellor had no difficulty in persuading herself that persons doing the high intellectual and moral work to which the two young ladies in Charles St were now committed owed it to themselves, owed it to the groaning sisterhood, to cultivate the best material conditions. . . . Her house had always been well regulated, she was passionately clean, and she was an excellent woman of business. Now, however, she elevated daintiness to a religion; her interior shone with superfluous friction, with punctuality, with winter roses. (184)

From its opening pages, the novel establishes the "cushioned feminine nest" (47) of Olive's Back Bay house as furnishing an interior life that, so far from undermining her feminist principles, enables their freest expression, functioning as a counterdiscourse to marriage and its underpinning of the ideology of separate spheres. It is, after all, "such a house, inhabited in such a way by a quiet spinster" (46) that enables Olive to live alone (with her servants), to invite Verena to come and live with her, and to imagine their eventual feminist triumph. Boasting views of the river and yet at once so inwardly turned that Basil's first impression is that "he had never seen an interior that was so much an interior" (45), the opening descriptions of Olive's house confirm its inside-out character, the way in which its supposed privacies take on their meaning and value in relation to the cultural and political organization of the public world. The reverse inversion also holds: The public discourse of Olive's feminism—for all the narration's poking fun at its melodramatic overwroughtness and wrongheadedness—is a muscular attempt to redefine the cultural space on which it is most often perceived to have turned its back—the space of the home, of domesticity.

"There is nothing more public than privacy."[40] Although Olive struggles against this formulation, wanting more than any other thing to enjoy Verena "secure from interruption" (184), "to keep her precious inmate to herself" (186), her attempts to resist its lesson only serve as further illustration of the elasticized reach of its jurisdiction. Although Olive desires her house to function as an impermeable zone of privacy, a bounded space that both figures and protects her affective and ideological distance from the world at large, all too often she must play host in her "queer corridor-shaped drawing room" (45) to the very people from whom she most seeks to take refuge. Just as her first visit from Verena is drawing to a pleasurable close, the parlor maid ushers in Basil, and Olive feels that "he had taken a base advantage of her, stolen a march upon her privacy"

(108), that "she had never seen anyone so free in her own drawing-room as this loud Southerner" (110). The formalized and regulatory mechanisms of polite society—the leaving of cards, the reciprocity of visits, the instigation and maintenance of social connections—work against Olive's sense of her household as sovereign and her cherished hope that she and Verena might knit up for themselves a sustaining world.

Caught out in her own home by the mannerly rituals of a social intercourse whose designs favor the married and the marriageable—favor, that is, the production of households where the consolidation of familial reproduction, kinship networks, property, and lines of inheritance do not stop short of a desire to reproduce *themselves*—Olive protects her hard-won and unrecognized domestic intimacy with an incivility that is harder on her than the unwanted visitor it is designed to discomfort. Not wanting to further Basil's suit with Verena at the expense of her own, "for the first time in her life, Olive Chancellor chose not to introduce two people who met under her roof" (109). This and other similarly calculated instances of rudeness—failing to invite Matthias Pardon to take a chair (154), for instance, or leaving the parlor each time Henry Burrage was announced (180)—are matched by Basil's equally aggressive and pointed instances of politeness. Seeking to learn Verena's temporary New York address, Basil applies directly to Olive, the codes of civilized intercourse greasing his wheels:

> He couldn't, of course, call upon Verena without [Olive] knowing it, and she might as well make her protest (since he planned to pay no heed to it) sooner as later. He had seen nothing, personally, of their life together, but it had come over him that what Miss Chancellor most disliked in him . . . was the possibility that he would interfere. It was quite on the cards that he might; yet it was decent, all the same, to ask her rather than anyone else. It was better that his interference should be accompanied with all the forms of chivalry. (276)

The way in which Basil trusts in the procedures of polite society to choreograph his interference in Olive and Verena's life together is most dramatically rendered in the novel's final scene at the Music Hall. Taken aback to see a policeman guarding the door to the anteroom in which Verena and Olive are waiting, Basil puts aside any thoughts of a "public tussle" (417) long enough to hand the officer his calling card with the request that " 'I should like very much to see Miss Tarrant, if you will be so good as to take in my card' " (418). The overdetermination of the codes of civility in favor of the marriageable mean that the very worst of Olive's rude behavior is insufficient against the onslaught of Verena's suitors, whose dumb confidence that the very least of them can make a claim on Verena that eclipses any of Olive's prerogatives finds knowing articulation in the sharp-tongued rebuke of Mrs. Burrage: " 'Don't you think it's a good deal to expect that, young, pretty, attractive, clever, charming as [Verena] is, you should be able to keep her always, to exclude other affections, to cut off a whole side of life . . . ?' " (308). Unable to authorize its own coherence, to give Olive and Verena's union the heft of legitimization, the domestic sanctuary of Olive's Charles Street household comes unstuck with a string of marriage proposals for Verena. Despite the intensity with which "she hated Europe" (109), Olive removes herself and Verena there for a year, as "on that continent of strangers they would cleave more closely still to each other" (182). This flight from households under siege marks not only the narrative's progress but the novel's formal division into three books: If the escape to Europe marks the end of the first book and the tearful decamping from New York concludes the second, so the conclusion of the third book, Basil's flight with Verena, is the dénouement that all the previous flights were designed, yet failed, to prevent.

Despite its undefended aspect, its constant vulnerability to intrusion, and its failure to claw to itself the sustenances and sanctions of marriage, the domestic architecture of Olive's house enables the production and maintenance of a homosocial intimacy from where she is able to assess the dominant sexual organization in terms that seem almost anthropological, quaintly without substance or effect. Noting how eagerly Verena is sought by a number of single men and allowing that Verena herself is fond of company, Olive reassures herself that "the friendship of a young man and a young woman was, according to the pure code of New England, a common social tie" (180) that Verena might consequently be allowed to pursue without incident. Moreover, Olive is confident that the program of feminist education that has come to constitute much of Verena's everyday home life on Charles Street will inoculate her against even this innocent pursuit, for it was her "optimistic contention that it was a 'phase,' this taste for evening-calls from collegians and newspapermen, and would consequently pass away with the growth of [Verena's] mind" (154). Olive's inversion of what patently remains the ruling sexual order of Boston seems immensely fanciful—a fancy whose only support is afforded by the beleaguered space of her Charles Street home. It is at odds with the proprieties of Boston society, which considers Olive's home life so negligible an impediment to the ambitions of the marriageable that its own comparable aspirations go unrecognized. Olive's passion for Verena and the organization of her household as their enabling context cannot alleviate either Mrs. Tarrant's complacent conviction that she "would occupy agreeably such an interval as might occur before Verena should meet her sterner fate" in marriage (117–18) or Matthias Pardon's harsher assessment that Olive is "right-down selfish" (158) in preventing Verena from becoming his wife and the darling of the American public. The narrative voice is no more accommodating, offering up again and again the spectacle of Olive's desire to be "inseparable" (254) from Verena as a delusion so singular that its full extent is no more reciprocated than fathomed by its object. "Olive would never get over the disappointment. It would touch her in the point where she felt everything most keenly; she would be incurably lonely and eternally humiliated" (376). As ludicrous as Olive's desires are made to seem and as devastated as she will assuredly be for having entertained them, there remains something monumental about her attempt to resignify the forms of domestic life. Olive's fostering of an intimacy via the public discourse of feminism, like her wresting from the marriageable the culture-shaping privileges of recognition and intelligibility, figures the potential, eclipsed as it is in the novel, for other sexual cultures, other interiorities, that contest heteronormativity's proprietary claims to love and marriage, to home and family, to community and collectivity, to public space and public knowledge, to memory and imagination—in short, to sexual culture.

FOUR

Remembering and Forgetting

The Memorialization of Homosexuality in Mrs. Dalloway

Set in London, on a single day in June 1923, the narration of *Mrs. Dalloway* again and again recalls another place and time, Bourton some thirty years earlier, when Clarissa Dalloway—then Clarissa Parry—was just eighteen and walked the terrace in the moonlight as if it were the off-stage space of some adult life in which at any moment she must take her part, a part as yet unimaginable, its potential shape only hinted at by the desirous presence of her rival suitors Peter Walsh and Richard Dalloway and Sally Seton, with whom she was in love. Yet the potential of these various narratives of romance is already compromised because, before the novel identifies the stakes of each, Virginia Woolf's very title, with its patronymic stitching up of Clarissa, confirms their outcome. While the remembered Bourton scenes replay the incompatible conflicts of amatory interest that once circulated about Clarissa—Peter's love for Clarissa, Clarissa's love for Sally, Richard's deus ex machina proposal to Clarissa—the novel's title, with its extradiegetic compass of the events of the novel, indicates, through its reproduction of the patronym, that the future belongs to heterosexuality.

Given critics' frequent argument that the novel as a generic form is indentured to the narrative of heterosexuality, the couple formation, and the marriage plot, this thumbnail reading of *Mrs. Dalloway* has the weight of predictability. Yet a reading that takes *Mrs. Dalloway*'s title as an anticipation and condensation of its narrative closure and that reconstructs the novel as strung across the straightforward sequence of past and present appears not to have read the novel very closely. Such a reading seems indifferent to the very characteristics of *Mrs. Dalloway*'s experimental form—its intercutting of time frames, the repetitive and cyclic forms of its plotting, its refusal of character as a distinct consciousness or perspective—that distinguish it from the traditions of the realist novel, including the latter's reification of heterosexuality *as* narrative. In this chapter, however, I argue that *Mrs. Dalloway* is as wedded as the most conventional marriage plot to the concept of heterosexual transcendency and that, moreover, this commitment is secured by precisely those "so queer and so masterful" modernist techniques of representation that would seem to eschew it.[1] Although Elizabeth Abel praises Woolf's novel for breaking free from the novelistic narrative's "tyranny of sequence," the compositional techniques of *Mrs. Dalloway* that work against the temporal linearity of the realist novel are the very mechanisms that reinforce those persistent and influential cultural narratives of sexual succession that Abel herself notes Freud is simultaneously working out in relation to femininity's risky passage from homosexuality to heterosexuality.[2] A queer counterpoint to Freud's theorization of the homosexual subject, the temporal logics of *Mrs. Dalloway*—most notably, the novel's governing trope of memory—struggle to render as chronological the distinction between homosexuality and heterosexuality.[3]

Freudian Memory: Homosexuality as Recollection

At the novel's opening, as Clarissa makes her way from her Westminster home to Bond Street where she will buy flowers for her party that night, her consciousness orders the world through which she passes, the narrative fashioned after her mental associations and asides. Even more than it bears the imprint of her idiosyncratic perception of the present scene— "life; London; this moment of June" (6)—the narrative's description of her simple errand is amplified by her capacity not simply to record but to recall. Woolf records in her diary that the compositional technique of *Mrs. Dalloway* imitates memory's tunneling back into the past from the present: "It took me a year's groping to discover what I call my tunnelling process, by which I tell the past by instalments, as I have need of it. This is my prime discovery so far."[4] Woolf couches her discovery of a nonsequential narrative organization in archaeological terms: "I dig out beautiful caves behind my characters; I think that gives exactly what I want; humanity, humour, depth. The idea is that the caves shall connect, & each comes to daylight at the present moment."[5] *Mrs. Dalloway*'s present is founded on these catacombs of memory. Held fast to a single day in June, the novel's present is balanced by a similarly condensed past, a summer in Bourton, memories of which are so comprehensive and sustained that they seem to hijack momentarily the momentum of the novel's narrative. The novel's stream-of-consciousness style greases the almost imperceptible slide between present and past, between description and recollection, which characterizes the novel both as a whole and at the level of a sentence.[6] Not restricted to Clarissa's perspective, but looped through the subjectivities of even very minor characters, the novel's stream of consciousness enables memory, the act of recollection, to stand as the naturalizing figure for the narrative's crosshatching of present and past.

If recollection naturalizes the narrative's temporal disjunctions, if it provides the explanatory frame for the novel's often imperceptible shifts between present and past, then recollection in turn is naturalized in large part by being housed in character, by proceeding from a single consciousness.[7] Woolf makes precisely this naturalizing claim in her 1919 manifesto "Modern Fiction," the opening exhortation of which anticipates the technical strategy of *Mrs. Dalloway*:

> Examine for a moment an ordinary mind on an ordinary day. The mind receives a myriad impressions—trivial, fantastic, evanescent, or engraved with the sharpness of steel. From all sides they come, an incessant shower of innumerable atoms. . . . Let us record the atoms as they fall upon the mind in the order in which they fall, let us trace the pattern, however disconnected and incoherent in appearance, which each sight or incident scores upon the consciousness.[8]

Woolf's advocacy of modernism's textual innovation over the familiar conventions of the nineteenth-century realist novel, characterized as complacently taken with the solid pleasures of the material and the external, rests on her confidence that the former is capable of rendering more accurately the workings of consciousness, the exterior world as it is refracted through the interior.

Moreover, in her insistence that the most irregular and irrational mental abstractions might yield up some design, that the apparent substance or ephemera of the near infinity of the mind's impressions cannot be used to distinguish between them, that the order in which ideas occur to the mind speaks of some organization beyond logic or chronology, Woolf's literary manifesto is startlingly close to Freud's formulation of free association, which he identified as the "fundamental technique of analysis": "We instruct the patient to put himself into a state of quiet, unreflecting self-observation, and to report to us whatever internal perceptions he is able to make—feelings, thoughts, memories—in the order in which they occur to him. . . . We urge him always to follow only the surface of his consciousness and to leave aside any criticism of what he finds, whatever shape that criticism may take."[9]

Woolf's hostile relationship to psychoanalysis—a hostility unalleviated by Bloomsbury's public identification as the second home of psychoanalysis—is so well documented it might seem at first unproductive to trace the similarities between her techniques for the textualization of human consciousness and Freud's principle of free association. Although I am not making an argument about influence or causality, in this chapter I nevertheless do pull together the representational economies of Woolf and Freud, arguing that their mutual fixation with memory as the trace architecture of human subjectivity produces as its compromised subject the figure of the homosexual. I trace in *Mrs. Dalloway* a narrative system whose reliance on memory is at once abetted and sabotaged by homosexuality; that is, I trace in Woolf's novel a mnemic economy we might equally call Freudian.

The homosexual comes to stand for Freud as a specifically mnemic problem, discredited as remembering subject yet somehow the subject of memory par excellence. In an essay that anticipates for clinicians common difficulties arising in the psychoanalytic relation, Freud foregrounds one category of person unresponsive to free association's imperative to recall. Despite Freud's impressing on his patients that the successful outcome of the treatment depends entirely on their adherence to the fundamental technique of free association and his reassuring them that nothing is "too *disagreeable* or too *indiscreet*," "too *unimportant* or *irrelevant*," or too "*nonsensical*" for articulation, he nevertheless finds, contrary to his initial expectations, that a certain kind of patient, having been invited to say anything whatsoever, has nothing at all to say: "When one has announced the fundamental rule of psycho-analysis to a patient with an eventful life-history and a long story of illness and has then asked him to say what occurs to his mind, one expects him to pour out a flood of information; but often the first thing that happens is that he has nothing to say. He is silent and declares that nothing occurs to him."[10]

Freud's interpretative confidence is unchecked by his patient's reluctance to knuckle under to the requirements of the fundamental technique of analysis: "This, of course, is merely a repetition of a homosexual attitude which comes to the fore as a resistance against remembering anything."[11] The patient's silence is nevertheless articulate about the origins of his analytic resistance to remembering: The disinclination to remember is, Freud tells us, "of course" and "merely," a homosexual one.[12] Yet while the will not to remember announces itself as homosexual, it also transpires that, when they do recollect, the memories of homosexuals are not to be trusted. In his writing up of "The Psychogenesis of a Case of Homosexuality in a Woman," Freud notes that "the analysis was broken off after a short time, and therefore yielded an anamnesis not much more reliable than the other anamneses of homosexuals, which there is good cause to question."[13] Although here it is ostensibly the brevity of the treatment that renders the anamnesis problematic—Freud terminates the analysis, recommending to the girl's parents that the therapy continue with a female doctor—the unreliability of this case history brings it into line with the questionable "anamneses of homosexuals" more generally. Reluctant to remember and unreliable when they do, the problem of homosexuality is for Freud a problem of memory.

It is not only that, for Freud, homosexuals have a troubled relation to memory but also that homosexuality is figured *as* memory, as the earliest and repressed record of the subject's sexual development.[14] For Freudian psychoanalysis, homosexual libidinal impulses are the persistent memory trace of heterosexuality—straightened out in the Oedipal narrative of sexual identification and desire, homosexuality nevertheless marks the prehistory of the heterosexual subject, the primacy of homosexuality perversely ensuring its secondariness.[15] As many theorists have noted, Freud's theorizations of normative sexuality derive from his prior analyses of perversions and neuroses.[16] Nowhere is this more marked than the ways in which Freud's conception of female sexuality is underwritten by his ongoing work on female homosexuality. In Freud's 1931 essay "Female Sexuality," it is his discovery of a phase preceding the Oedipal, in which the little girl enjoys an intensely passionate "exclusive relationship to her mother," which confirms the developmental trajectory of heterosexuality's evolution from homosexuality already implied in his earlier work. While Freud's unearthing of the existence of the little girl's early attachment to the mother is figured famously as an archaeological find, the following sentence characterizes that work as a figure for another kind of uncovering, the remembering of a repressed memory, distanced from the subject both by time and repudiation:

> Our insight into this early, pre-Oedipus, phase in girls comes to us as a surprise, like the discovery, in another field, of the Minoan-Mycenaean civilization behind the civilization of Greece.
>
> Everything in the sphere of this first attachment to the mother seemed to me so difficult to grasp in analysis—so grey with age and shadowy and almost impossible to revivify—that it was as if it had succumbed to an especially inexorable repression.[17]

Always a return to a previous state, female homosexuality is itself structured like a memory: Like Freud's hysterical patients, it seems that female homosexuals also "suffer from reminiscences."[18] Loath or unable to access their own memories, homosexuals in Freudian psychoanalysis come to represent memory itself. Properly contained in the past as the prehistory of heterosexuality, for Freud, homosexuality—and particularly female homosexuality—is fashioned after recollection: That is, homosexuality is committed to memory.

The psychoanalytic conception of the individual as "a cluster of mnemonic operations and transformations" might equally describe the construction of character in *Mrs. Dalloway*, where memory, ostensibly sourced in character, produces character as its heightened effect.[19] Like Freud's patients, Woolf's characters are animated by recollection, their memories enabling less a reproduction of past events than a transformation of those events in the present. While recollection is identified as the crucial narrative mode for *Mrs. Dalloway*, underwriting each character's claim to the present, its burdens fall most heavily on the novel's representations of homosexual desire. A novel of remembrance, *Mrs. Dalloway* ultimately confines homosexuality to the register that enables its most voluble articulation—that of memory. For Woolf's *Mrs. Dalloway*, as for Freud, the remembering homosexual subject is invariably recast as the homosexual subject of memory. Increasingly, homosexuality is confined to the mnemic register, its surfacing in the present a temporary glitch in that future-directed temporality that is, as the novel's closure attests, contracted to heterosexuality.

THE TWIN MECHANISMS OF MEMORY

From its opening lines—its description of preparations for Clarissa's party that June evening of 1923—*Mrs. Dalloway* identifies memory as the mechanism that sutures past and present, then and now, structuring not simply the constitutive settings of its story but the innovations of its technical form, the very logics of its narration:

> Mrs Dalloway said she would buy the flowers herself.
>
> For Lucy had her work cut out for her. The doors would be taken off their hinges; Rumpelmayer's men were coming. And then, thought Clarissa Dalloway, what a morning—fresh as if issued to children on a beach.
>
> What a lark! What a plunge! For so it had always seemed to her, when, with a little squeak of the hinges, which she could hear now, she had burst open the French windows and plunged at Bourton into the open air.[20]

The ease of the narrative's transition in this passage as elsewhere, the unmarked effortlessness with which it plunges Clarissa from her immediate present to her recollected past, frequently provokes some readerly confusion in distinguishing between now and then, for while the sentence's end confirms that Clarissa remembers the squeaking hinges on the French windows at Bourton, it seems at first that another set of squeaking hinges "which she could hear now"—perhaps those of the doors Rumpelmayer's men were coming to remove—recall them to her across a thirty-year gap.[21] Yet despite these sometimes disorienting effects of the narrative's cross-cutting of its advance with the detailed retrospection of its characters' reminiscences, the narration does not so much shuttle between different locations—London and Bourton—or even between different temporalities—1890 and 1923—as open itself up to a continuing process of recollection in which memory incorporates the past as an integral part of the present.[22] This symbiotic relationship between past and present knits up an everyday for the characters of *Mrs. Dalloway,* in which "the present, for them, is the perpetual repetition of the past."[23] The work of recollection—both the boomerang trajectory of the present through the past and the technical innovation of the narrative form that delivers it—can be seen in the continuation of the opening passage just cited. With its hesitations and repetitions, its parenthetical asides, its excavation of the present for the past, its strings of present-participial phrases and the elaborate nip and tuck of its punctuation luring the reader through the lengthy unraveling of its almost impossibly sustained sentences, Woolf's prose exemplifies many of the signature stylistics of *Mrs. Dalloway*'s modernist project to represent consciousness:

> How fresh, how calm, stiller than this of course, the air was in the early morning; like the flap of a wave; the kiss of a wave; chill and sharp and yet (for a girl of eighteen as she then was) solemn, feeling as she did, standing there at the open window, that something awful was about to happen; looking at the flowers, at the trees with the smoke winding off them and the rooks rising, falling; standing and looking until Peter Walsh said "Musing among the vegetables?"—was that it?—"I prefer men to cauliflowers"—was that it? He must have said it at breakfast one morning when she had gone out on to the terrace—Peter Walsh. (5)

Despite the characteristic easy plunge from present to past, the novel does not represent memory—the mechanism that naturalizes that transition—as a straightforward process but one characterized by partiality and unreliability. Reminded of Bourton some thirty years ago by nothing more than the freshness of the morning, Clarissa's recollections falter with her memory of Peter Walsh's interruption of her reverie at the open window. Although she remembers the flowers and the smoke-wreathed trees, the flight patterns of the rooks, even the precise tone of the squeaking hinges on the French doors, Clarissa cannot remember what it was that Peter said to her on the terrace: " 'Musing among the vegetables?'—was that it?—'I prefer men to cauliflowers'—was that it?" Moreover, it is precisely this amnesia she forgets when she goes on to characterize the peculiarly selective nature of recall: "It was [Peter's] sayings one remembered; his eyes, his pocket-knife, his smile, his grumpiness and, when millions of things had utterly vanished—how strange it was!—a few sayings like this about cabbages" (5). Musing on the selective character of memory, its imperfect reconstruction of the past, Clarissa perversely identifies her recollection of Peter's sayings, one of which she has only just forgotten, as evidence of the retentiveness of memory, contrasting them with those "millions of things [which] had utterly vanished."

Clarissa's thinking about the internal processes of memory as significantly divided between those things it maintains as recollections and those "millions of things" of which it bears no perceptible trace is soon put aside for a second division—that between memory as a whole and present experience. "But every one remembered;" Clarissa thinks to herself, disparagingly cutting short her reminiscences, "what she loved was this, here, now, in front of her; the fat lady in the cab" (11). Devaluing her memories on the basis of the democratic ubiquity of the faculty to remember, Clarissa refocuses her attention on the woman before her, a chubby stand-in for the idiosyncratic pleasures of the present moment. Through her prioritization of experience over memory, Clarissa not only distances herself from the processes of recollection but from her earlier speculations about the forked nature of memory itself, its twin modalities of remembering and forgetting. Although *Mrs. Dalloway*, like Clarissa, hinges memory more on recollection than amnesia, I want to return to Clarissa as she forgets what she nevertheless claims to remember, to her inability to recall whatever it was that Peter said to her on the terrace all those years ago.

For forgetting something is not the reverse of remembering something: That is, remembering does not restore what forgetting misplaces. Rather, the mechanisms of forgetting, like those of remembering, are the psychically invested recordings of the past. There can be no doubt that for Freud the significance of memory can be traced both in what is remembered as well as in what is forgotten. In his *Psychopathology of Everyday Life*, published first in 1901 and translated into English in 1914, Freud identifies forgetting—the forgetting of proper names, the forgetting of foreign words, the forgetting of impressions and intentions—as symptomatic of some repressed knowledge: "Analysis of the examples of forgetting that seem to require a special explanation reveals that the motive for forgetting is invariably an unwillingness to remember something which can evoke distressing feelings."[24]

While *Mrs. Dalloway* makes considerably more of remembering than forgetting, Clarissa's disavowed lapse in memory is connected to her recollection of what, thirty years later, still stands as "the most exquisite moment of her whole life" (40). Her forgetting of what Peter said to her on the terrace, her uncertain recall of two possible statements, allows her to pass from her recollection proper to a consideration of the tendentiousness of memory itself. The painful content of Clarissa's memory of Peter, from which she is protected by her forgetting of Peter's words, concerns his interruption of her on the terrace, a scene that threatens to recall another traumatic scene that is also and not incidentally another interruption staged on the same terrace:

> They all went out on to the terrace and walked up and down. Peter Walsh and Joseph Breitkopf went on about Wagner. She and Sally fell a little behind. Then came the most exquisite moment of her whole life passing a stone urn with flowers in it. Sally stopped; picked a flower; kissed her on the lips. The whole world might have turned upside down! The others disappeared; there she was alone with Sally. And she felt that she had been given a present, wrapped up, and told just to keep it, not to look at it—a diamond, something infinitely precious, wrapped up, which, as they walked (up and down, up and down), she uncovered, or the radiance burnt through, the revelation, the religious feeling!—when old Joseph and Peter faced them:
>
> "Star-gazing?" said Peter.
>
> It was like running one's face against a granite wall in the darkness! It was shocking; it was horrible! . . .
>
> "Oh this horror!" she said to herself, as if she had known all along that something would interrupt, would embitter her moment of happiness. (40–41)

Here, lesbianism is enjoyed on borrowed time. It has no continuity of its own and, as if temporality has been conclusively indentured to heterosexuality, is always vulnerable to interruption. Yet it is not lesbianism but its interruption that is the traumatic event, an interruption whose traumatic force is registered in the transferal of its temporal modalities to lesbianism itself. By being hardened into memory, lesbianism itself comes to figure interruption: More traumatic than Peter's interruption of Sally and Clarissa's walk on the terrace is the force with which the persistent memory of Sally and her kiss interrupts the smooth chronologies of Clarissa's everyday life.

Considering her love for Sally from the vantage point of the present, Clarissa identifies as definitive the necessarily temporary status of the relationship, its inevitable suspension with the advent of marriage whose claims on futurity are institutional: "The strange thing, on looking back, was the purity, the integrity, of her feeling for Sally. It was not like one's feeling for a man. It was completely disinterested, and besides, it had a quality which could only exist between women, between women just grown up. It was protective, on her side; sprang from a sense of being in league together, a presentiment of something that was bound to part them (they spoke of marriage always as a catastrophe)" (38–39).

Clarissa's figuring of lesbianism as an interlude—that brief moment unannexed to childhood or adulthood "between women just grown up"— is another example of her motivated forgetfulness. Her retrospective insistence on the discontinuous and interruptible character of lesbianism functions as her defense against a lesbianism that, avowed only in the register of recollection, has annexed to itself the violent force of interruption. Not only do the events of the past—her affair with Sally being the event most sedimented as Clarissa's past—refuse to be corralled to history, continuing instead through memory to interrupt the present, but Clarissa's feeling for women is neither restricted to the past nor indeed to Sally: "She could not resist sometimes yielding to the charm of a woman, not a girl, of a woman confessing, as to her they often did, some scrape, some folly. And whether it was pity, or their beauty, or that she was older, or some accident—like a faint scent, or a violin next door (so strange is the power of sounds at certain moments), she did undoubtedly then feel what men felt" (36).

"As if she had known all along that something would interrupt": Clarissa's fearful bracing of herself against the inevitability of interruption comes to consolidate itself as a central aspect of her personality, although the interruption she most defends herself against is the rupturing into her adult life of lesbian affect.[25] Hypersensitive to interruption, Clarissa experiences at the heart of her own life "an exquisite suspense" (34), profound enough to affect even her perception of the regularities of clock time: "For having lived in Westminister—how many years now? over twenty,—one feels even in the midst of traffic, or waking at night, Clarissa was positive, a particular hush, a solemnity; an indescribable pause; a suspense (but that might be her heart, affected, they said, by influenza) before Big Ben strikes. There! Out it boomed. First a warning, musical; then the hour, irrevocable. The leaden circles dissolved in the air" (6). The chimes of Big Ben, so central to the plotting of *Mrs. Dalloway*—for many months the novel's working title was *The Hours*—both interrupt and advance the narrative action. Big Ben's striking of the hours—like the repetition across the novel of the sentence "The leaden circles dissolved in the air"—is generally discussed in terms of the novel's many connecting devices, which function to draw together in imagined community diverse characters, some of whom never meet, through the simultaneity of their experience.[26] Yet Clarissa experiences her anticipation of the clock's chime idiosyncratically and, moreover, as a moment of disengagement from the immediacies of everyday life, as time out of time. Her speculation that the suspenseful pause she detects before Big Ben strikes the hour might have less to do with the clock than the syncopation of her influenza-weakened heart incorporates as a somatic symptom her fearfulness of interruption, of time. No organic cause need be sought for Clarissa's symptoms, although her heart, as she guesses, is undoubtedly its seat. Clarissa's recurrent memories of her love for Sally pull like an undertow against the progressive advance of narrative temporality such that "she feared time itself" (34). Like the "indescribable pause" Clarissa hears before Big Ben's magisterial chiming of the hour, the alibi of recollection forces an opportunistic gap in the chronological unravelings of story that repudiates even as it maintains Clarissa's lesbian affect, animating it in the present in order to confirm its location in the past.

Stream of Consciousness: The Subject in Memory

One of the most sustained effects of *Mrs. Dalloway*'s literary-technical experiments with stream of consciousness is its representation of homosexuality as always already in the past. As a technology of memory, *Mrs. Dalloway*'s stream-of-consciousness technique complicates, while attempting to regulate, lesbianism's time frames, its mediation of the relations between past and present. Not first a literary but a psychological concept, stream of consciousness was defined by William James, in his 1890 *The Principles of Psychology*. "Consciousness," he writes, "does not appear to itself chopped up in bits. Such words as 'chain' or 'train' do not describe it fitly as it presents itself in the first instance. It is nothing jointed; it flows. A 'river' or a 'stream' are the metaphors by which it is most naturally described. In talking of it hereafter, let us call it the stream of thought, of consciousness, or of subjective life."[27] In arguing for a stream, rather than a train or chain, as the foundational metaphor for human consciousness, James refers his reader to the illustrative circumstances of what two men—or boys—waking up in bed together, can remember of the night before. In part because I am charmed by the way in which James's scenario of two men in the same bed exemplifies for the modern reader less the workings of recollection than the spectacle of two men in bed together, in part because *Mrs. Dalloway*'s representation of same-sex desire depends crucially on the breaking of the rule James's scenario strives to enforce, I cite James here at length:

> When Peter and Paul wake up in the same bed, and recognise that they have been asleep, each one of them mentally reaches back and makes connection with but *one* of the two streams of thought which were broken by the sleeping hours. As the current of an electrode buried in the ground unerringly finds its way to its own similarly buried mate, across no matter how much intervening earth; so Peter's present instantly finds out Peter's past, and never by mistake knits itself on to that of Paul. Paul's thought in turn is as little liable to go astray. The past thought of Peter is appropriated by the present Peter alone. He may have a *knowledge*, and a correct one too, of what Paul's last drowsy states of mind were as he sank into sleep, but it is an entirely different sort of knowledge from that which he has of his own last states. He *remembers* his own states, whilst he only *conceives* of Paul's.[28]

Earlier in his discussion, James summarizes the rule of which his example of Peter and Paul is a demonstration: "Neither contemporaneity, nor proximity in space, nor similarity of quality and content are able to fuse thoughts together which are sundered by this barrier of belonging to different personal minds. The breaches between such thoughts are the most absolute breaches in nature."[29]

Of course, Woolf's novel is noted for its vaulting of such impediments, its fusing of consciousnesses precisely on the grounds of temporal or spatial proximity, likeness of type or nature.[30] While *Mrs. Dalloway* licenses the temporal disjunctions of its narrative by fashioning them after the disjunctions of characters' reminiscences, equally the novel's representation of a collective consciousness puts pressure on the coherence of this system of characterization, in which each proper name lays a claim to an individuated sentience. At these moments, Woolf does not naturalize stream of consciousness by confining it within the bounds of character but turns its untrammeled and associative rhythms to the task of animating quicknesses or affinities between characters, in a stylistic reinforcement of Clarissa's belief that her self exceeds her materiality, "that somehow in the streets of London, on the ebb and flow of things, here, there, she survived, Peter survived, lived in each other, she being part, she was positive, of the trees at home; of the house there, ugly, rambling all to bits and pieces as it was; part of people she had never met" (11).

The wash of consciousness that throughout the novel pulls Clarissa into alignment with Septimus Smith, a traumatized war veteran who takes his own life toward the novel's end, is perhaps the purest example of Woolf's representation of a consciousness in excess of a subjectivity. While other simultaneities and coincidences that might equally seem to violate the coherence of character can be attributed, within the novel's networks of friendship and acquaintance, to shared memories or sympathetic rapport, Clarissa and Septimus never meet. Clarissa's posthumous reconstruction of Septimus's consciousness in the novel's climactic penultimate scene is widely assumed to index both Woolf's technical virtuosity and Clarissa's transcendence of her own history. Licensed across a range of embodied narrative perspectives yet seeming to belong to no one, this collective consciousness is pressed at *Mrs. Dalloway*'s close into the service of the novelistic drive to render heterosexuality and homosexuality chronologically distinct.

Woolf was anxious enough about critical assessments of Clarissa and Septimus's remoteness from each other at the level of the narrative's action to proffer, as if casually, in her introduction to the novel's 1928 Modern Library edition a detail "of little importance or none perhaps" in order to contextualize their relationship—namely, that "in the first version Septimus, who later is intended to be her double, had no existence; and that Mrs Dalloway was originally to kill herself, or perhaps merely to die at the end of the party."[31] Like many another obedient reader, I want here to consider Clarissa and Septimus as each other's double not simply in their shared homoeroticism but in the doubled ways in which their homosexuality is played out in relation to trauma, to the violent simultaneity of past and present: in short, to memory.

Shell Shock and Homosexuality: The Dislocations of Memory

Septimus Warren Smith is first described standing in the crowd that gathers—within sight of Mrs. Dalloway, who is now looking out on to the street from the window of Miss Pym's flower shop—to speculate about the identity of the personage obscured inside the impressive motorcar that backfires and then is caught momentarily in traffic outside Mulberry's shop window: "Septimus Warren Smith, aged about thirty, pale-faced, beak-nosed, wearing brown shoes and a shabby overcoat, with hazel eyes which had that look of apprehension in them which makes strangers apprehensive too" (17). The extremity of Septimus's apprehensions derange the world around him. Although "every one looked at the motor car," he fancies himself the object of each staring eye and even the impediment to the car's progress: "It is I who am blocking the way, he thought" (18). He struggles against some unspecified but repressed knowledge, "some horror . . . come almost to the surface and . . . about to burst into flames"

(18). His frequent imaginings of suicide—under the wheels of a cart, a train, an omnibus—are a relief to him in a world come unhinged, straining to communicate with him via the sky-writing airplane, the sparrows that sing to him in Greek, even the black tracery of branches against the sky.

The free availability of Septimus's symptoms has not facilitated his literary critical diagnosis. While it is widely agreed that he is mentally disturbed, there is some dispute as to the origins of his derangement, opinion being divided as to whether his trauma stems from his experiences of the war or his guilty disavowal of his love for his officer, Evans, a man "undemonstrative in the company of women" (96). David Dowling favors the shell shock theory, pointing out that Septimus first enlisted because of his passion for Miss Isabel Pole, his lecturer in Shakespeare; that his relationship with Evans was "not necessarily homosexual," and that his phobia about heterosexual intercourse and intimacy with his wife might be a consequence of "the suppression of the libido" consistent with the trauma of shell shock.[32] Mitchell Leaska claims that "nowhere in the novel is there any evidence that Septimus's psychological state is the result of shell shock," arguing instead that Septimus's "psychic paralysis" is the consequence of the taboo nature of his love for Evans.[33] The critical reception of *Mrs. Dalloway* demonstrates that the novel's opaque referentiality affords both readings: There is, of course, no sense in which the possibility of Septimus's postwar trauma cancels the possibility of his homosexuality, no sense in which his psychotic homosexual panic might be said at least to protect him from the equally brutalizing symptoms of shell shock.[34] Reading Septimus as equivalently traumatized by his sexual inclinations and his experiences of war enables a consideration of Woolf's mnemic representations of homosexuality as crucially amplified by the medicalization of shell shock. Shell shock, then, becomes the framing discourse for Septimus's homosexuality, its clinical presentations slantingly addressing the particularities of Clarissa's lesbian bent, which is also characterized by a traumatized relationship to time and chronology.

Mrs. Dalloway's characterization of shell shock reinforces the novel's representation of homosexuality as a disordering of chronology. In prominent circulation during the years of *Mrs. Dalloway*'s composition, psychoanalytically informed understandings of shell shock articulate symptoms in which a subject, through conscious or unconscious recollection, remains traumatized in the present by his permanent vulnerability to his past—symptoms that the novel in turn hollows out for the representation of homosexuality. Shell shock, then, is not only the defining context for *Mrs. Dalloway*'s representation of Septimus's homosexuality; it is equally a neurotic intensification of those anxieties of chronology that characterize Clarissa's lesbianism. Even allowing for their considerable differences (the most articulable of these might be age, gender, and—not least—class), the character in *Mrs. Dalloway* most like Septimus is Clarissa.[35]

Despite Dr. Holmes's bluff diagnosis that "there was nothing the matter with [Septimus]" (27), nothing could be more immediately obvious to the reader than the spectacular cluster of his symptoms: his pathological feelings of dread; the deadening of the register of his empathetic emotions; his inability to hold himself distinct from the world of everyday objects; his delusions of his own messianic importance. While the severity of Septimus's derangement outstrips the symptoms commonly attributed to shell shock—"paralyses and muscular contractures of the arms, legs, hands and feet, loss of sight, speech and hearing, choreas, palsies and tics, mental fugues, catatonia and obsessive behaviour, amnesia, severe sleeplessness, and terrifying nightmares"—the novel persistently locates his experience of the war as the explanatory site for his psychotic transformation.[36] Yet *Mrs. Dalloway* has next to nothing to say of the war as an event, almost nothing to say of the shellings, the battles, the conditions of trench life, the minutiae of everyday army life that might be understood to be the catalyst for Septimus's shell shock—a significant gap in a novel so characterized by the deftness of its characters' allusive reconstructions of their pasts.

Deprived of any content, the recurring allusions to "the war" come to seem almost symptomatic, as when Sir William Bradshaw, the Harley Street specialist, observing Septimus's repetition of the same word, notes that "he was attaching meanings to words of a symbolic kind. A serious symptom to be noted on the card" (106). The repeated nominal references to the war that recycle the most pared-down account of Septimus's combat career—"Septimus had fought; he was brave" (27)—only once open out into an extended account of the details of his experience of war:

> There in the trenches . . . he developed manliness; he was promoted; he drew the attention, indeed the affection of his officer, Evans by name. It was a case of two dogs playing on a hearth-rug; one worrying a paper screw, snarling, snapping, giving a pinch, now and then, at the old dog's ear; the other lying somnolent, blinking at the fire, raising a paw, turning and growling good-temperedly. They had to be together, share with each other, fight with each other, quarrel with each other. But when Evans . . . was killed, just before the Armistice, in Italy, Septimus, far from showing any emotion or recognising that here was the end of a friendship, congratulated himself upon feeling very little and very reasonably. The War had taught him. It was

> sublime. He had gone through the whole show, friendship, European War, death, had won promotion, was still under thirty and bound to survive. He was right there. The last shells missed him. He watched them explode with indifference. (95–96)

Here, with the theater of war contracted to the domesticated spread of "a hearth-rug," the obliqueness of Woolf's representation of the war constitutes the account of Septimus's combat experience through an equally oblique account of his love for and loss of Evans.[37] Initially bolstered by his display of soldierly composure, his emotional battening down comes to undo Septimus—"For now that it was all over, truce signed, and the dead buried, he had, especially in the evening, these sudden thunderclaps of fear. He could not feel" (96)—and, in a panic, he proposes to Rezia, an Italian milliner.

Septimus's marriage and his return to London with his wife are no protection against his wretchedness. He is seized alternately by two neurotic states, oppositional in their affect if not their intensity: aggrandizement and guilt. In the grip of the former, he imagines himself entrusted with "the supreme secret [that] must be told to the Cabinet; first, that trees are alive; next, there is no crime; next, love, universal love," a revelation that he jots down in the shorthand form "no crime; love" (75); in the throes of the latter, he knows himself to have "committed an appalling crime and been condemned to death by human nature" (107). As symptoms, both of these psychotic conditions gesture associatively less to the war itself than to Septimus's ungrieved loss of his relationship with Evans. Both index the criminal nature of any sexual connection between men: the one to overturn it in favor of a revised parliamentary legislation that has nothing against any of love's forms; the other to nail it more firmly to a punitively heterosexual natural order.

In Septimus's moment of greatest ascertainment, and hence his moment of greatest insanity, Evans appears to him in his rented lodgings: "It was at that moment . . . that the great revelation took place. A voice spoke from behind the screen. Evans was speaking. The dead were with him" (103). Septimus's perception of the apparitional Evans raises to the second power memory's more recuperable disruptions of the relationships between past and present so characteristic of the novel's narration. More than a figure from the past, Evans in his resurrection from the dead marks the extremity of the novel's figuring of the permeability of the present, its saturation with the past. Septimus's hallucination of Evans not only literalizes the raising of the dead that, as Miller argues, structures the narration as a whole—"*Mrs. Dalloway* has the form of an All Souls' Day in which

Peter Walsh, Sally Seton, and the rest rise from the dead to come to Clarissa's party"[38]—but it also emphasizes as homosexual the flashback of desirous identification that runs a line between present and past.[39]

The disorderings of propriety, of human nature, of "marrying ... [and] having children" (13) that homosexuality might be said to effect is figured in *Mrs. Dalloway* as the disordering of temporality itself. When Rezia says " 'It is time' " (78), reminding Septimus of their midday appointment with Bradshaw, the very word *time* detonates for Septimus an associative explosion that ends predictably with the reappearance of Evans: "The word 'time' split its husk; poured its riches over him; and from his lips fell like shells, like shavings from a plane, without his making them, hard, white, imperishable, words, and flew to attach themselves to their place in an ode to Time; an immortal ode to time. He sang. Evans answered from behind the tree" (78).[40] Septimus's psychotic meditation on time conjures up his beloved Evans, restoring the dead not to life but to the living and marking the furthest reach of *Mrs. Dalloway*'s homosexual disruptions to chronology.

The Death of Homosexuality

Just as Septimus's temporal disorders inevitably take on a homosexual cast, so his restoration to an ordered world of rationality is marked by a recuperative heterosexuality. After days of sustained madness culminating in Evans's resurrection from the dead, Septimus's recovery is measurable in the extent to which he puts aside his earlier phobic conviction that "love between man and woman was repulsive" and recognizes himself not simply within the particulars of his own marriage but within the institutionalized protocols of marriage itself (99). The first description of Septimus restored to health seems almost unremarkable:

> Through his eyelashes he could see her blurred outline; her little black body; her face and hands; her turning movements at the table, as she took up a reel, or looked (she was apt to lose things) for her silk. She was making a hat for Mrs Filmer's married daughter, whose name was—he had forgotten her name.
> "What is the name of Mrs Filmer's married daughter?" he asked. (155–56)

Here, the return of the real, steeped as it is in the everyday banalities of married life, undercuts the distorted grandeur of Septimus's previous derangement. Unperturbed by the once-horrifying sight of his wife, his perception of the conventionality of the scene is evidence of his recovery. The very ordinariness of Septimus's inquiry about a forgotten name is at once evidence of his recovery and of what he has recovered from. The first category in Freud's discussion of everyday parapraxes is the forgetting of proper names, among which he notes "there is a type of forgetting which is motivated by repression."[41] An indication of Septimus's return to health—Freud's fondness for parapraxes depends on the fact that their occurrence is "very common and very familiar" and "since they can be observed in any healthy person, have nothing to do with illnesses"—his forgetting of a woman's married name is recognizable as a defense against the knowledge of institutionalized heterosexuality, a displaced refusal to consider the mechanisms of patronymic reproduction.[42]

As the objects of his previous fancy reveal themselves as everyday items, now solid and unalarming in their domesticity—a bleak crag resolves into a sofa; the faces of the dead into patterns on a dividing screen—Septimus's horror of marriage reorganizes itself as a pleasure and a contentment. It is this scene, constituted in the name and place of heterosexuality, that Dr. Holmes intrudes on in order to have Septimus committed, and it is his fear of its being disbanded that has a reluctant Septimus—"he did not want to die"—throw himself out the window to his death on the railings below (164). Septimus's suicide, the repeated threat of which once had marked his alienation from his wife, now speaks to his desire not to be separated from her. As Septimus lies "horribly mangled" on the street below, his wife hears him in the anthropomorphic tolling of Big Ben—"The clock was striking—one, two, three: how sensible the sound was . . . like Septimus himself"—the heterosexual restitution of his death figured in his posthumous synchronization with the real of clock time (165).

In terms of the simplest sequence of plot events, Dr. Holmes is to blame for Septimus's death, his ascent of the staircase to the Warren Smiths' room propelling Septimus out the window as surely as if the two men had been hydraulically connected. Holmes's blustering incredulousness at this outcome—"Who could have foretold it? A sudden impulse, no one was in the least to blame"—only serves to implicate him more thoroughly in those networks of culpability whose existence he denies (165). While the likelihood of Septimus's death has hovered over *Mrs. Dalloway* as the overdetermined closure of that line of narrative—he threatens suicide a number of times; he is identified with homosexual desire—there is something in me that shares Holmes's dumb amazement at Septimus's final plunge: "And why the devil he did it, Dr Holmes could not conceive" (165). However alarming Septimus finds Holmes, his death is caused not by the doctor but by the requirements of the representational field of the novel itself. That is, the hydraulic system that has Holmes climbing as Septimus plunges is but an effect of the novel's more comprehensive "organiz[ation] around the contrary penchants of rising and falling."[43] It is this larger novelistic patterning that underwrites the near-critical consensus that Septimus is a scapegoat for Clarissa; that, through their counterweighted narratives, his death makes hers unnecessary.[44] Yet, better placed than Holmes to apprehend the doubling of Septimus and Clarissa, something still disquiets me about Septimus's dying for Clarissa, something that jars the logics of substitutability that underwrite the scapegoat's efficacy.

Clarissa herself, while able to reconstruct without being told the precise means of Septimus's death, cannot initially say why Septimus has died: "He had killed himself—but how? Always her body went through it, when she was told, first, suddenly, of an accident; her dress flamed, her body burnt. He had thrown himself from a window. Up had flashed the ground; through him, blundering, bruising, went the rusty spikes. Then he lay with a thud, thud, thud in his brain, and then a suffocation of blackness. So she saw it. But why had he done it?" (202). Her inexplicable ability to recall the details of Septimus's death, from his plunge out the window to his penetration on his landlady's area railings, is the most extreme demonstration of their figural twinship in the representational economy of *Mrs. Dalloway*. It is the cumulative weight of their frequent doubling—"She felt somehow very like him—the young man who had killed himself" (204)—that licenses Clarissa's subsequent interpretation of Septimus's death.

"Why had he done it?" Of her three speculations—to preserve the integrity of his homosexual desire; to escape the bullying of his specialist, Sir William Bradshaw; to lighten the pressures of life itself—it is the first and most speculative that is prioritized not only by the novel but in subsequent critical readings: "But this young man who had killed himself—had he plunged holding his treasure? 'If it were now to die, 'twere now to be most happy,' she had said to herself once, coming down in white" (202–203). Clarissa's attribution of homosexual cause to Septimus's death is made through associative reference to her feelings for Sally at Bourton, as an earlier passage, whose play on the oppositional movements of rising and falling finds its final expression in Septimus's jump, makes clear:

> She could remember going cold with excitement and doing her hair in a kind of ecstasy... with the rooks flaunting up and down in the pink evening light, and dressing, and going downstairs, and feeling as she crossed the hall "if it were now to die 'twere now to be most happy." That

was her feeling—Othello's feeling, and she felt it, she was convinced, as strongly as Shakespeare meant Othello to feel it, all because she was coming down to dinner in a white frock to meet Sally Seton! (39)[45]

Just as they have tended to accept, despite Septimus's own more prosaic account, Clarissa's numinous gloss of his death as an "attempt to communicate," an "embrace," so critics have tended to follow Clarissa's interpretative lead on the homosexualization of Septimus's suicide (202).[46] Yet the immediate context for his death is not homosexual but heterosexual: His brief recovery is measurable in terms of his heterosexual acculturation, evidenced in both his newfound affection for his wife and his inhabitation of the conventions of patronymic transmission.

As one schooled in the narrative grammar of homosexuality and death, which enables not only Clarissa's speculation about the cause of Septimus's suicide but also its scholarly attribution to the higher authority of the novel itself, I detect something excessive, almost luxuriously wasteful, in the way in which *Mrs. Dalloway* restores Septimus to heterosexuality only to have him jump to his death some few paragraphs later. Even if Clarissa's evaluation of Septimus's death is written off as an educated guess or a sympathetic hunch that, in falling short of the mark, registers the limitations of the knowledge of characters and not the diegesis, there is still something overcompensatory about the novel's handling of Septimus, his repudiation of homosexuality and his death—two narrative twists that should neutralize rather than secure each other. Although there seems something almost contradictory in *Mrs. Dalloway*'s curing and killing of Septimus (with him being made to wear both the classic literary punishments for homosexuality, as if they did not underwrite two counterpoised economies of redemption and reprobation), the underlying logic that rationalizes the excessiveness with which he is written out of the narrative is the novel's desire to fix homosexuality in the past. E. M. Forster's first reading of *Mrs. Dalloway* was so attuned to this imperative, most legible in the novel's articulation of homosexuality as memory, that he misread Clarissa's end in Septimus's: "Does [Clarissa] likewise commit suicide? I thought she did the first time I read the book."[47]

If critics have tended to follow Clarissa in reading Septimus's suicide in terms of homosexuality's dying fall, then equally they have interpreted her reaction to his death as abreactive. Even relatively oppositional readings of the novel's treatment of Clarissa's same-sex desire agree on the cathartic effect of Septimus's death. Consider, for instance, Emily Jensen's and Elizabeth Abel's readings of *Mrs. Dalloway*, the former seeing Clarissa's passage from Sally to Richard as a "respectable suicide," the latter as "a developmental turn."[48] Jensen argues that Clarissa's thirty-year repression of her lesbian feeling for Sally has been more rather than less successful until Septimus's suicide figures for her "the self-destruction involved in her own life": "she recognizes that she has committed her own kind of suicide: she has in fact committed one of the most common of suicides for women, that respectable destruction of the self in the interest of the other."[49] With a changed emphasis, Abel reads the same scene differently. Like Jensen, Abel reads Septimus's suicide as a psychodramatization of Clarissa's own lesbian loss—"Septimus's death evokes in Clarissa the knowledge of what death saves and what she has lost; her grief is not for Septimus but for herself"—but one that enables her to break her developmental impasse and move toward a heterosexual orientation: "By recalling to Clarissa the power of her past *and* the only method of eternalizing it, Septimus enables Clarissa to acknowledge and renounce its hold, to embrace the imperfect pleasures of adulthood more completely."[50] Despite the marked differences in their interpretations, both Jensen and Abel, like many other critics, identify Clarissa's recognition of the loss of her adolescent love for Sally as the repressed knowledge that, once brought to consciousness, facilitates her psychological transformation at the close of the novel.[51]

Yet could anything be less repressed than Clarissa's passionate and frequent memories of a love lost—memories in which the intense registration of the love is held in precise balance against the intense registration of its loss? Her imaginative veneering of Septimus's suicide with his homosexuality speaks not only of the widespread cultural assumption of the doomed trajectory of same-sex desire but also of her own necrophiliac investment in homosexuality as a past event. It is not the loss of lesbianism but its continuous interrupting presence that is repressed in Clarissa's repeated remembering of Sally, as evidenced in her insistent framing of that love *as* memory—that is, in her memorialization of lesbianism. Only once does Clarissa acknowledge the persistence into adulthood of her lesbian desire. In one of the novel's most cited passages, she gives opaque account of her adult feeling for certain women, comparing this expansiveness with the confines of her attic bedroom with its single bed and her nocturnal readings of Baron Marbot's *Memoirs*:

> She did undoubtedly then feel what men felt. Only for a moment; but it was enough. It was a sudden revelation, a tinge like a blush which one tried to check and then, as it spread, one yielded to its expansion, and rushed to the furtherest verge and there quivered and felt the world come closer, swollen with some astonishing significance, some pressure of rap-

ture, which split its thin skin and gushed and poured with an extraordinary alleviation over the cracks and sores. Then, for that moment, she had seen an illumination; a match burning in a crocus; an inner meaning almost expressed. But the close withdrew; the hard softened. It was over—the moment. Against such moments (with women too) there contrasted (as she laid her hat down) the bed and Baron Marbot and the candle half-burnt. (36)

For all its opacity—its retreat into the unindividuated pronominal form of "one," its stream of suggestive verbs (*yielded, rushed, quivered, gushed,* and *poured*) that can barely lay claim to a subject, its evocative indeterminacy bearing down eventually on the weird specificity of the match in the crocus—Clarissa denies the homoeroticism of this passage, her parenthetical aside—"(with women too)"—disavowing, by seeming belatedly to allow, its lesbian cast.

Clarissa's repression of any possibility of sexual desire between women articulated in the present is marked by her symptomatic relapses into that almost historic period monumentalized by Sally Seton, her flashbacks to Bourton regular enough to seem finally metronomic. Sally, for instance, provides the means by which the unbounded blushing, rushing, and gushing of lesbian affect in the present is immediately channeled back into the past: "But this question of love (she thought, putting her coat away), this falling in love with women. Take Sally Seton; her relation in the old days with Sally Seton. Had not that, after all, been love?" (37). With the persistence of some fantasized origin that will write itself across each subsequent scene, "her relation in the old days with Sally Seton" comes to stand not just as an exemplification but the imaginable limit of "this falling in love with women," the latter collapsing back into the former as if there was nothing to distinguish between them.

Clarissa's insistent re-creation of same-sex desire as a past event underwrites her identification of Septimus's suicide as homosexual. The affinity she feels for the dead man is based on her perception that her homosexuality, like his, is a thing of the past: "And once she had walked on the terrace at Bourton" (203). Clarissa's swift reconception of death—"Oh! thought Clarissa, in the middle of my party, here's death, she thought" (201)—as the death of homosexuality facilitates her return, unchanged, to the party: "The clock was striking. The leaden circles dissolved in the air. But she must go back. She must assemble" (204–205). Far from abreactive, far from shocking her into the realization of lesbian loss, the knowledge of an adult world recognized in its here and now, Clarissa's imagining of Septimus's homosexual death provides another support to her continuing fantasy of homosexuality as quarantined from the present moment, defined in relation to a temporality that is not, that cannot be, this one. Boasting a prodigious memory—"she could remember scene after scene at Bourton": Sally's way with a cigarette; Sally's naked run along the upstairs corridor; most memorably, Sally's kiss—Clarissa forgets one thing: Memory is not the securing of the present against the past, the proof of their distinction, but the transformation of the past brought to bear on the present, the sign of their cohabitation (8). Clarissa's attempt to characterize same-sex desire as historical, no longer present, as something only available through recollection, is undone by the very mechanism that enables it, the doubled figure of memory itself, its hybridization of chronology continually rewriting the past into the present.[52]

Don't Forget Miss Kilman

In a novel whose tender representations of homosexual affect are legitimized by homosexuality's confinement to the past, Miss Kilman is, if not actually the exception that proves the rule, the excessively unpalatable figuration of homosexuality in the present tense. In love with Clarissa's seventeen-year-old daughter, Elizabeth, and unable to detain her a moment longer at their afternoon tea table at the Army and Navy Stores, the ardent Miss Kilman presses herself on the departing young woman in the only way she can, hoping at least to inhabit her in the form of a memory: " 'Don't quite forget me,' said Doris Kilman" (146). But who could forget Miss Kilman? Who could forget the crude connotation of lesbianism encoded even in Miss Kilman's name, its lack of subtlety little alleviated by the etymological disclosure that the family name was spelled "Kiehlman in the eighteenth century" (136)? Unlike any of *Mrs. Dalloway*'s other characters, less in her idiosyncrasies than her falling outside the narrative's fairly elasticized sympathies, Miss Kilman moves through the world savaged by her sense that "she had been cheated," the privileges and pleasures of life going instead to the undeserving—the frivolous, the rich, the complacent (136).[53] "Bitter and burning" (137) and "degradingly poor" (136), Miss Kilman's moral superiority is underwritten by her religious conviction, neither of which can deliver her from "that violent grudge [she has] against the world which had scorned her, sneered at her, cast her off, beginning with this indignity—the infliction of her unlovable body which people could not bear to see" (142).[54]

"Had Stein written *Mrs Dalloway*," speculates Kevin Kopelson, "Miss Kilman might be its heroine."[55] As fascinating as it is to imagine the contours of a novel that might take Miss Kilman as its center, her abiding sense that "she had been cheated" is borne out even in her being elbowed out of the narrative sympathies, her cameo appearance two-thirds through the novel emphasizing the ways in which her story is already in the service of another, whose name is, of course, also the novel's: Mrs. Dalloway. More even than Septimus, Miss Kilman is whittled down to the single narrative function of doubling Clarissa, recalling not only her adolescent passion for Sally but also what she might have become "if she could have had her life over again" (13).[56] "A monster grubbing at [Clarissa's] roots," Miss Kilman is the distorted figure of Clarissa's repression of her knowledge of lesbianism as a mode of being, a passionately affective inclination, habitable in the present (15). "Ah," thinks Clarissa in the middle of her party, "how she hated [Miss Kilman]—hot, hypocritical, corrupt; with all that power; Elizabeth's seducer; the woman who had crept in to steal and defile.... She hated her: she loved her" (192). The violence of her loathing for Miss Kilman flipping unexpectedly into an equally passionate affection, Clarissa's memorialization of her lesbianism ensures that her identification with Miss Kilman is profoundly ambivalent.[57]

While Miss Kilman "despised Mrs Dalloway from the bottom of her heart," her rigorous program of self-discipline and religious fervor only diluting that emotion to a savage pity, Clarissa's equally violent hatred for Miss Kilman is always pitching into its opposite emotion, the disavowed possibility of her love for Miss Kilman a powerful fantasy of lesbianism in Clarissa's present: "For it was not her one hated but the idea of her, which undoubtedly had gathered in to itself a great deal that was not Miss Kilman; had become one of those spectres with which one battles in the night; one of those spectres who stand astride us and suck up half our life-blood, dominators and tyrants; for no doubt with another throw of the dice, had the black been uppermost and not the white, she would have loved Miss Kilman! But not in this world. No" (14–15). Framed in the conditional and further alienated from the present by its imaginary location in some parallel world, the possibility of Clarissa's love for Miss Kilman is repeatedly raised in a demonstration of its impossibility. For all that Clarissa fancies her as "some prehistoric monster," Miss Kilman's monstrousness derives not from her remoteness to but her immersion in the present, from the contemporaneity of her lesbianism (139). Saddled with "her unlovable body" and the more cumbersome burden of inhabiting a sexuality by herself, Miss Kilman is the novel's homeopathic rendering of that possibility it is always defending itself against—the possibility of homosexuality in the narrative present, its ambitions, indistinguishable from those of narrative more generally, bearing down on the future.

FIVE

First Wife, Second Wife

Sexual Perversion and the Problem of Precedence in Rebecca

In the anxious field of sexual identification, sequence is its own alibi. Purporting to do nothing more than take instruction from the principles of temporal order, sequence underwrites those regulatory narratives that establish heterosexuality as the most developed form of sexual identification and homosexuality as a not-quite heterosexual disposition that is nevertheless not only held distinct from heterosexuality but also constituted as its repressed origin.[1] In this charged context, sequence—what comes before and what comes after—often tips into precedence—what comes first and what comes second—as the logics of causality it allegedly secures mark themselves as already in the defensive service of heterosexuality.[2] Although the magisterial reification and mutually exclusive, hierarchical definition of heterosexuality and homosexuality is perhaps the most recognizable effect of the ideological work of sexual sequence, the cultural insistence on the sequential nature of sexuality—its preconditions and its final outcomes, its causally connected development—defends less against homosexuality per se than against an undifferentiated sexual desire—the polymorphous drives and impulses of which exceed easy narrativization.[3]

I want to chase these thoughts about sexual sequence and the ideological work it does in framing sexualities as, on the one hand, coherent and distinct, and on the other differently valued across a series of texts that take Daphne du Maurier's 1938 novel, *Rebecca*, as its lynchpin: du Maurier's novel itself; Alfred Hitchcock's 1940 film adaptation, *Rebecca*; subsequent readings of Hitchcock's film in feminist film criticism; and Susan

Hill's 1993 sequel to the original novel, *Mrs. de Winter*. The highly charged effects of sexual sequence and the even more electrifying possibility of its failure continually rehearsed in du Maurier's *Rebecca*—perhaps nowhere more evident than in the narrative's anxious exploration of serial matrimony, the second Mrs. de Winter's uneasy succession of the first—equally structure the novel's spin-offs, not only their diegetic struggles to secure a heterosexual femininity against a previous sexual ambivalence but also their complex serial relationship to each other and the text they take as their point of narrative origin. Reading across this textual sequence with its varying investments in *Rebecca*, I want to analyze in relation to female sexuality something that exceeds the specificity of the *Rebecca* sequence, something I might yet in this context call the *Rebecca*-effect: the confounding of—by attempting to make a sequential distinction between—legitimate and illegitimate forms of female sexuality. Not in the hope of resolving questions of sexual nomination or taxonomy, but in order to specify further the narrative workings of cause and effect, of before and after, of first and second, of homosexuality and heterosexuality, I trace across that textual series an increasingly neurotic interest in recuperating an authoritative and unidirectional narrative of sexual sequence.

Reading du Maurier's *Rebecca*

Precisely because the overt and, in the end, futile representational struggle of *Rebecca* is to quarantine perverse sexuality within the confines of character, I am not interested in reading *Rebecca* as a novel that corrals sexual perversity at the level of the proper name, that depicts Mrs. Danvers and the dead Rebecca as excessively but, in terms of the novelistic narration, superfluously pathological. Instead, I read *Rebecca* as a novel undone by its obsession with plotting and replotting the coordinates of a sexual field, the representational strategies and effects of which are less about registering the specific formations of a given sexual perversion than about rehearsing the persistent yet vain attempts to define and enforce sexual registration itself through the regulatory technologies of sequence.

Dead before the diegetic frame of the novel, Rebecca is very much alive in terms of its narrative representation of a feminine sexuality governed by the principles of sequence. The ambivalent mark of a perverse anteriority—abnormal, promiscuous, infertile, diseased, masculine, misanthropic in the literal sense—Rebecca is the fantasized center of a nimbus of sexual degeneracy that, recognizable in the novel's narrative structure, its metaphorical language, and its unresolved teetering between the gothic and the romance, anticipates but equally defers the naturalized legitimacy and authority of her successor's heterosexuality. This nonspecific sexual perversity, nowhere named in du Maurier's novel, at certain narrative moments comes to intimate a very specific sexual perversity—homosexuality—also figured culturally as unfeminine, nonreproductive, and unnatural, the historic specification of which, moreover, has not required its nomination. *Rebecca*'s nonspecific but, for that very reason, horrific representations of female perversity, framed by a novel obsessed with questions of precedence and sequence, attempt to distinguish but in the end muddy beyond recognition the culturally overdetermined line between good and bad female sexuality, heterosexuality and homosexuality, the desire to be a woman and the desire to have one.

Although du Maurier resisted such a labeling, *Rebecca* was both marketed and critically evaluated as a gothic romance. In prepublication publicity, Victor Gollancz, du Maurier's publisher, promoted the novel as "an exquisite love story" with "a brilliantly created atmosphere of suspense," and reviewers in both England and America frequently compared the novel to the classic of its genre, Charlotte Brontë's *Jane Eyre*.[4] The plot of *Rebecca* is widely known not only because of the canonic stature of its presumed antecedent or its own initial success and continued reprinting but also because of its stage and film adaptations and its more recent sequelization. Plot summaries, of course, weigh against more readerly pleasures, as anyone knows who has ever anxiously had to cut someone short with "Don't tell me what happens."[5] Not assuming universal familiarity with *Rebecca*'s plot, and because my argument rests on a distinction between a blandly chronological arrangement of its events and the forward and backward working of them in the narration, the precise textual calibration of anticipation and suspense through the registers of before and after, past and future, I venture a plot summary here.

A young woman, unnamed throughout the novel, working in Monte Carlo as the paid companion to a vulgar American, Mrs. van Hopper, meets and falls in love with the brooding and recently widowed Maxim de Winter. Hearing that she is leaving Monte Carlo with her employer, Maxim asks her to marry him, and they return to England, to his ancestral home of Manderley, as husband and wife. Painfully conscious of her unworldliness and sure that Maxim's remoteness is due to the grieving love he still feels for his first wife, Rebecca, the second Mrs. de Winter falls prey to the manipulative cruelties of the housekeeper, Mrs. Danvers, and her unyielding passion for Rebecca. Close to killing herself at Mrs. Danvers's suggestion, the second Mrs. de Winter is interrupted by a commotion from the bay where a boat has run aground. Although previously

Maxim had identified another drowned body as being that of his wife, in the subsequent diving explorations Rebecca's body is discovered inside her yacht sunken at the same site. Maxim confesses to his current wife that he did not make the misidentification in error but in order to conceal the fact that he had murdered the depraved Rebecca, on learning that she was pregnant, and stowed her body in her yacht before scuttling it in the bay. Thrilled to find that Rebecca was morally corrupt and moreover that Maxim never loved her, the second Mrs. de Winter supports him through the subsequent police investigation into the circumstances of Rebecca's death. After a suspenseful coronial inquiry, Rebecca's death is declared suicide, and Maxim is cleared of all suspicion. The case threatens to reopen, however, when Rebecca's cousin and former lover, Jack Favell, confronts Maxim, his second wife, and the local magistrate with fresh evidence—a note from Rebecca, written on the eve of her death—suggesting murder rather than suicide. This evidence causes the party to trace Rebecca's business on the last day of her life and, working through her appointments diary, they go to London to interview the doctor she consulted that afternoon. Expecting that he will confirm Rebecca's pregnancy and consequently strengthen the hypothesis of murder, the de Winters are surprised but relieved to find that Rebecca had lied about her condition and was instead terminally ill with a malignant uterine growth, a discovery that bears out the coroner's finding of suicide. As they drive home, off the hook at last, the de Winters find that Manderley is on fire, burning on the horizon. They retreat off shore, to some unspecified Mediterranean island, where—never mentioning the chain of events that delivered them to this condition—they live out a reassuringly dull exile.

What this plot summary does not catch at—as is the nature of plot summaries—are the temporal dislocations of the novel's narration. As its famous and often-quoted first line suggests—"Last night I dreamt I went to Manderley again"—*Rebecca* is largely a retrospective narration.[6] The most recent events in *Rebecca* constitute the opening chapters of the novel as the narrator describes her and her husband's self-imposed exile from England "on this indifferent island" (10). In the straightforward order of the plot summary, the retrospective narration of the rest of the novel specifies the series of past events that necessitated the de Winters' flight from and their nostalgic inclination toward England. Securing at its outset the heterosexual outcome of its plot, the retrospective weight of *Rebecca*'s narration is entirely formulaic: "memory spanning the years like a bridge," the narrator recalls the events in her past that account for her present condition (13). It would be a dull reader who missed her cues in the opening chapters—"Well, it is over now, finished and done with. I ride no more tormented, and both of us are free" (12)—who failed to recognize that here, as elsewhere, "we would do best to speak of the *anticipation of retrospection* as our chief tool in making sense of narrative, the master trope of its strange logic."[7] Yet the Russian formalist distinction between *fabula* and *sjuzet*—that is, the distinction between the ordering of events represented in the narrative and the narrative's own ordering of them—does not recuperate the novel's peculiar temporality, its frequent and proliferating switch points between tenses, its diegetic prioritization of the unstable, tumbling relationships among past, present, and future.

Less anticipated than the retrospective narrative is the narrator's inability to sustain herself in any temporal framing for long, her pitching back and forth between the scene she describes and those she imagines might precede or follow it, as she is processed, as if unwillingly, by the fantasies of an imagined past and future.[8] Not attributable to plot, these secondary switches in tense reinforce the narrator's frequent descriptions of herself as uncertain, transitional, and anxious. The attempt to imagine herself inhabiting more reassuring versions of her marriage—or, as I will shortly argue, more reassuring versions of her heterosexuality—no less than her painful reconstitution of a past she did not inhabit, emphasizes the narrator's position as the heroine of a gothic romance: frightened, unknowing, and powerless. Yet even more than it reinforces the narrator's generic function, the novel's fascinated shuttling between the past and the present is symptomatic of its continued yet failed attempt to secure the sequence of its own story, where that temporal obsession is the alibi for a sexual one, worked across the always-crumbling distinctions between the first and second Mrs. de Winters, between a perverse and a normative sexuality, between homosexuality and heterosexuality.[9] If the narrator's imaginary forward projections articulate her unambitious but tellingly unrealized hopes for her future—happily married, children—her equally imaginative plunges into the past implicate her in a series of desiring identifications with the sexually corrupt Rebecca, where the latter threatens to undermine any possibility of securing the former.[10]

Of all the many scenes in *Rebecca* in which the narrator, tremulous, with heightened senses and flagging confidence, puts herself in Rebecca's place—"Another one had poured the coffee from that same silver coffee pot, had placed the cup to her lips, had bent down to the dog, even as I was doing" (83)—the much-discussed scene in which Mrs. Danvers shows her Rebecca's bedroom condenses the ambiguous workings of desire that drive all of the narrator's identifications with the first wife. Letting herself into Rebecca's room for the first time and finding to her surprise that it is not swathed in dust-cloths like the other disused rooms of the west wing, the narrator predictably registers her momentary confusion as a temporal disturbance:

> For one desperate moment I thought that something had happened to my brain, that I was seeing back into Time, and looking upon the room as it used to be, before she died. . . . In a minute Rebecca herself would come back into the room, sit down before the looking-glass at her dressing-table, humming a tune, reach for her comb and run it through her hair. If she sat there I should see her reflection in the glass and she would see me too, standing like this by the door. (173; ellipsis in original)

This palimpsest effect—in which one time frame is superimposed on another—and the queer effect of that doubled image reflected in a further frame, that of the dressing-table mirror, is the novel's most concentrated remembering of that primal scene that spooks the narrative all the more efficiently for being nowhere spoken: the first and second Mrs. de Winters in their bedroom, at last, alone. Although she casts herself at this moment as an "uninvited guest" who "had strolled into my hostess's bedroom by mistake" (forgetting for the moment the determination with which she had made her way there), the narrator eclipses her first indiscretion with a second, taking a seat at the dressing-table, handling the hairbrushes, and looking at herself in the mirror (174). The mirror giving herself back nothing but her own, now solitary, reflection, "sallow and plain," she finds herself prey to "a growing sense of horror, of horror turning to despair" (174) and consoles herself as best she can by fingering Rebecca's dressing-gown, her slippers, and the bed quilt, tracing the monogrammed *R de W* on the nightgown case, pulling out the sheer nightgown, neither "touched [n]or laundered since it was last worn," and pressing it to her face to inhale its scent (174–75).

There is a kind of built-in exhaustion to these scenes in which the narrator hunts up traces of Rebecca, less like a detective than a lover bereft. The trawling of Rebecca's bedroom is a more conventionally eroticized experience than the previous wiping of fingers on her lipstick-stained handkerchief (125), wearing her clothes (113), and sitting in the imprint she left on the cushions of an armchair (83), as the arrival of Mrs. Danvers confirms. Always more than anyone bargains for—"triumphant, gloating, excited in a strange unhealthy way" (175)—Mrs. Danvers triangulates the scene, hot-wiring the traditional geometry of erotic desire. Like many another, Mrs. Danvers is a different woman in the bedroom than she appears in more public spaces: "her manner, instead of being still and unbending as it usually was, became startlingly familiar, fawning even"

(175–76). Smiling close, breathing on the narrator's cheek, taking hold of her arm and speaking in a newly "low and intimate voice," Mrs. Danvers runs her through her paces again: She shows her the bed, has her handle the nightgown and hold the dressing-gown against her as if for size; she forces Rebecca's slippers over her hands, instructs her to imagine Rebecca lying in bed, shows her the hairbrushes, opens Rebecca's wardrobe and has her feel the sable wrap and then press some scented velvet against her face; finally she shows her Rebecca's underclothes.

Although in this passage the narrator describes herself in the terrified thrall of Mrs. Danvers's pathological fixation with Rebecca—"I wanted to run away, but I couldn't move" (176)—what she is forced to do here, right down to the most intimate smelling of Rebecca's unwashed clothes, is no different from what she has just done in private of her own volition. The difference, then, is less one of agency than spectatorship. Forced to consider herself observed by Mrs. Danvers in these poses—just as Mrs. Danvers compels her to imagine herself the object of Rebecca's spectral gaze ("Do you think the dead come back and watch the living?" [181])—she is obliged to think those postures peculiarly hers. It is the confirming gaze of the other woman that authenticates those desiring identifications as—however fleeting, however partial—identity. When the silent narrator finally makes her noncommittal answer—repeating "I don't know" (181)—she fancies that this shift registers in the grain of her voice, which is newly "high-pitched and unnatural. Not my voice at all" (181). Having represented to herself her interest in Rebecca as a consequence of her jealous rivalry with her for Maxim's affections but finding herself pulled into a different triangulation, separated from Mrs. Danvers by nothing more than Rebecca's gossamer-thin, apricot nightdress, the narrator, released from that bedroom, stumbles to her own, locks herself in and lies on her bed feeling "deadly sick" (181).[11]

Discussing the classic romance's narrative of deferral—achieved largely through the heroine's imperfect understanding of the hero, which has her misrecognizing his unspoken but, as it invariably turns out, ardent interest in her as indifference or even cruelty—Tania Modleski speculates that the romance genre functions to instruct female readers in the benevolence of heterosexual masculinity.[12] She argues that the hero's declaration of love and brief explanation of his past actions, which mark the genre's narrative closure, retrospectively rewrite the heroine's—in some cases, quite elaborated—fears as groundless, demonstrating instead the symbiotic dovetailing of masculine and feminine desires in heterosexuality. According to Modleski's argument, then, the didactic function of the romance genre is to arouse in order to allay in its female readers a fear of heterosexual masculinity. Of all the romance subgenres, the gothic romance is most extravagantly patterned after this cycle of threat and reassurance, as the usual impediments to the romance's narrative closure here take on a monstrous cast, as the heroine's paranoid fantasy—only revealed as such in the closing pages—misrecognises the hero as the villain. While *Rebecca*'s narrative can be plotted according to this template, the reassurance of its romance story never loosens the more muscular grasp of what constitutes its threat. Much more emphatic in its representation of the horrific muddling of sequence than its resolution, *Rebecca*'s past continues to bulge into the present like some ghastly prolapse. The sexual perversity, which—while most obviously coagulating with Mrs. Danvers and Rebecca—equally casts its lines around the novel's narrator, never gives way to that heterosexuality which claims to succeed it. Following Modleski's argument that the form of the romance is shaped by its function as psychic defense against patriarchal power structures, *Rebecca* can be read as a story in which the form of its defense dwarfs its function, in which the narrative of heterosexual reassurance never succeeds the narrative of perversion's threat.

For the novel's passion—like its horror—continues to be articulated in terms of female perversity: The heterosexuality that would cinch the novelistic economy of sequence remains secondary to the perversion it allegedly succeeds, not only because it is never half as plausible or interpellating but also because the former remains constitutionally dependent on the latter. If Rebecca's sexuality, even posthumously, has temperatures rising and falling, blood climbing to and draining from faces accordingly flushed or bleached, has hearts quickening and slowing, gives rise to adoring devotion and murderous rage, what effects might be attributed to the heterosexuality that purports to be its full and true measure? Practically none. Casting itself as the final word in the developmental teleology that structures not only the romance genre but the avowedly evolutionary relationship between perversion and heterosexuality, heterosexuality in *Rebecca* turns out to be next to nothing: attenuated, hyperdomesticated, passionless, a pallid imitation of the dangerously elemental force that refuses to relinquish its claim to the shape of sexuality itself. It is not only that the narrator recognizes that her husband treats her as he treats his dog, Jasper, handling them both with the same distracted affection. It is not even that her single claim to have known her husband "as a lover" (74) during the weeks of their honeymoon is efficiently capsized by Mrs. Danvers's contemptuous " 'Well, he's a man, isn't he? . . . No man denies himself on a honeymoon, does he?' " (252). Rather, it is that while Maxim claims Rebecca has come between him and his second wife, stymieing their chances of a happy marriage—" 'Her shadow between us all the time. . . . Her damned shadow keeping us from one another' " (277)—it is only in the sheltering overhang of her shadow that any uxorious passion is articulated at all. After all, it is talk of Rebecca's murder and the perversities that seemed to license it that galvanize Maxim to hold the narrator, to kiss her as he had not kissed her before, to declare his love for her. Moreover, the long-awaited knowledge of her husband's love produces in the narrator a reaction whose cool depiction almost licenses as frigidity: "He went on kissing me, hungry, desperate, murmuring my name. I kept on looking at the patch of curtain, and saw where the sun had faded it, making it lighter than the piece above. 'How calm I am,' I thought. 'How cool' " (280).

Far from enabling a mutually satisfactory heterosexuality, the removal of the threat of Rebecca—Maxim's getting away with murder—initiates for the narrator and her husband an exiled existence whose overwrought dullness stands as antidote to the more carnal excitements that energize the bulk of the novel and its representations of the disordering of chronological and hence sexual sequence. Knitted together by the small rituals of afternoon tea, English mail, and old copies of *Field*, the de Winters gently decompose on their rented balcony, a couple of prematurely aged expatriates: "Oh, the Test matches that have saved us from ennui, the boxing bouts, even the billiard scores" (10). No longer electrified by danger, the companionate nature of their relationship stands in the place of sexuality. Playing out their charades of self-satisfaction—the taking of buttered bread and China tea, the reading aloud of journalistic accounts of county cricket matches—the de Winters give themselves up to a "boredom [that] is a pleasing antidote to fear" (9). Predictably enough, that fear held in check by boredom finds its articulation in the chaotic disordering of timeframes, in memory's drift to the past and imagination's anticipation of the future. Once again those deformations of precedence and temporal order speak more pertinently of a monstrous usurpation of propriety, of sexual perversity's overturning of heterosexual supremacy, as is everywhere apparent in the botanical fantasy of interbreeding, the vile clashes between nature and culture that open the novel.

"Last night I dreamed I went to Manderley again." As a figure for the heterosexual investment in patronymic reproduction, the ancestral home is monumentally weighted for the gothic romance.[13] *Rebecca* opens with Manderley in ruins. Tellingly, for a novel obsessed by sexual sequence, that ruin is represented in terms of the deposition of any taming or civilizing impulse, in terms of a persistently anarchic force that triumphs over the order that claimed to succeed it: "Nature had come into her own again and, little by little, in her stealthy, insidious way had encroached upon the drive with long, tenacious fingers" (5). There is a pornographic detailing to the narrator's wet dream, her fevered imagining of heterosexuality's before and after; what proceeds from, which is also what precedes, heterosexual legitimacy, the patronym, and civilized reproduction. The overgrown garden marks a sexual relapse where the "white, naked limbs" of beeches "intermingled in a strange embrace" (5), "things of culture and grace" had blown into "jungle growth" (6 and 5), monstrous rhododendrons "had entered into alien marriage with a host of nameless shrubs, poor, bastard things" (6), and the wanton "half-breed from the woods, whose seed had been scattered long ago beneath the trees and then forgotten," advances on what was once lawn (6–7). The histrionically mixed metaphors of miscegenation, masturbation, monstrousness, and primitivism, with their insinuation of homosexuality, that sexual depravity which is best told slant, do not anticipate simply the reversal of sexual sequence—perversion's triumph over heterosexuality—but the incoherent jumbling of the oppositional terms that govern sequence's operation: before and after, past and future, first and second. Cast as a return, a backwards movement, the passage back to Manderley is nevertheless also an advance, as the dreaming narrator imagines the dilapidated estate in years to follow. This cross-cutting of past and future maps on to a series of oppositions in the dream—purity and contamination, culture and nature, pedigree and half-breed, civilized and savage, legitimate and illegitimate—whose resonance with the bifurcated field of sexuality is reinforced by the ways in which they anticipate the novel's vain attempt to order female perversion and heterosexuality sequentially, the ways in which each pair rehearses the horrific, even nightmarish overthrow of precedence, the proper order of things.

Reading *Rebecca* as a narrative in which heterosexuality is the result of a strenuous—and alarmingly reversible—turning away from a more foundational and polymorphous perversity is to describe a field, not unlike the psychoanalytic, in which sexual desires and sexual identifications—to the extent that they can be distinguished—cannot be rendered in terms of the sexual identities from which they allegedly proceed. *Rebecca*'s determined but failed project is to force a sequential distinction between the sexually perverse and the heterosexual, to represent an unambiguous female heterosexuality succeeding that mire of perversity. The novel's overinvestments in sequence and precedence—specifically, its anxious attempts to quarantine the first Mrs. de Winter from the second, to narrativize the trajectory of feminine sexuality from sexual perversity to marital heterosexuality—defends against a knowledge that sexual desire might not be choreographed by some developmental narrative, that the wash of identification might animate, across the clearly stipulated fields of sexual identification, vagabond desire.

READING HITCHCOCK'S *Rebecca*

As an adaptation, a second-generation repetition of the same story, Hitchcock's 1940 *Rebecca* raises to the second order the fraught logics of sexual sequence prominent in du Maurier's novel. Revisiting the intricate and chronologically articulated problems of feminine identification in du Maurier's *Rebecca*, Hitchcock's adaptation labors to establish as irreversible heterosexuality's romantic ascendancy over perversity. Relying on similar, although more emphatically worked, techniques of sequential distinction, the narrative development and most particularly the final frames of Hitchcock's film struggle to close down on the ungovernable and multivalent lines of female identification and desire—the very aspects of du Maurier's novel that prove most resistant to the regulatory orderings of chronology and precedence. Partly because Hitchcock's adaptation, more than du Maurier's novel, structures its own closure in relation to the union of the heterosexual couple, reifying heterosexuality as the only sexuality with a future, and partly because, in order to shore up the ideological claims of its representations of a naturalized heterosexuality, the well-known stringencies of the Production Code required, even more than homosexuality's banishment from the screen, its periphrastic representation, sexual perversion in the film version of *Rebecca* frequently congeals as homosexuality.[14] In comparison to the novel, the film makes infrequent mention of Rebecca's alleged illegitimate pregnancy or her heterosexual promiscuity—her plays for Maxim's estate manager, Frank, and his brother-in-law, Giles, are not represented at all, and her sexual relationship with her cousin, Favell, is only briefly alluded to. The film's veiled representation of sexual perversity, then, battens on to homosexuality—that sexuality whose cultural recognizability is often indexed to allusion, inference, and connotation.

Although Hitchcock's producer, David Selznick, was committed to maintaining a fidelity to the novel in the film adaptation of *Rebecca*, many of the changes—determined both by the Motion Picture Association Production Code and the less specific stylistic patterns of the classic Hollywood film—work against the sexual ambivalence that structures the novel so prominently.[15] While the film opens with Joan Fontaine's retrospective voiceover that follows quite closely the novel's narration, there is no suggestion of her and Maxim's lackluster exile. Instead, the film reinstalls that romance closure so notable by its absence in the novel, ending with the de Winters in each other's arms before the flaming ruins of Manderley. In the novel, Mrs. Danvers sends her boxes to the station and is thought to have sneaked away for the train after setting the fire; in the film, she is upstairs in Rebecca's bedroom, burned alive outside the safety of heterosexuality's mutual embrace, her grotesque destruction installing her as a sexually eccentric figure outside, yet crucial to, the sacrificial order of Hollywood cinema, where, more often than not, the death of the homosexual secures the film's closure.[16]

The way in which the film lays to rest the ghost of Rebecca with the same efficient purpose as Mrs. Danvers is consigned to the flames, its closing delivery of the second Mrs. de Winter, backlit against Manderley's blaze, into the arms of her husband (house ruined, marriage saved), showcases a developmental sequence that prioritizes the future over the past, heterosexuality over other forms of sexual affiliation. While the full gratification of romantic convention in Hitchcock's adaptation attempts to close down the ambivalent vicissitudes of feminine identification and desire that structure the novel's circular narrative, what reinscribes these identificatory circuits as problematic still is the film's strategic reliance on point-of-view editing and spectator-identification techniques that maintain the mobile field of a desiring identification as a critical issue. *Rebecca*'s famously paranoiac atmosphere is in large part generated and sustained through subjective camera-work that encourages spectatorial identification with the heroine—a heroine, moreover, whose own anxious narrative trajectories are structured by what are represented as problems of identification.[17] The representational field of the film, then, keeps alive the infinitely various and unregulatable processes of identification and desire against which its literal narrative strenuously works.

In its drive for closure, its drive to secure heterosexuality as chronology's triumph, the film adaptation of *Rebecca* reauthorizes the sequence of before and after so discredited in the novel's frequent temporal switchbacks, its substitution of foreign exile for ancestral home, its prioritization of the gothic past over the romantic future. By fashioning itself as a romance in the classic Hollywood tradition, Hitchcock's *Rebecca* credits sequence with an interpretative weight, licensing the allegedly developmental relationships between sexual perversity and heterosexuality. While there is little doubt that the film defends itself much more efficiently against female perversion than does the novel, much post-Mulvey feminist film criticism, concerned with the explication of female subjectivity and desire, overlooks or marginalizes the film's vestigial but still quite potent flickerings of same-sex desire. In this regard, feminist analyses of the film have tended to be susceptible to the rewards of sexual sequence that *Rebecca* showcases. While critical of the film's representations of female subjectivity, much feminist discussion of *Rebecca* relies on fixed categories of sexual identification governed by the now-familiar logics of sequence and precedence. Explicitly or implicitly, these analyses' reliance on psychoanalytic models of sexual development and their resolution of Oedipal dilemmas inadvertently coincides with what is ostensibly being critiqued—the film's ideological prioritization of heterosexuality, perhaps most apparent in its drive for closure.[18]

In his essay "Primal Scenes and the Female Gothic: *Rebecca* and *Gaslight*," John Fletcher argues for the cultural primacy of fantasy in loosening up the gender-bound scripting of the Oedipal narrative. His emphasis on fantasy's unhooking of identity and desire, his alertness to the constraints of any deterministic understanding of gender, have the potential to articulate sexuality as mobile and unrestricted, as having a wider definitional ambit than the hegemony of sexual object choice can allow. Yet when Fletcher comes to read the scene in Rebecca's bedroom between Mrs. Danvers and Fontaine's character as "localizing the fantasy of the phallic mother in her very absence," it becomes clear that his prioritization of the destabilizing work of identification and fantasy has no purchase on his understanding of sexuality, which continues to be—even in the most unpromising circumstances—unequivocally heterosexual.[19] In the name of freeing up gender, Fletcher commits himself to a battening down of sexuality:

> The sequence's boldest tactic in dramatizing the fantasy of the all-desired and all-possessing phallic woman comes in the moment with the negligee. Transfixed by her husband's photograph on Rebecca's dressing-table, Fontaine hears Mrs. Danvers intone: "Then she would say 'Good-night Danny' and step into her bed." Fontaine is then beckoned to witness the unimaginable scene hinted at by a chain of metonymic connections—Maxim's photograph, Rebecca in bed, the transparent black negligee so tantalizingly displayed to the reluctant Fontaine: "Look! You can see my hand in it!"[20]

The unimaginable and metonymically framed scene that Fletcher refers to here (and that elsewhere he describes as "the compellingly implied marital scene" or "the off-camera scene of [Maxim and Rebecca's] implied lovemaking") struggles to eclipse some other scene—namely, the lovemaking of Rebecca and Mrs. Danvers, which might be considered easier to imagine here, and only in part because homosexuality is conventionally called to mind through the trope of unimaginability.[21] Fletcher argues that, both for Fontaine's character and the cinematic spectator, the metonymic chain of the husband's photograph, the wife in bed, and the housekeeper's display of the wife's negligée calls to mind the de Winter's marital conjunction. No doubt it might. Yet (is it just me?) another scene seems to be being avoided here—one that is, moreover, secured as the much more straightforward representational effect of Mrs. Danvers's hand inside Rebecca's transparent black negligée: namely, Mrs. Danvers's hand inside Rebecca's transparent black negligée.

It is not that I think the literal has more sway than the metonymic, that I want to install the homosexual possibility at the expense of the heterosexual.[22] Rather, I want to correct Fletcher's favoring of a heterosexual fantastic in order to keep afloat the notion that the energy of the bedroom scene, what marks it as a space of horror, is its refusal to choose between—let alone offer as coherent alternatives—the ciphers of sexual outcome: Maxim's photograph or Rebecca's negligée.[23] The installation of Maxim's portrait— an attempt to dilute the horrific effect of the bedroom scene's all-female coordinates—does not secure heterosexuality against the specific perversity of homosexuality but, rather, insinuates that sexual perversity is itself nonspecific, indifferent to the regulatory blandishments of sexual object choice.[24] Despite his critique of determinism and hypostatization, Fletcher's representation of Rebecca as the phallic woman, "narcissistically complete in herself, both sexual object and subject," and his rescuing of her from the Oedipally gendered script is heterosexually presumptive insofar as it assumes that the refusal of heterosexuality requires the refusal of sexuality itself.[25] While Rebecca's sexual self-sufficiency removes her from those circuits of heterosexual exchange for which the Oedipal narrative traditionally readies the little girl and consequently might be said to complicate the film's "drive towards narrative closure with its Oedipal satisfactions," this defense against heterosexuality places her beyond sexuality altogether, most notably beyond the homosexuality that continues to invigorate her posthumous relationships to Mrs. Danvers and the second Mrs. de Winter.[26] In Fletcher's reading, far from animating the sexuality of other women, Rebecca's proximity leaches it from them. Describing the scene in Rebecca's bedroom, Fletcher argues that Fontaine's character "is never more childlike and desexualized than when, with her Alice-band and her short-sleeved, buttoned-up blouse, she is made to stand or sit in the place of Rebecca," while Mrs. Danvers is victim to a "projective identification with the all-powerful Mistress of the House [that] cancels her own sexuality in a gesture that cedes it to the figure she serves."[27] In arguing that "the conservative Oedipal fantasy of *Rebecca*" is arrested by the fantasy of the phallic woman, in not considering the film's equally arresting articulation of homosexual identifications,

Fletcher's avowedly feminist project has a narrower enunciation, a narrower spectrum of identification and disidentification, than the film itself.[28]

I have considered Fletcher's argument in relation to *Rebecca* at some length because its securing of a female sexuality and subjectivity outside the conventional scriptings of the Oedipal narrative at the expense of female homosexuality, far from being idiosyncratic, replicates in broad stroke the work Hitchcock's film has frequently been called on to do in feminist film theory. While ostensibly resisting the ideological patterning of Hitchcock's film, feminist criticism of *Rebecca*—like the film itself— tends to close down against the sexual ambivalence that enables its progress, not only by constituting the entire field of sexuality as parceled out between the distinct and mutually exclusive categories of heterosexuality and homosexuality but—more galling—by ruling against homosexuality as a viable or sustaining model for critical thought.

Rebecca's almost iconic status for feminist film theory is made apparent by two books, published in the late 1980s by leading theorists in the field, that take stills from Hitchcock's film for their cover illustration. Mary Ann Doane's *The Desire to Desire: The Woman's Film of the 1940s* has a close-up of Fontaine, half of her face almost overexposed, the other half nearly lost in shadow, from the introduced scene where she and Maxim watch themselves in a home movie sequence. Tania Modleski's *The Women Who Knew Too Much: Hitchcock and Feminist Theory* has an imperious Mrs. Danvers and a schoolgirlish Fontaine in the minstrel's gallery before an enormous portrait of Caroline de Winter, the sister of Maxim's great-great-grandfather.[29] The influential interventions of both books in debates about female spectatorship and subjectivity take *Rebecca* as their most public face. Both Doane and Modleski read *Rebecca* in ways that are enabling for a feminist film theory grappling with gender-bound understandings of identity, desire, and spectatorship. Both read the film as complicating or interrupting the smooth-running machinery of the monolithically masculinist classic narrative cinema, as figuring—however incompletely—feminine desire.[30] Yet, in different ways, both essays are derailed by the specificity of female homosexuality, their elaborations of desire and identification finally coming down on the side of a femininity that is always—but without acknowledgment—heterosexual.

Although Doane has nothing to say about female homosexuality per se, it stands in a metaphoric relationship to what she describes as the problems of female spectatorship: That is, within the figural logics of Doane's essay, female homosexuality emerges as that which impedes "the emergence . . . of female subjectivity, the articulation of an 'I.' "[31] Representing female spectatorship as profoundly complicated by an inability to distinguish adequately between subject and object, as governed by the operations of paranoia and narcissism, Doane's account is ghosted by psychoanalysis's account of that other impossibility, even more strongly indexed by undifferentiation, paranoia, and narcissism—the lesbian. Within psychoanalytic frameworks, it can be said of the female homosexual, as it can of Doane's female viewer, that "what she lacks, in other words, is a 'good throw.' "[32] This connection is made more explicit when Doane, casting about for some parallel for "the contradictions and convolutions of female spectatorship," argues that these "are analogous to those described by Julia Kristeva as 'the double or triple twists of what we commonly call female homosexuality': 'I am looking, as a man would, for a woman'; or else 'I submit myself, as if I were a man who thought he was a woman, to a woman who thinks she is a man.' "[33] Leaving aside the extraordinary contortions that Kristeva identifies as definitive for the female homosexual, Doane's metaphoric use of Kristeva not only positions the lesbian as emblematic of the impossibility of female spectatorship but also implies that any possibility of the latter requires the exclusion of the former.[34] Despite the fact that *Rebecca*, and its charged circuits of female-female looks and desires is the occasion for these speculations, Doane's argument assumes that female spectatorship, like feminine desire and identification, is a heterosexual affair.

Modleski's essay gives female homosexuality a more central position, identifying its importance both in the paths of female identification traced in *Rebecca* and the film's own narrative development. Reading *Rebecca* as "a film that follows quite closely the female oedipal trajectory outlined by Freud" and consequently opposing the influential assumption that "all Hollywood narratives are dramatizations of the male oedipal story," Modleski's essay argues that "there is something more at stake here, something potentially more subversive, though it is treated by the film, as it is treated by psychoanalysis, as a 'problem': that is, the desire of women for other women."[35] Modleski refuses the literal sequence of the film's diegesis, arguing insightfully that while Rebecca's perversity impedes the film's conservative closure, requiring her violent erasure, the strength of her already-absent presence throughout the narrative suggests that "there is reason to suppose we cannot rest secure in the film's 'happy' ending."[36] What complicates Modleski's persuasive critique of *Rebecca*'s overarching Oedipal narrative is her inadvertent collusion with it. Modleski frames the desire of women for other women as a feminine desire for the mother and, in tamping lesbianism back into the developmental telos of heterosexual femininity, authorizes those strange—if strangely recognizable—relationships between female homosexuality and heterosexuality in which the former's before enables the latter's after: "Finally it becomes obvious that the two desires cannot coexist: the desire for the mother impedes the progress of the heterosexual union. Ultimately, then, the heroine disavows her desire for the mother, affirming her primary attachment to the male."[37] What is even more obvious than the impossibility of homosexuality and heterosexuality's coexistence is their lack of equivalence. Modleski's vocabulary gives her game away. While desire between women is always infantile and best kept in the family, the mother's counterpart—her competition, if you like—is not, as might be expected, the father but any representative of his gender, "the male." Under these conditions, the mother will never be sufficient as a lure against the mature blandishments of heterosexuality.

To a large extent, Hitchcock's adaptation of du Maurier's narrative—the removal or minimization of references to Rebecca's heterosexual perversities, the casting of the lesbian-inflected Judith Anderson as Mrs. Danvers, the reviving of that well-worn coincidence between heterosexuality and the happy ending—closes down on the mobility and unparticularized character of female perversion in the original novel.[38] Perhaps less expected is the tendency of feminist film criticism to follow Hitchcock's lead, even while arguing against the ideological consequences of his representations of femininity. The invocation of female homosexuality functions in Doane's and Modleski's essays much as it does in Hitchcock's film: It is that which enables the narrative in the first place but whose destruction is required by its closural economy. It must—either through inevitability or compulsion—be succeeded by female heterosexuality, these two marking out first and last positions like those photographs of a fat woman and a thin woman in weight-loss advertisements, the before and after of some narrative of improvement.

READING *MRS. DE WINTER*

Billing itself on its cover as "the sequel to Daphne du Maurier's *Rebecca*," Susan Hill's *Mrs. de Winter* authorizes its relationship to its predecessor according to precisely those logics of sequence so compromised in the original novel.[39] Kitted out as loyal to its antecedent—the inside cover blurb recklessly claims "Daphne du Maurier would approve"—the sequelizing force of *Mrs. de Winter* is more recognizable as a defense against the way in which *Rebecca*, despite its apparent overdetermination of the generic promise of romance, refuses to structure its closure in terms of an unambivalent prioritization of heterosexuality. Despite the avowed commitment to continuity and coherence, which the very notion of a sequel puts into circulation, *Mrs. de Winter* takes up *Rebecca*'s narrative only to close it down again, this time for good, in a demonstration that the most consequential narratological effect of the sequel is its retrospective capacity to rewrite the original narrative closure as provisional. Its own intelligibility determined by the relationships between first and second, before and after, *Mrs. de Winter* consequently functions as a disavowal of those knowledges about the unreliability of sequence that structure *Rebecca*. The narrative preposterousness of *Mrs. de Winter*, then, is not that it is a sequel to *Rebecca* but that it imagines it might set straight the terms of du Maurier's closure by resuscitating the very principles of precedence whose demonstrable exhaustion enable *Rebecca*'s closural economy.

If there seems a kind of logic, even an inevitability, to a cinematic Hollywood remake of *Rebecca* one year after its successful publication as a novel, it is harder to naturalize in terms of literary production or consumption Hill's sequel to du Maurier's novel, published more than fifty years after the original in 1993. After all, the specific cultural and sociohistoric configurations of femininity, marriage, and sexual dissidence that enable the gothic horror of the original novel are so altered in themselves and their relationship to each other by the late twentieth century that their as if continuous unraveling in the shape of a sequel—even one that labors to establish its own immediately postwar setting—cannot lay a claim to the readerly effects of thrilling fascination for which *Rebecca* is famous. Perhaps attuned to such implausibilities, the dust jacket flap offers its own naturalizing explanation: "What happened after that fatal fire at Manderley? What happened to Max de Winter and to his second wife? What, for that matter, happened to Mrs. Danvers and Jack Favell? Millions of readers have wondered. Now it can be told."[40] Projected onto "millions of readers," the interest in continuity and serialization evidenced here is more properly symptomatic of *Mrs. de Winter*'s anxious desire to move beyond *Rebecca*'s narrative and, most particularly, its troubling point of narrative closure.

In describing the last five sentences of *Rebecca* as "intriguing," *Mrs. de Winter* claims as its authoritative inspiration the narrative insufficiency or, at least, the open-endedness of its predecessor.[41] Yet this account of its own evolution is implausible given the quite striking way that none of the three questions asked on the dust jacket of Hill's novel have any purchase on the narrative economy of du Maurier's. Bluntly, *Rebecca*'s readers already know what happened to Max de Winter and his second wife—they live quietly on a Mediterranean island—and they do not care what happened at Manderley after the fire or for the fate of Mrs. Danvers or Jack Favell.[42] Doubtless, narrative has an infinite potential to generate further narrative, and the childlike prompt of *What happens next? What happens next?* might continue any story indefinitely. Nevertheless, in the sequential unraveling of any given novelistic field, within the warp and weft of suspense and its satisfaction in any particular novel, all questions are not due equal consideration. Hill's interest in du Maurier's novel is, in the end, an interest in what constitutes for *Rebecca* the nonnarratable—those aspects of the novel that have no "narrative future."[43]

Under the guise of picking up where *Rebecca* left off, Hill's novel has a much greater investment in writing du Maurier's novel beyond its own ending.[44] The nonnarratable elements of *Rebecca*—Maxim's being found not guilty of Rebecca's death, the destruction of Manderley, the de Winters' Mediterranean exile—are precisely what the narrative line of *Mrs. de Winter* is structured by and that it in turn oversteps in order to advance a different story, in order to satisfy some reservoir of curiosity whose origin, while claimed as *Rebecca*, is entirely elsewhere. As a sequel, as the imagined aftermath of some previous narrative, *Mrs. de Winter* is undone by the slipperiness of those very terms—first and second, before and after—it wishes to fix in order to adjudicate differently *Rebecca*'s representations of female perversity and heterosexuality. While Hill's narrative becomes pointlessly mired in many affectless repetitions of *Rebecca*'s plot, it concertedly works against any reiteration of the coordinates of *Rebecca*'s closure and its bathetic installation of heterosexuality in exile. Moreover, Hill's determined and uninspiring de-perversion of du Maurier's gothic romance that reframes the story as overwhelmingly heterosexual (albeit tragic) repeats the mistake of *Rebecca*'s narrator, imagining that the smooth unravelings of after could supersede the jagged promontories of before.

It is difficult to understand quite how, when it relies so heavily on the vocabulary, the figurings, and even entire scenes from *Rebecca*, but *Mrs. de Winter* manages from the start to still any sexual eddies or undercurrents that might toss the narrator up against the disconcerting sexualities of Rebecca or Mrs. Danvers. Indeed, twelve years on, Rebecca and Mrs. Danvers seem no longer to have any sexuality, disconcerting or not. Rebecca is here reduced to a "single handwritten letter, black and strong, tall and sloping. R.," which appears mysteriously and—the narrative would have us believe—terrifyingly on a wreath laid at the grave of Maxim's sister, while Mrs. Danvers is a spayed shadow of her former self, and not simply because she—as Hill pedantically relates about nearly every character—"looked a little older" (77 and 279). Having persuaded the narrator by some unlikely contrivance to come and see her in her present and modest situation as housekeeper to an elderly lady in Fernwode, Mrs. Danvers—like some pathetically aging film star with no sense of the limits that now constrain her performances—again attempts Rebecca's bedroom routine. Once again, although only with the meager props she had been able to carry away from Manderley, Mrs. Danvers shows the narrator Rebecca's hairbrushes, her "underwear, nightdresses, stockings, a fur trimmed wrap, a pair of gold slippers" (309). She might be a proficient shop girl for all the sinister effect she manages to rake together. If Mrs. Danvers is still a perverse figure, she is no longer sexually perverse, and, more important, the narrator herself stands well clear of any sexual identifications Mrs. Danvers had once brought into play. Although the narrator doggedly declares herself "terrified, fascinated," it seems more like some bad habit she has fallen into, not the effect of anything *Mrs. de Winter* can articulate (310).

While Mrs. Danvers still poses a threat to heterosexual happiness, it is not by standing in for any alternative economy of excitations and their satisfaction but, more expediently, by threatening to have Maxim exposed as a murderer. Although it is his wife who has been suffering the threats of Mrs. Danvers and Jack Favell, Rebecca's double-crossing cousin, Maxim decides, in the name of justice, to confess to his crime. Efficiently and predictably enough, as he is driving to make his confession, he is killed in a road accident, "crushed against a tree, down on one of the narrow, twisting lanes not far from Manderley" (371). Although the narrator declares that she "could not understand why he was dead," it is plain enough to anyone familiar with the closural demands of the novel, of which death, like marriage, is a nonnegotiable sign (371).[45] *Mrs. de Winter*'s commitment to writing *Rebecca* beyond its own ending can be seen in the extent to which Hill manages to press-gang death into the service of heterosexuality, making it seem like just another word for marriage.[46]

Perhaps the most striking formal problem with *Mrs. de Winter* is that, despite its nearly 400 pages, it has nothing to say. As one reviewer concludes, "the novel's lavish expenditure of banality in its descriptive passages seems designed to camouflage the fact that it hasn't got much of a plot."[47] Nothing to say, not much of a plot: These deficiencies are not—or not solely—attributable to Hill's vacuous development of storyline, but derive from the disavowed desire to reinscribe as authoritative the workings of sexual sequence, to rescript *Rebecca*'s closure as narrative middle. So far from being an extension of *Rebecca*'s narrative, the story of *Mrs. de Winter* acts in the service of an even more compelling cultural narrative, the hierarchical categorization of sexuality according to taxonomies of sexual object choice. Determined to recapture for heterosexuality the ideological work of closure, *Mrs. de Winter* demonstrates a desire to succeed—that is, both to follow and supplant—*Rebecca*.

After Before

Without doubt, the narrative orderings of female sexuality, which allows other forms of sexual affiliation, most notably homosexuality, but only to consolidate the sequential heft of heterosexuality, circulate with considerable authority in a range of cultural discourses other than those which animate the texts under discussion here.[48] Yet the *Rebecca* texts—and the sequential logics that govern their own intertextuality—exemplify a persistent cultural narrativization of the forms of female sexuality that determines not only their hierarchical relationship to one another but also the way in which that hierarchy is secured by lines of temporality, by sequence and chronology. The laws of precedence that purportedly distinguish between female perversion and heterosexuality have little purchase on *Rebecca*'s temporally fractured plot. Yet the heterosexually licensed logics of sequence in large part eschewed by du Maurier's novel are variously taken up in the frequently homophobic orderings of before and after that prominently structure subsequent attempts to retell *Rebecca*. The numerous attempts to rewrite, to reread, and to remake *Rebecca* are recognizable as a defense against that novel's failure to end, where that defense is motivated less by narratological than sexual anxiety: All *Rebecca*'s afters try to recuperate her before.

SIX

Wild Life Photography

Pulp Sexology and the Camera

Throughout this book I have taken late-nineteenth-/early-twentieth-century sexology as a crucial grounding discourse for female homosexuality, contending that the persistent association of lesbianism with invisibility, no less the etiological description of lesbianism via figures of derivation and belatedness, take on a definitional force in the sexological production of specific sexual taxonomies. In this last chapter, I turn to the more recent genre of what might be called pulp sexology—the 1950s and 1960s post-Kinsey proliferation of sexological paperbacks. I do so less to suggest historical continuity than to trace the transformed yet perseverant logics of sequence that frame lesbian invisibility as a problem to be solved, even while producing it as their naturalized effect. My argument turns on a close reading of Frank Caprio's *Female Homosexuality: A Psychodynamic Study of Lesbianism*, both because it is a representative and influential example of its genre and because its belatedly 1970s Australian edition, the edition I first encountered, contains a photographic essay of a sexual encounter between two women—the sixteen consecutive images of which literalize the cultural reliance on sequence in rendering visible lesbian subjects.[1] Moreover, because the photographs demonstrate that in the end this confidence in the visibilizing capacities of sequence is misplaced, testifying more explicitly to the failure of sequence to distinguish between homosexuality and heterosexuality, I recuperate the photographic essay here as a better, more apt illustration for my book than for Caprio's.

The opening shot; the opening door. A medium long shot in which the white strip of the edge of the door bisects the frame vertically, the brunette on the left-hand side, the blonde on the right. The brunette wears white; the blonde a darker, geometric print. Their oppositional codings of dark and light are reinforced by the relatively hard frontal lighting that lightens the stairwell of the apartment building while throwing the shadow of the blonde woman behind the open door. If I offer here a few technical terms for describing this photograph—the composition of the frame, medium long shot, frontal lighting—it is not because I imagine this tells us anything much. On the contrary, I think it is clear, even from a cursory glance, that a formalist approach has little to say to or about these photographs. The fairly consistent use of medium long or medium shots, frontal lighting, and an unchanging camera angle and height is not without its charm. Still, rather than naturalize itself, this mise-en-scène testifies to the endearing gaucheness of amateur photography or amateur pornography to the extent that the two are almost indistinguishable here. Quite predictably, the lures of formalism are effaced here for me by the greater lures of narrative. Let me say this instead: Here the protagonists meet. Separated still by the front door of the apartment, they will not stop touching each other for the duration of the narrative.

Pulp Sexology: Knowledge and Pleasure

Caprio's text is an early example of pulp sexology's persistent focus on homosexuality or lesbianism, these works coming to constitute a significant subgenre of pulp sexology.[2] Consider as exemplary Dr. Benjamin Morse's *The Lesbian: A Frank, Revealing Study of Women Who Turn to Their Own Sex for Love*.[3] Managing at once to be both forthright and euphemistic, Morse's title promises a revelation, a disclosure of the hidden facts of lesbianism: "Who is this woman, this lesbian? Where does she live? How does she love? And most important, what made her the way she is? This book is designed to give the answers to these questions. Its

As if it were a couch, they sit on the foot of the bed, legs crossed at the knee, glasses of something in each hand, cigarettes in the other, feet entwined. The bed is covered with a chenille bedspread, the pillowcases and sheets printed with an American quilt pattern. The wall behind the headboard is covered in partially obscured posters. The women look at each other, and the brunette rests her cigarette hand on the blonde's knee as casually as if it were her own. More than anything, here it is the glasses and the cigarettes, the very symmetry of them, that moves me. It is hard to say what function they serve. Certainly, they allude to a sociality in excess of the sexuality they nevertheless seem also to promise. They are gestural, decorative, ritualistic. Two women smoking and drinking on a bed seems at once innocent and perverse. The glasses are full, the cigarettes only drawn on once or twice.

aim is the lighting of a darkened area."[4] The list of questions—rhetorical insofar as they are seldom conclusively answered in the texts that they nevertheless inaugurate—and the figuring of lesbianism as a darkness or an obscurity that might be illuminated by the dissemination of knowledge are recognizable staples of the genre.[5] So, too, is a certain historical or ethnographic reach whose almost encyclopedic categorization of lesbianism works against the definitive specification it seems to promise. Typifying the lesbian across a broad range of categories—not only sexual but occupational, affective, and lifestyle—Morse's exhaustive delineation of the lesbian type defers any precise definition, encompassing as readily the masculinity of the tomboy and the femininity of the eternal female, the educational or career ambitions of the college or working girl and the domestic appetite of the bored matron, the celibacy of the frigid abstainer and the promiscuity of the prostitute. [6] Individual pulp sexology texts—the field of pulp sexology more gener-

And then the cigarettes are gone, not to be seen again. A slightly tighter, high-angle but still symmetrical shot. The women's hands touch, each resting her free hand on the other's shoulder. There is here a sense of suspension, attributable partly no doubt to the photograph's arrested temporality but, more significantly, to a sense of the two women hesitating on the brink of an action that will disclose itself as sexual, the counterbalancing symmetry of their grip on each other neither quite a fending off nor an embrace. I recognize this hold from my childhood judo. It is the preliminary grip for a basic throw called osotogari.

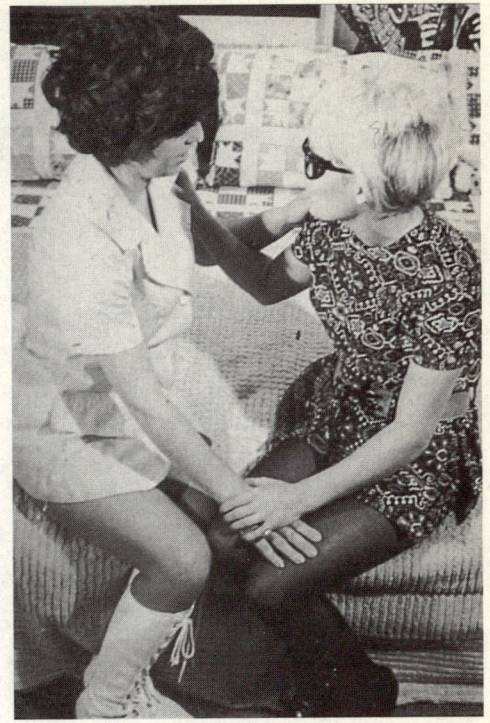

ally—often attest to this internally conflicted relationship to their production of knowledge: Unable to articulate its content with any specificity, they fetishize its form.

While the prolific and often contradictory information disseminated by pulp sexology never quite congeals as coherent knowledge, knowledge about lesbianism is nevertheless represented as not only desirable for the general reader, routinely interpellated as "the student," but essential for the young person—here, the young woman—who would otherwise fall victim to her own ignorance. Typically, this authorization of sexological knowledge is reinforced by the further narrative strategy of the case history, a familiar formal characteristic of late-nineteenth-century sexology, which in pulp sexology closely resembles the novelistic and avowedly unscientific pulp fiction from which it barely distinguishes itself. Accordingly, Morse concludes one of his case histories by casting it as a cautionary tale:

The brunette relinquishes her hold even though I judge that she has the slight weight advantage. The blonde begins to unbutton her jacket.

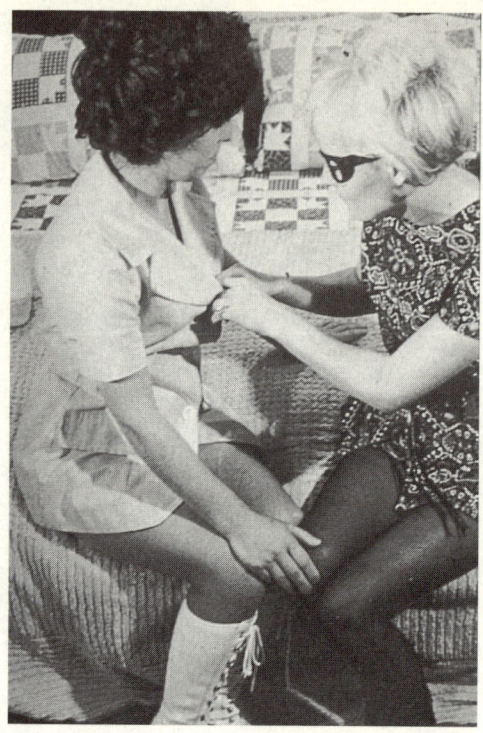

Angela's own lack of knowledge was the greatest contributing factor to her descent into lesbianism.

To state this more pointedly: *if Angela Pierce had read this book during her senior year at high school, she would never have found herself in bed with Lucia Whitcomb.*[7]

This emphasis on the young person and the prophylactic nature of sexual knowledge, so routinely evoked in pulp sexology, takes its discursive force from the rhetorical function of the young person in definitions of and debates about the regulation of obscenity. Given the long-standing tradition in American obscenity law of taking as the measuring stick for what might be considered obscene the young person, whose innocent potential it threatens to destroy, pulp sexology's avowed commitment to the moral health of the young person is a cannily strategic justification not for the suppression of explicit information about lesbian sexual practices but for its widespread circulation.[8]

Given recent considerations of the genre, which range from dismissals

The jacket is off and cast to one side. A pillow from the head of the bed has been placed under the brunette's head and shoulder. The blonde woman, her face held close over the face of the other, unzips the brunette's shorts. They look smilingly into each other's faces as the brunette slides the blonde's sleeve down from her shoulder, exposing a black bra strap.

of its scientific authority to camp reclamation, perhaps my tracing of the sexological project across the more often than not pseudonymous names of pulp sexology's authors and the hoary promises of their titles might seem at best naive. It might seem, that is, to miss what is frequently taken as the most obvious generic characteristic of pulp sexology—that the sexological cast of these works is no more than the slightest of alibis that enables the circulation of materials otherwise deemed obscene.[9] Without disregarding the legitimizing framework afforded the obscene by sexological discourses—a legitimacy particularly salient after the 1957 U.S. Supreme Court rulings that defined obscenity "as utterly without redeeming social importance"—there is some critical advantage to be had in not distinguishing too quickly or absolutely between the sexological and the obscene.[10] Although sexology has long derived its cultural authority by defining itself in opposition to the obscene, this legitimizing gesture cannot produce even as an effect the opposition it claims as its original distinction. The long-standing anxiety that the sexological and the obscene

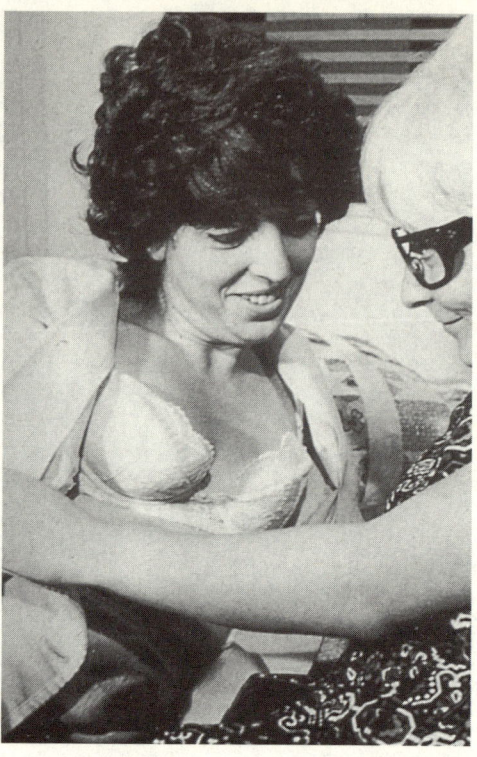

Unexpectedly, in the next medium close-up, the brunette has her jacket on again and the blonde holds the unbuttoned sides open to reveal a scalloped lace bra. They smile at each other with what seems like pride and satisfaction.

might not be readily distinguished rests on the fact that both the sexological and the obscene can be productively understood as articulating systems of sexual science, as bringing to visibility certain forms of sexual knowledge. However much sexology has marshaled itself under the rubric of science, claiming an objective, even disembodied, stake in the scientific accumulation of knowledge, the specifically sexual nature of that knowledge always threatens to draw it back into the realm of the obscene and its putatively nonproductive, pleasure-oriented economies of sexual arousal. For example, while the case history is the privileged form for sexology's etiological project, the narrative modality for its most persuasive diagnostic tracing of lesbianism's origin, the very conventions that establish its clinical authority ensure that it functions equally as an erotic set piece. The case history's inaugural, frequently first-person description of the subject's sexual history; its specification of pathological identifications; its narration of sexual opportunities and behaviors; its confidence that etiol-

The camera shifts in relation to the figures, who are shown now from the head of the bed. This new perspective offers up a further, yet incomplete, glimpse of the room—the bottom edge of a batik wall hanging, a pair of cupboard doors with perhaps a bag hung over its handles—a backdrop that seems, as in a snapshot, incidental to the claims of the central subject and, for that reason, continues subsequently to catch at the viewer's attention. The brunette, jacket off again, reclines on a pillow and slides the blonde's sleeve down from her other shoulder. The blonde rests on her right elbow, her floral belt discarded on the bed beside her.

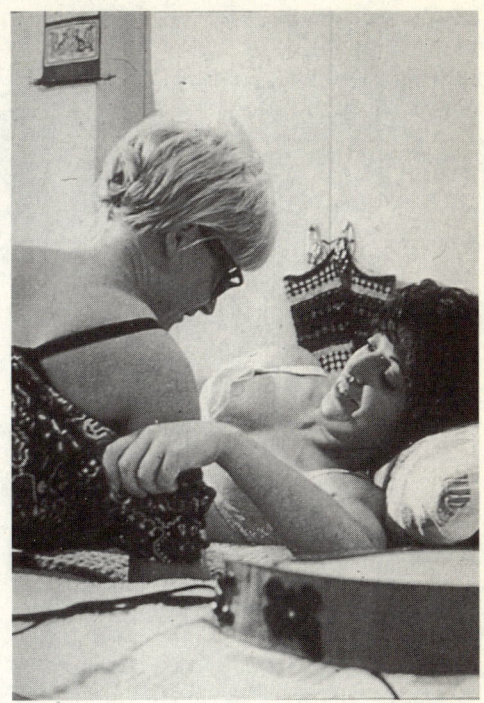

ogy can be established by nothing more than narrative causality recall the novelistic pleasures of character and plot while working toward a satisfaction that is, at least potentially, masturbatory. Rather than eschew this connection entirely, pulp sexology registers an ambivalent fascination with its own function as a hinge between scientific or medical and obscene or pornographic discourses. The hybridized form of pulp sexology, then, is not simply an obscenity masquerading as an intelligence but a genre in which both sexological and pornographic knowledge is crucially articulated. Its adaptation of the case history, its ethnographic revelation of sexual subcultures, and its production, recitation and transmission of sexual truths play not simply on the disparity between cultural valuations of scientific knowledge and sexual pleasure but on the engrossing spectacle of a copulative pleasure-knowledge, the energies of which are derived from being routed through both the cognitive and the erotic.

In part because of the split register of pulp sexology's scholarly and pornographic framing, in part because of the consequent disjunctions be-

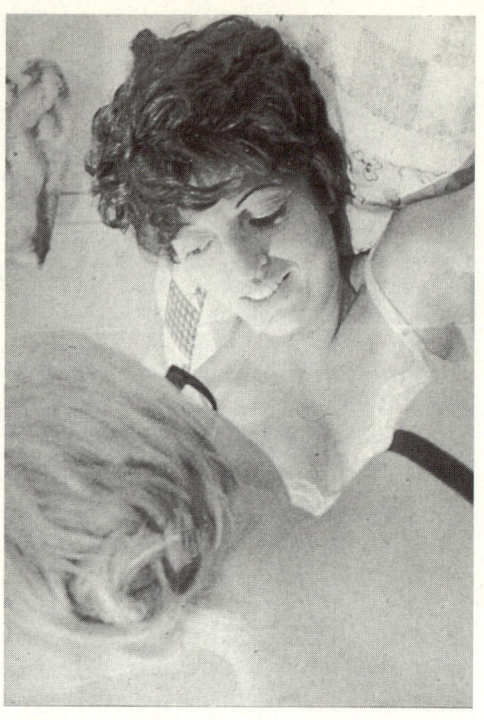

A medium close-up over the shoulder shot of the brunette. This is the only horizontal, landscape alignment in a sequence that is otherwise made up of vertical, portrait shots.

tween textual intention and readerly use, the ideological effects of pulp sexology are difficult to calibrate.[11] Far from coherent as a genre—argumentative or conceptual incoherence seems almost to have been a generic requirement of individual works—pulp sexology cannot simply be dismissed as homophobic (even if it can't either be recuperated as antihomophobic).[12] While pulp sexology is easy to ridicule, I want to take seriously its sexological framing; that is, I want to think about its intellectual and carnal investments in the sexual taxonomies of heterosexuality and homosexuality, particularly its attempt to bring lesbianism to cultural visibility by distinguishing it from female heterosexuality. In a post-Kinsey sexological world in which sexual identity is newly figured as distributed across a spectrum of possibilities slung between the oppositions of what were formerly acknowledged as the only games in town, heterosexuality and homosexuality, pulp sexology is newly energized in its negotiation of a distinction, however blurred that differentiation may prove to be, between heterosexual women and lesbians.[13] Moreover, the rhetorical function of that distinction is not only to hold the two sexual economies sepa-

Both women are upright in the next back- and side-lit medium shot. Their bras removed, they hold each other at the hip, hands clasping each other's shorts. The left breast of the brunette catches the light.

rate but also to assert, through the naturalizing effects of that discrimination, the hierarchy of heterosexual precedence over lesbian secondariness. If that strategy complacently depends on the self-licensing logics of sexual sequence—heterosexuality first; lesbianism second—then it does so in order to circumvent a further sequential narrative that also figures heterosexuality first, lesbianism second—namely, the narrative of sexual conversion, the ubiquitous specter of heterosexuality's degenerative fall into lesbianism. As such, pulp sexology functions as a significant cultural site for the fraught working out of the problem of lesbian invisibility through the logics of sexual sequence.

Frank Caprio's *Female Homosexuality*

Caprio dedicates his book "To Alfred C. Kinsey and his workers with deep respect and esteem for their successful efforts to bring to the attention of the public the need for a more realistic and scientific understanding of sex."

In a longer shot, both women are standing on the bed. The blonde woman rests her hands on the other's shoulders, while the brunette, naked, peels back her companion's black pantyhose, exposing her buttocks. This seems a tricky maneuver—trickier for being executed on the unstable surface of a bed. Its motivation appears to be the display of the bohemian collage of the posters at the head of the bed, their juxtaposition of modernist and psychedelic styles offering an ethnographic context for the imminent spectacle of lesbian sex.

Despite aligning his sexological project with Kinsey's, however, Caprio deviates from it in significant ways, most notably in his desire to divide cleanly the field of sexual registration, to fix the definitional limits of lesbianism. Critical of the ways in which female homosexuality has been subject to what he calls "prejudiced censorship for the past half century," Caprio, in seeking to define and specify lesbianism, to fix it as a category, is nevertheless compelled by his belief in lesbianism's transmissibility: "To conquer a disease, knowledge limited to physicians regarding its cure is not sufficient. The public must be educated as to its cause, symptomatology and ways of preventing its development" (8). That public evoked in Caprio's dedication as newly attentive to the necessities of "a more realistic and scientific understanding of sex" is soon recruited to a most un-Kinsey-like project—the prevention of lesbianism. The fantasized, nearly primal, scene for Caprio's narrative is the scene of sexual conversion, the point at which a young, always heterosexual, woman declines into lesbianism. It is with the intention of preventing this occurrence—the moment when the first-second logics of

The eleventh frame of a sixteen-frame sequence and both women are naked at last, if we don't count those glasses. Heavily framed, they never appear to have any lenses in them. They remind me of the safety glasses we had to wear at school in the metalwork workshop when drilling or using the lathe. Or are they, like the blonde's hair with its obviously dark roots, a disguise? And if the glasses seem oddly to promise a protection of some sort, a safety, what are we to make of the unexplained appearance of the leopard-skin rug? Covering but not obscuring the chenille bedspread, the leopard-skin rug barely manages to get into circulation its connotations of wildness, the exotic, bestiality. Reinforcing this exoticness is the "primitive"-style fetish-head necklace that hangs on a beaded string on the back wall. Shaped like a skull, its wooden eyes stare across the bed, reversing the direction of the camera's sight lines. The pillows have been banked at the head of the bed under the leopard skin, and the brunette lies back, the blonde kneeling at her far side, one hand under the other's breast.

sexual hierarchy are overturned by the first-second logics of sexual succession—that Caprio disseminates accessible knowledge regarding female homosexuality, as "many of the naive and ill-informed are initiated into lesbian practices because of their complete ignorance, which enhances their susceptibility to the advances of the older and experienced invert" (8). If Caprio counters this scene of sexual initiation with his own scene of sexual instruction, both are equally figured around the eroticized—that is, the failed—distinction between heterosexual and homosexual women.

Caprio's persistent and unsuccessful attempts to define and identify in order to contain female homosexuality are marked by the compulsions, even the pleasures, of repetition. Again and again his various chapters on the diverse but sexologically perennial topics of female homosexuality across cultures and history, female homosexuality as a theme in literature, female homosexuality among prison inmates, and the differences and similarities between male and female homosexuals rehearse the same problem of representation—namely, the securing of lesbian legibility inside a visual field in-

Another medium close-up, with the brunette's head cropped at the left hand side of the frame. Almost centered in the frame and looked at by both women, the brunette's left nipple is held between the blonde's thumb and middle finger.

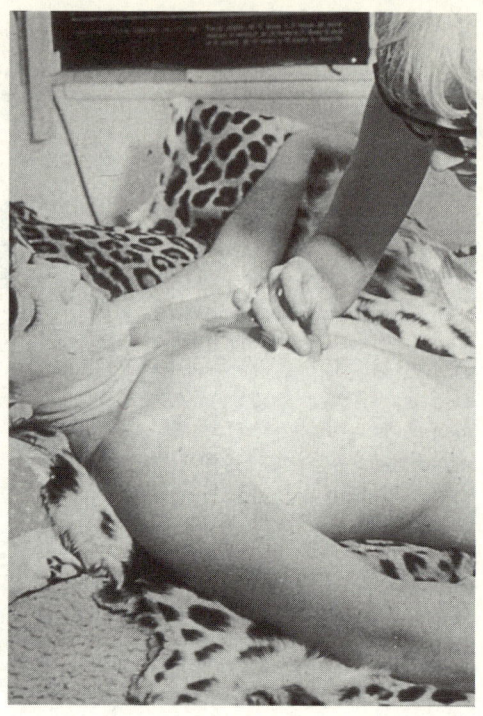

dentured to the gendered grammar of heterosexual difference. Consider as exemplary the chapter titled "Lesbian Practices among Prostitutes in Various Parts of the World," in which Caprio describes the extensiveness of his research: "In the spring of 1953, I returned from a tour around the world during which I interviewed prostitutes in the following cities: Havana, Cuba; Panama City, Panama; London, England; Paris, France; Venice, Genoa, Naples, Rome, Isle of Capri, Italy; Vienna, Austria; Honolulu, Hawaii; Tokyo, Japan; Manila, Philippine Islands; Singapore, Penang, Malay; Hong Kong; Bombay, India; Cairo, Egypt." "Prostitutes for the major part," he writes disarmingly, "are lesbians in disguise" (104). Referring to the staging of lesbian performances described as providing for brothels "a lucrative source of income" (110), Caprio observes that sometimes these performers are not only lesbians but lovers in everyday life; sometimes they are heterosexual women performing lesbianism for an audience that—like Caprio and, as it turns out, the rest of us—cannot tell the difference. Moreover, for Caprio, the problem of not being able to tell the difference between lesbian and hetero-

The blonde licks the brunette's nipple—or, rather, she has her tongue just behind it. Like the earlier fingers either side of a nipple and the even earlier hand splayed beneath a breast, this act reveals itself more properly as a pose, something staged for maximum visibility. Despite the erection of her nipple, the brunette seems deadened to this scene. Not simply passive but disengaged, her gaze drifts over the blonde woman's shoulder and out of the frame.

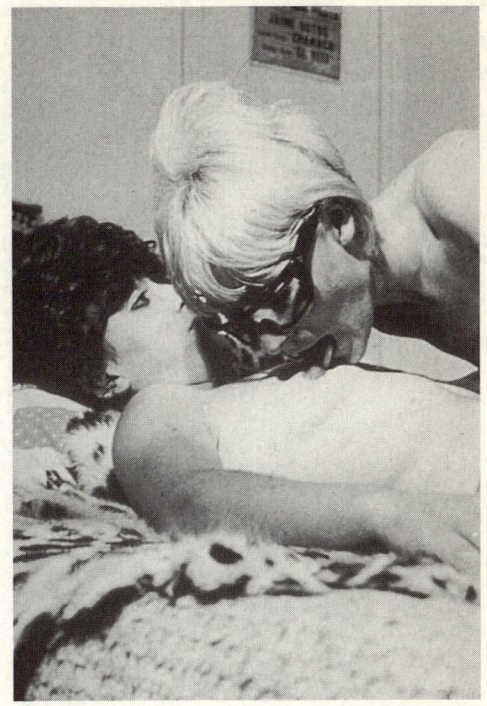

sexual women is not simply a spectatorial one, for his emphasis on what he calls latent or unconscious homosexuals ensures that very often even lesbian self-identification is problematic. As he observes, "Many prostitutes are latent homosexuals insofar as they resort to sexual excesses with many men to convince themselves that they are heterosexual. A large number of them become participants in lesbian activities, never suspecting originally that some day they would ever indulge in homosexual practices" (104).[14]

But if for some prostitution is an escape from the horrors of lesbianism, for others lesbianism is an escape from the boredom of prostitution. As Caprio notes, "The incidence of lesbianism among prostitutes is especially high in countries where competition for business is keen and where many of them do nothing else but wait for an occasional patron. This, I was told, was an important factor accounting for widespread lesbianism among prostitutes in Tokyo and Bombay" (107). When free time is all that stands between heterosexual women and lesbianism, when a gap between clients is enough to turn heterosexual women into lesbians, Caprio's attempt to

The blonde is almost in the same position as before, supported by her elbows, but the brunette is now on top of her, lying against her back and holding the blonde woman's breast so that the nipple is visible between her thumb and index finger. The brunette again looks out of the frame and her tongue is held oddly—and, it has to be said, un-photogenically—between her teeth and lower lip.

specify lesbianism demonstrates the impossibility of that task. Moreover, this dangerous slithering between heterosexuality and homosexuality is not limited to the brothel's lesbian performers but also their male spectators. Caprio observes,

> There is a class of men who attend these lesbian performances quite regularly. They rationalise their desire to see two women engage in sexual acts by stating that sheer curiosity prompts them. Psychoanalysts have discovered, however, that in reality this represents the unconscious projection of their own latent homosexual tendencies. For them to see two men in homosexual activity would create a severe mental conflict enhancing their feelings of guilt. By seeing two lesbians perform, they are able to appease their conscience while at the same time vicariously gratifying their homosexual yearnings. (110)

Although Caprio is careful to distinguish between that class of men and those like himself "who visit these performances for the purpose of gath-

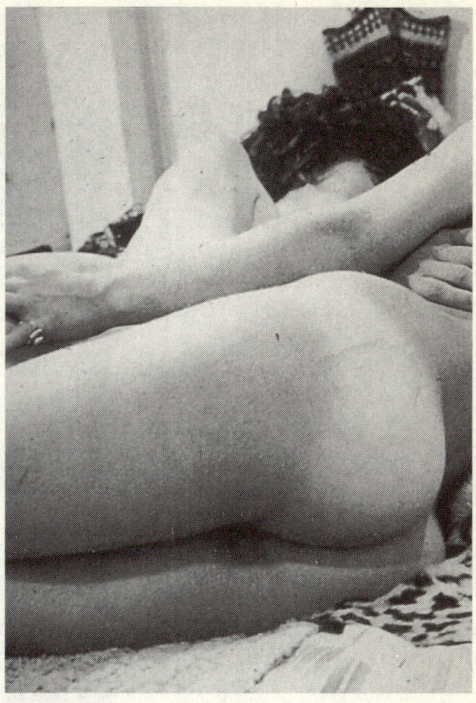

A curious photograph. In the foreground the buttocks, legs and distinct tan line of the blonde, whose torso and head is cropped from the picture. Behind her, the brunette lies, her right hand at the blonde woman's waist, the blonde woman's hand on her thigh.

ering scientific data," once again it is hard to tell the difference between them (110). Caprio's stated intention of specifying lesbianism in order to prevent its spread has instead enumerated the prolific potential of homosexuality. Following Caprio's analysis, what seems impossible is any sense of what he most hopes to secure—a stable or assured heterosexuality defined in strict opposition to a stable, albeit second-order, homosexuality.

Furthermore, remembering that Caprio seeks to define and specify lesbianism in order to curb it, his cure seems to resemble closely, too closely, the epidemiological modes of transmission of the very disease it is meant to curtail. For the sexual knowledge that Caprio identifies as transmitting lesbianism seems not unlike the scientific knowledge he promulgates in heterosexuality's defense. He writes, "An 'innocent' girl has sex with another experienced lesbian. She in turn seduces the next. It is this kind of cycle or chain of seduction that accounts for the increasing incidence of lesbianism in our midst" (152). This kind of sexual knowledge is represented as irreversible; the vampiric touch of the lesbian is utterly seductive and permanent in its effect: "Once a woman is seduced by [a lesbian],

The shower scene, the wash up, the end. Both women stand in a white-tiled shower cubicle, looking down at their own bodies. The blonde woman still wears her glasses. They are almost in the same physical relation to each other as they were in the opening shot, although here it is not the door but the white spray of water that falls between them. The blonde washes the inside of her leg; the brunette directs water on to her pubic hair, seen here for the first time in the last frame. The brunette caresses the blonde's breast. They do not look at each other.

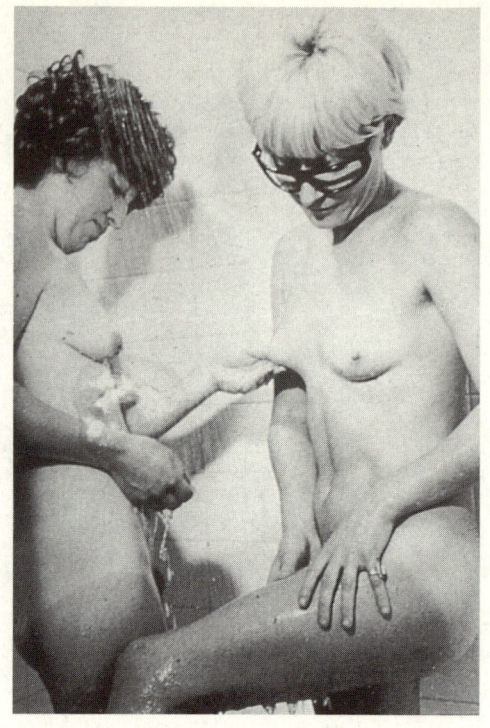

it is almost impossible for any man or lover, to win back his wife or sweetheart from the fascinating toils of these perverts. No man stands any chance against an active Sapphist once she has properly seduced a woman with her own wiles."[15] Caprio would save these innocent women from the contaminating touch of sexual knowledge by informing them in advance and in scientific detail of what the lesbian is, what she looks like, where she can be found, what her sexual practices are. It is hard always to remember that this almost obsessive specification of lesbianism is designed to protect women from its otherwise tempting prospects. Caprio's zeal to protect heterosexual women from lesbian temptation further complicates the already fraught distinction between homosexual and heterosexual populations insofar as it destabilizes the presumptive heterosexuality of his own medicalized authority. After all, in his preface, chiding those who would suppress the results of his research, Caprio cites the psychoanalyst Dr. Ernest Jones as his support: "It is people with secret attractions to various temptations who busy themselves most with removing those temptations from other people; really they are defending themselves under the pretext of defending others, because at heart they fear their own weakness" (9). I am not suggesting that Caprio is in some sense really a homosexual (neither, of course, am I suggesting that he isn't). Rather, I am noting that the urgency with which he seeks to render lesbianism visible is most obviously countered by his failure to do so. Far from fixing the object of his inquiry, Caprio demonstrates the difficulty of determining once and for all the specificity of lesbianism, even implicating himself in the spread of the homosexuality he desires to contain. Moreover, the naturalized narratives of sexual sequence that assert the precedence of heterosexuality are destabilized by heterosexuality's susceptibility to lesbianism, the chronologies of sexual conversion reworking the putatively self-evident claims of sequence. In this, the narrative of *Female Homosexuality* repeats but does not resolve what I have been calling the problem of lesbian representation.

LESBIANISM AND THE EVIDENTIAL EROTICS OF PHOTOGRAPHY

My argument here, but equally throughout this book, is that the logic of sexual sequence, through its insistence on the derivativeness of lesbianism, keeps alive the very problem it claims to lay to rest: the problem of lesbian representability. This conundrum is productively dramatized in the unnamed and uncredited photo-essay that appears in the 1971 Australian edition of *Female Homosexuality*. Not included in the first edition, the photographs draw attention to their supplementary nature, the way in which they function as a supplement to Caprio's text. In the contradictory—which is to say, Derridean—sense, the supplement functions both as something extra and something required to make up a lack. Radically unlike the rest of Caprio's book, most obviously in terms of medium but also in its structures of address, the photo-essay is at once the mark of both the excessive and the deficient. However old-fashioned its pornographic conventions now appear—or, perhaps I should say, however its pornographic charge is now routed through retrospection—its early-1970s addition supplements the erotic potential of Caprio's 1950s text, enabling its continued circulation under the sign of contemporaneity. Yet despite signaling an excess, an abundant addition, the photo-essay's supplementarity also registers an inadequacy, not only in the textual insufficiency that requires its addition but also in its own mimetic relationship to the text it supplements. If, despite its urgent identification of the need to disseminate knowledge about what the lesbian is, to fix lesbianism in a secondary relationship to female heterosexuality, Caprio's *Female Homosexuality* is a more successful demonstration of the impossibility of doing so with any authority, then the supplementary sequence of photographs is caught up on precisely, if perhaps predictably, the same problem.

The impossible bind of lesbian representation offers itself up as the interpretative context for the supplementary photo-essay. There is no acknowledgment or mention made of the photo-essay's appearance in this edition. It is simply spliced into the original edition of Caprio's book, the sixteen photographs appearing on eight unnumbered pages inserted between pages 112 and 113. Unanchored by any contextualizing captions that might broker to the reader the experience of looking, the photo-essay offers itself as a purely visual record that speaks for itself, an ob-jective and analogical capture of a material reality.[16] The putatively "evidential force" of photography is here in the service of an ethnographic pornography in which the sexual moves of the two omen, like the late-1960s stylings of their clothing and interior decoration, testify to the neutral, scientific, and uninvested documentary function of the camera.[17] The technological apparatus of the camera—particularly what Roland Barthes describes as its "power of authentication"—appears to resolve the long-standing problem of lesbian representability.[18] Of course, as Barthes has also taught us, the fantasy of photographic objectivity is itself the paradoxical effect of the photograph's connotative structures insofar as "the connoted (or coded) message develops on the basis of a message *without a code.*"[19] Accordingly, the photo-essay's documentary realism, unfolded across a series of consecutive photographs, is recognizable less as a sign of the minimal distinction between an actual event and its representation than an imperative to frame lesbianism through the disciplinary strategies of visibility and sequence.

I first saw this photo-essay in 1992, in the basement stacks of the Baillieu Library as part of the Willis Collection, an uncataloged gay and lesbian bequest to which I was allowed browsing access. The photo-essay I saw three years later, when I began working with it, was quite a different thing from the one I had been holding in the interim in my mind's eye. It surprised me to see what I had forgotten; surprised me more to see what I had remembered. I guess if that's the way with narrative, it is even more so the way with pornography. So I had remembered the cigarettes, the cameo ring on the blonde's left-hand little finger and how it is showcased in the unzipping of the white hot pants; I had remembered the white lace-up boots because they were uncannily like a stylish matching set that both my mother and four-year-old sister sported one ill-advised winter back home; I had remembered—of course—the black-rimmed safety glasses and the unforgettable shower scene. I had forgotten a great deal: who undressed whom; the sequence of sitting, standing, lying; the suggestions of interior decorating. I forgot about the leather and suede floral belt discarded on the bedspread—or, rather, I had misremembered it as an elaborate pair of underpants that I see now were nowhere in evidence.

Considering these photographs in their singularity and their narrative relationship to each other, it is possible to determine how the strategies of sequence and visibility work in this photo-essay—both in terms of its literal organization and its central themes—to articulate lesbianism as its scientific and pornographic subject. Insofar as it is radically removed from the clinical or avowedly illustrative style of photography associated with sexology, the photo-essay might seem more obviously recuperable to a pornographic impulse to register as a visual narrative sex between women.[20] However, my focus here remains on the imbricated drive of a pleasure-knowledge that registers the desire to see in both erotic and cognitive economies. Accordingly, I want to consider this photo-essay as consistent both with the fraught and long-frustrated sexological attempt to taxonomize female homosexuality as a distinct category and the pornographic acquisition of knowledge, where that knowledge is everywhere represented in terms of the visible.[21] There are any number of directions in which these photographs might be taken, but I want to think about the ways in which the photo-essay's naturalized reliance on the strategies of sequence and visibility rehearse the problems of lesbian representability they claim to resolve.

It is the sequential arrangement of the photographs, the way in which that sequencing supplements the photographic urge to documentary realism with the near-cinematic drive for continuity, that most tellingly speaks to the problem of lesbian representation. Arranged as a sequence, the photo-essay is marked by a desire to overcome what is a defining characteristic of the photograph—its capture of a moment in time, "a fragment of the spatio-temporal continuum."[22] As a sequence, the photographs work simultaneously in pornographic and sexological registers: On the one hand, they represent and induce the embodied rhythms of sexual arousal and satisfaction, and, on the other, they displace the desire for sexual etiology onto the techniques of continuity, the evidential proof of lesbianism no longer residing in the single frame of corporeal display but dispersed across the narratively organized spectacle of sex acts. Yet it is also as a sequence that the photographs fail. I am thinking here of that misordering of photographic frames that has the brunette's jacket inexplicably reappearing once it has already been taken off and laid aside; the single shot that is horizontally aligned requiring the viewer to turn the book or tilt her head; the appearance of the leopard-skin rug that, while possible to recuperate to some diegetic frame, marks as distinct the five subsequent photographs that constitute the overtly sexual but almost entirely unnarrativized sequence of sex acts.

These glitches in continuity attach themselves to—indeed, can be seen to dramatize—some larger failure of representation. It is not that these failures of sequence are unavoidable—how difficult would it be to have the photographs in the correct sequence and the same orientation? to do away with the leopard-skin rug and choreograph the sex acts more convincingly?—but that they demonstrate something in contradistinction to what they seem most obviously to be demonstrating. While each photograph overreaches its framing, aspiring to a narrative momentum not usually ceded to the photographic medium, the photo-essay as a whole cannot naturalize the narrative to which it lays a claim.[23] Without the twenty-four-frame-per-second slickness of continuity editing that underwrites cinematic realism, the photo-essay keeps breaking down into its sixteen constitutive images, its jerky claim on continuity, far from securing relations of causality, drawing attention to sequence as an organizing and regulatory technology. Of course, this might be said of any photographic sequence—Régis Durand suggests as much when he notes that "in spite of various attempts to give it, through sequencing or assemblage, some kind of diegetic quality, the photograph is arrested, suspended"[24]—but my point here is that both the desire for and the failure of sequence assume a particular pertinence in the vicinity of lesbianism, the disciplinary production of which has long relied on the self-authorizing logics of sequence.

It is no surprise, then, that when sequence fails in the sexological or pornographic specification of its subject the evidential lading falls to the single-frame knowledge and pleasures of visibility. The claims that visibility makes across these photographs and the failures enacted in its name are productively condensed in the one item whose appearance has from the first struck a jarring note, the one consistent prop across the narrative drama staged by the sequence of photographs: the blonde's black-framed glasses. As the singular supplement to nakedness, the prosthetic character of the glasses, their making up of a deficiency, recalls, in relation to Caprio's wider sexological project, the supplementary function of the photo-essay itself, its simultaneous registration as excessive and insufficient. I suggested earlier that perhaps the unexpected and inexplicable persistence of the glasses across every frame but one requires that they be read as a disguise; that is, as an impediment to full and final visual disclosure. Without letting go of the implications of this possibility, it is equally plausible to read the centrality of the glasses—their sidelong appearance at the front door, their tenacity when every other garment has been removed, and their final upstaging of the shower scene—as indexing the severity of the blonde's visual impairment.

As anyone who wears them will doubtless know, the remedial function of prescription glasses is always overwhelmed by their iconic one. In the world, as in this photo-essay, glasses stand in for a disability of vision even as they remedy it. When you are wearing glasses, everyone can see that you are visually impaired in those very instances when, through their prosthetic intervention, you aren't. If, through a curious disavowal of their function, glasses symbolically carry the sense of the visual impairment they ameliorate, through a similar putting aside of knowledge, the photo-essay works this disavowal in reverse. That is, while purporting to remedy a visual deficiency, the photo-essay more properly confirms the impairment itself—the well-known intractability of lesbianism in the visual field. The photographs' claim to visibility, then, does not escape but demonstrates again the impossible bind of lesbian representation: That is, the urgent cultural imperative to specify what lesbianism is and the recognition of the impossibility of doing so in any definitive way. Like any version of lesbian representation I might hold as an imaginary counter to this one, that I might fancy as more comprehensive, more accomplished, the photo-essay is inevitably structured by lesbianism's—which is also to say, sexuality's—resistance to knuckling under to the requirements of visual disclosure.

It comes to me before these photographs that lesbian visibility is a lure—one that is, moreover, whatever its more immediate impulses, also always in the service of a homophobic imperative to know and mark the lesbian as distinct and identifiable, as emblematic of a certain pathology, as a member of a fixed minority population in order to license as natural and in no need of explanation that heterosexual femininity which the lesbian dangerously imitates and from which she must therefore be distinguished.[25] If categories of gender are commonly understood to be eminently visible, both written on and underwritten by the body, then categories of sexuality, themselves constituted by the apparently ineluctable logics of gender, seem worryingly insensitive to the burdens of ocular proof. The lesbian body, even (and perhaps particularly) when naked, looks first and foremost like a woman's body. Nor is there much reassurance—although any amount of pleasure—in bringing two women's naked bodies together to represent lesbianism as a relational phenomenon, to define or capture lesbianism as this photo-essay does as the moment when one woman has her tongue at another's nipple.[26] Surely that seems the easiest thing, something that any woman could or might do, something that only an act of will or an orientation, once seemingly fixed and distinct but rendered newly precarious, defends her against.

What exactly does lesbian visibility make visible? Just as the photo-essay's claims on continuity draw attention to sequence as a disciplinary strategy, what each of these photographs strenuously makes visible is the very notion of visibility itself. What is not made visible, what we can say remains to be seen, is the evidential representation of lesbianism itself.

If, as I have argued throughout this book, the cultural narrativization of the relations between categories of sexual registration produce the lesbian as second best, requiring that figure to assume as its own the cultural burden of derivativeness that more properly characterizes sexuality itself, then those sequential logics maintain the epistemological problem they seem to resolve—the problem of lesbian representability. The first-order/second-order logic of sexual sequence that distinguishes between homosexuality and heterosexuality (but only by degree) consequently constitutes as its effect the difficulty of specifying lesbian difference—a difficulty that also functions as its motivation or inaugurating problem. Unless recognized as the paradoxical yet productive crucible of lesbian definition, this tightly worked relationship between sexual sequence and lesbian visibility—in which problem and solution, cause and effect repeatedly assume each other's form—continues to inhabit every intervention bent on resolving it. In my first chapter, I argued that the contemporary lesbian theoretical focus on lesbian invisibility mistakes its project to the extent that it imagines a refusal of the foundational grammars of sexual sequence, the derivative accounting for the lesbian in terms of her others, will secure lesbian visibility, the certified specification of lesbian difference. Although wired across the same questions of cultural legibility, sexual difference, and hierarchy—a set of concerns I have condensed under the rubrics of visibility and sequence—my project here has been to demonstrate the strategic value in lesbian derivation. Animating the same sequential logics that purport to demonstrate the imitative, second-order nature of lesbianism, my tactic throughout this book has been to put pressure on the sexualized coordinates of first and second, origin and outcome, heterosexuality and homosexuality, arguing that their slippery dialectic, most prominently in the service of heterosexual precedence, equally foregrounds the speciousness of that prioritization. Derivatively figured in terms of her others, the almost but not quite difference of the lesbian always threatens to return as resemblance—one, moreover, shot through with the disavowed knowledge that categories of sexual registration themselves, not lesbianism particularly, are always secondary, always back formations, always belated.

Notes

Preface

1. Judith Butler has argued for the productive potential in lesbian derivation, and my argument here is indebted to hers. In *Gender Trouble: Feminism and the Subversion of Identity* (New York: Routledge, 1990), Butler argues that homosexuality's putative imitation of heterosexuality might rather be read as a subversion of the conditions that enable the latter's naturalizing assumption of originality in the first place. Although the cultural practice of gay drag is her most extended and most cited metaphor of the ways in which an understanding of performativity works against the cultural choreography of sex and gender's pas de deux and its securing of heterosexuality as its natural effect, she also cites as exemplary the specifically lesbian production of butch/femme identities (123). In the chapters that follow, however, my argument takes a historically nuanced and literary or narratological framing in order to pursue in some detail the implications of primacy and derivation for categories of sexual identity, particularly lesbianism. See also Butler's "Imitation and Gender Insubordination," in *Inside/Out: Lesbian Theories, Gay Theories*, ed. Diana Fuss (New York: Routledge, 1991), 17.

2. Although her discussion takes quite a different turn from mine, Valerie Rohy in *Impossible Women: Lesbian Figures and American Literature* (Ithaca, N.Y.: Cornell University Press, 2000) argues that the trope of lesbian impossibility "describes the unacknowledged contradictions within hegemonic systems of sexuality, which patriarchal culture, in its will to meaning, displaces onto lesbian figures" (4).

3. Or is it, rather, as Eve Kosofsky Sedgwick suggests in *Epistemology of the Closet* (Berkeley: University of California Press, 1990), that the traditional literary canon has always played host to texts that work corrosively against its own monumentality? According to Sedgwick, "Canonicity itself then seems the necessary wadding of pious obliviousness that allows for the transmission from one generation to another of texts that have the potential to dismantle the impacted foundations upon which a given culture rests" (54).

4. Many commentators have noted that the teleological force of narrative itself is in the service of a heterosexuality that annexes to itself the cultural force of sequence.

See, for example, Judith Roof's claim that "narrative is heterosexual" (*Come as You Are: Sexuality and Narrative* [New York: Columbia University Press, 1996], 192n1) and Paul Morrison's that "the temporal art of narrative is itself both heterosexual and heterosexualizing" ("End Pleasure," *GLQ: A Journal of Lesbian and Gay Studies* 1, no. 1 [1993]: 54).

Chapter 1: First Things First

1. Terry Castle, *The Apparitional Lesbian: Female Homosexuality and Modern Culture* (New York: Columbia University Press, 1994), 2. In crucial ways, Castle's important book consolidates the critical field of lesbian studies as framed by the relation between lesbianism and invisibility. The representation of lesbianism as falling outside the limits of cultural visibility is a long-standing and persistent one. For example, describing the cultural production of lesbianism in late-nineteenth-century sexological and criminological discourses, Lynda Hart draws on the same contradictory sense of vision in excess of the visual: "Rather than an absent object being hallucinated as present, the formula for the secreting of lesbian sexuality was to produce its presence *as a hallucination*" (*Fatal Women: Lesbian Sexuality and the Mark of Aggression* [London: Routledge, 1994], 15). Similarly, Renée C. Hoogland argues that "the lesbian merely haunts the edges of the field of vision" (*Lesbian Configurations* [New York: Columbia University Press, 1997], 25).

A further consequence of the discursive production of the lesbian as invisible—her persistent association with what can't be seen—has meant that the lesbian is taken as a dense cipher for the limit conditions of cultural visibility. That is, the lesbian is not only constituted as a representational problem but equally stands as a potent figure for problems of representation more generally. See, for example, Bonnie Burns, "*Dracula's Daughter*: Cinema, Hypnosis, and the Erotics of Lesbianism," in *Lesbian Erotics*, ed. Karla Jay (New York: New York University Press, 1995), 197; Elizabeth Grosz, *Space, Time, and Perversion* (Sydney: Allen & Unwin, 1995), 158; and Judith Roof, *A Lure of Knowledge: Lesbian Sexuality and Theory* (New York: Columbia University Press, 1991), 5.

2. My foregrounding of the sexological consolidation of female homosexuality as a discursive identity is not intended to discount those presexological discourses—say, the juridical, the novelistic, and the pornographic—whose various figurations of desire between women crucially structured the epistemological foundations of sexology.

3. Castle, *The Apparitional Lesbian*, 2.

4. In a discussion of the cultural politics of outing, Judith Roof critiques the frequent lesbian and gay investment in visibility as a political end: "Predictably, the problem visibility appears to resolve, then, is invisibility—which is a product of the very same logic that produces visibility as an answer" (*Come as You Are*, 146). Writing of the double bind of visibility for the category of homosexuality, Guy Hocquenghem argues similarly for the necessary co-implication of visibility and invisibility: "Without a play with invisibility, visibility is no more than pointless foolishness, a false problem, second-rate psychology. Visibility is not an aim in itself" ("On Homo-Sex, or Is Homosexuality a Curable Vice," *New Formations*, no. 39 [Winter 1999–2000]: 74).

5. Although lesbian invisibility is most prominently structured by the axes of gender and sexuality, this logic presumes majoritarian identifications with other categories (say, of race or class) whose differentiated relations to the representational technologies of cultural legibility necessarily complicate any straightforward recourse to the notion of "invisibility." Lynda Hart observes, for example, that the sexological production of female homosexuality as an impossibility implicitly took as its subject the white

middle-class Englishwoman, whose racial, national, and class others were crucially and visibly perverted: "The distinction that was being made between heterosexuality and homosexuality was thus built on a prior division between white, middle-class women and other(ed) women" (Hart, *Fatal Women*, 4). Similarly, Judith Halberstam argues that the figure of lesbian spectrality overlooks the racialization of lesbian invisibility: "When white lesbians continue to invest exclusively in this construction of lesbian sex as elusive, apparitional, silent, and intangible, other hyper-visible lesbian sexualities with highly complex relations to silence and exposure are totally discounted" (*Female Masculinity* [Durham, N.C.: Duke University Press, 1998], 115).

In a slightly different context, Biddy Martin critiques several cinematic representations in which the racialization of lesbianism renders it visible. Discussing the trend to reinforce butch–femme relationality across racial difference, Martin writes, "Making lesbian desire visible as desire, rather than identification, requires an added measure of difference, figured racially. Disidentification from assigned gender is accomplished through darkness, as if whiteness and femmeness could not be differentiated and as if blackness were pure difference" (*Femininity Played Straight: The Significance of Being Lesbian* [New York: Routledge, 1996], 86).

6. Monique Wittig, "The Straight Mind," *Feminist Issues* 1, no. 1 (Summer 1980): 110; Castle, *The Apparitional Lesbian*, 12.

7. As Judith Halberstam argues, "Although it may ultimately prove unfruitful to theorize lesbianism and female masculinity synonymously, it is important to acknowledge that historically within what we have called lesbianism, masculinity has played an important role. Masculinity often defines the stereotypical version of lesbianism . . . ; the bull dyke, indeed has made lesbianism visible as some kind of confluence of gender disturbance and sexual orientation" (*Female Masculinity*, 119).

8. To compare the sometimes distinct, sometimes synchronized discursive effects of the inadmissibility of male homosexuality and the impossibility of female homosexuality, consider two British libel prosecutions, both unsuccessful: Oscar Wilde's famous 1895 case against the Marquis of Queensberry for accusing him of "posing as a Somdomite" and Maud Allan's lesser-known 1918 prosecution of Noel Pemberton-Billing, an Independent MP and editor of *Vigilante*, a newspaper that published an article linking Allan to the "Cult of the Clitoris." In both cases, the obliqueness of the allegedly libelous description functioned as a strategic mechanism less for obscuring than for securing the homosexuality of its referent. Queensberry's allegation—clear enough despite his famous spelling mistake—that Wilde posed, without necessarily being, a sodomite hardly alleviated its libelous force; the notions of theatricality and imitation implicit in "posing" served to index homosexuality almost as securely and certainly as incoherently as the older catalog of sodomitical acts that they here reinforced. A similar kind of heat-seeking indirection governs the *Vigilante*'s metonymic substitution of the clitoris for lesbianism—a convenient and historically practiced sleight-of-hand that allows an anatomical feature common to women as a class nevertheless to delineate from that group an unimaginably perverted subcategory about whose identity, practices, and distinguishing marks swirls as much epistemological doubt as exists in relation to the significance, location, and function of that body part that is here its stand-in.

Despite the slanted reference to homosexuality in both allegedly libelous statements, the progress and outcome of both cases demonstrate the different discursive relations of male and female homosexuality to the horizons of cultural possibility—the former forbidden, the latter unthinkable. For while their unsuccessful prosecutions marked the end of both Wilde's and Allan's theatrical careers, the forbidden—literally illegal—status of male homosexuality proved spectacularly damaging in Wilde's case, as his unsuccessful prosecution of Queensberry provided the legally incriminating evidence for Queensberry's successful prosecution of Wilde for "acts of gross indecency." In Allan's case, lesbianism remains strategically undefined. Not predicated on sexual acts between women or even the desire for such acts, the unspecified possibility of lesbianism rests on inappropriate sexual knowledge—namely, Allan's familiarity with the specialist medical terminology of the "clitoris." Implicitly charged not with possession but knowledge of a clitoris, it is Allan's understanding of the derogatory weight of Pemberton-Billing's reference to that anatomy that prevents his article from being libelous. The different ways in which the two trials specified and elaborated the "slur" of homosexuality that instigated the prosecution in the first place is reminder enough that the discourses of the forbidden and the unthinkable are not entirely distinct, not in their tactical outcomes for instance. It is the frightful but describable visions of male homosexuality that enable the defense-about-to-turn-prosecution to overturn Wilde's case while the opposite—the inability to imagine two women in any productive or pleasurable conjunction—is what enables a different court to make what amounts to the same ruling against Allan.

My accounts of Wilde's and Allan's libel cases are dependent on the critical commentaries of Lucy Bland, "Trial by Sexology? Maud Allan, *Salome*, and the 'Cult of the Clitoris' Case," in *Sexology in Culture: Labelling Bodies and Desires*, ed. Lucy Bland and Laura Doan (Chicago: University of Chicago Press, 1998), 183–98; Ed Cohen, *Talk on the Wilde Side: Toward a Genealogy of a Discourse on Male Sexualities* (New York: Routledge, 1993); Laura Doan, *Fashioning Sapphism: The Origin of a Modern English Lesbian Culture* (New York: Columbia University Press, 2001); and Jennifer Travis, "Clits in Court: *Salome*, Sodomy, and the Lesbian 'Sadist,' " in *Lesbian Erotics*, 147–63.

9. No more than a glance at *The Penguin Book of Australian Slang: A Dinkum Guide to Oz English* confirms this suspicion. Under its entry for homosexuality, which includes more general terms such as *fag, fruit, poofter*, and its rhyming *wooly woofter*, is a list of slang terms whose extensiveness—the singular *cocksucker* notwithstanding—cannot conceal its dogged fixation on the definitiveness of a single sex act, whether actively or passively conceived. Alphabetically then: *bum bandit, dinter, dung-puncher, bender, chocolate bandit, intestinal tourist, mattress-muncher, pillow-biter, poo-jabber, ring jockey, shirt lifter* (to) *shit doughnuts, shit puncher, shit stabber, turd bandit, turd burglar, turd dinter*, and *turd puncher*. While innovation and irreverence have long been hailed as two of the defining characteristics of white Australia's national identity, which might make slang something Australians fancy themselves particularly good at, this hardly explains the mean clutch of terms for lesbian, all of them simply diminutive plays on the word itself: *les-be-friends, lesbo, leso, lesso, lezzy*. See *The Penguin Book of Australian Slang: A Dinkum Guide to Oz English*, ed. Lenie Johansen (Ringwood: Penguin, 1988; rpt., 1996).

10. Conventionally, this refusal to entertain the plausibility or even possibility of sex between women has been characterized as a peculiarly Victorian disavowal—one apocryphally attributed to no less a representative of the Victorians than Queen Victoria herself who, when consulted as to whether the Criminal Law Amendment Act might be extended to include acts of gross indecency between women, declared such acts impossible and hence in no need of legislation. Still, male and female homosexuality's differentiated relations to representation have not fallen away as we put a distance between ourselves and the Victorians. Never quite superceded, always available for reactivation, Judith Butler ("Sexual Inversions," in *Discourses of Sexuality: From Aristotle to AIDS*, ed. Domna C. Stanton [Ann Arbor: University of Michigan Press, 1992]) finds the same discrimination operative in the medico-juridical AIDS discourses that pathologize "the [male] homosexual subject as a bearer of death" while raising to the second power the impossibility of lesbianism: "One might ask here whether lesbian sexuality

even qualifies as *sex* within hegemonic public discourse. 'What is it that they do' might be read as 'Can we be sure they do anything at all?' " (346).

11. I am thinking here of the numerous ways in which vaginal intercourse comes to occupy the place of naturalness and rightness: the Freudian account of the young girl's normative repudiation of her clitoris for her vagina; the first-base/second-base calculation of degrees of sexual activity that, momentarily, enabled Bill Clinton's claim that he and Monica Lewinsky had not had sex; the legal distinction between sexual assault and rape; the confusion and uncertainty among even feminist doctors regarding protocols (say, the necessity of cervical smears) for patients whose sexual history and current practice falls outside the presumptive model of heterosexuality.

12. As Lauren Berlant and Michael Warner argue in "Sex in Public" (*Critical Inquiry* 24, no. 2 [Winter 1998]), the privatization of heterosexuality's sex act marks it as the definitional heart of a heterosexual culture that nevertheless annexes for itself in no less defining ways a series of acts whose avowed asexuality territorialize a whole world: "The sex act shielded by the zone of privacy is the affectional nimbus that heterosexual culture protects and from which it abstracts its model of ethics, but this utopia of social belonging is also supported and extended by acts less commonly recognized as part of sexual culture: paying taxes, being disgusted, philandering, bequeathing, celebrating a holiday, investing for the future, teaching, disposing of a corpse, carrying wallet photos, buying economy size, being nepotistic, running for president, divorcing, or owning anything 'His' and 'Hers' " (555).

13. For theoretical elaborations of this model, see Rosi Braidotti, *Patterns of Dissonance: A Study of Women in Contemporary Philosophy*, trans. Elizabeth Guild (Cambridge: Polity Press, 1991); Luce Irigaray, *Speculum of the Other Woman*, trans. Gillian Gill (Ithaca, N.Y.: Cornell University Press, 1985); Marilyn Frye, *The Politics of Reality: Essays in Feminist Theory* (New York: Crossing Press, 1983); and Adrienne Rich, "Compulsory Heterosexuality and Lesbian Existence," in *The Lesbian and Gay Studies Reader*, ed. Henry Abelove et al. (New York: Routledge, 1993), 227–54.

14. For theoretical elaborations of this model, see Lynda Hart, *Fatal Women*, 92–93, and Monique Wittig, *The Straight Mind and Other Essays* (Boston: Beacon Press, 1992).

15. Eve Kosofsky Sedgwick, *Epistemology of the Closet* (Berkeley: University of California Press, 1990), 86–90.

16. Ibid., 47.

17. Rosi Braidotti, "Revisiting Male Thanatica," *Differences: A Journal of Feminist Cultural Studies* 6, nos. 2–3 (1994): 203. Braidotti's essay is a response to Trevor Hope's "Melancholic Modernity: The Hom(m)osexual Symptom and the Homosocial Corpse" (*Differences: A Journal of Feminist Cultural Studies* 6, nos. 2–3 [1994]: 174–98). Hope's essay, Braidotti's response, and Hope's reply ("The 'Returns' of Cartography: Mapping Identity-In(-)Difference," *Differences: A Journal of Feminist Cultural Studies* 6, nos. 2–3 [1994]: 208–11) constitute a productive rehearsal of the tensions that have marked attempts to theorize lesbianism and male homosexuality both together and apart.

18. Hart, *Fatal Women*, 92–93.

19. Randolph Trumbach argues in *Sex and the Gender Revolution* (vol. 1 of *Heterosexuality and the Third Gender in Enlightenment London* [Chicago: University of Chicago, 1998]) that the role of the sodomite emerges substantially earlier and has more social significance than that of the sapphist. For Trumbach, the sodomite and the sapphist bookend the eighteenth century—the former appearing around 1700 and the latter not until the 1770s. Moreover, in Trumbach's account, the advent of the sodomite, defined by his effeminacy, gave rise to a three-gender system—"(man, woman, and sodomite)"—that in turn inaugurates male heterosexuality and homosexuality. "Men

had entered a new gender system by changing the nature of their sexual relations with each other: men no longer had sex with boys or women—they now had sex either with females or males. They were now supposed to be exclusively homosexual or heterosexual" (9). By comparison, for Trumbach,

> For most of the century there was no exclusive sapphist role against which the majority of women could define themselves as heterosexual. And after 1770 when it becomes possible to document a sapphist role among some aristocratic and middle-class women, it is hard to see that it had on women's behavior anything like the effect that the sodomite role had had on men since the beginning of the century. Throughout the century most women did not have an exclusive heterosexual identity (which is not to say they were not attracted to men), and they experienced the new male heterosexuality mainly as its victims. The sexual behavior of women was therefore defined by their relationship to men and not in opposition to a sapphist minority. (429)

This is not the place—I am not the scholar—to dispute the accuracy of Trumbach's findings. The terms of Trumbach's argument, however, raise the suspicion that the cultural inconsequence or invisibility of sexual relations between women, which he argues pertains for most of the eighteenth century, licenses his retrospective reading of the sapphist as a kind of belated sodomite. For more authoritative rebuttals of Trumbach's argument that critique, among other things, the belatedness of his sapphist, see George E. Haggerty, "Heteromachia," *GLQ: A Journal of Lesbian and Gay Studies* 6, no. 3 (2000): 435–37, and Valerie Traub, *The Renaissance of Lesbianism in Early Modern England* (Oxford: Oxford University Press, forthcoming).

20. Despite the apparent anachronism of the concept of heteronormativity in this context, I am following the lead of Theresa Braunschneider ("The Macroclitoride, the Tribade, and the Woman: Configuring Gender and Sexuality in English Anatomical Discourse," *Textual Practice* 13, no. 3 [1999]), who, in the context of her discussion of seventeenth-century tribadic discourses, argues persuasively for a sense of heteronormativity—the normative framing of "potentially reproductive male-female copulation" (530n12)—that precedes the emergence of heterosexuality as sexual taxonomy. The way in which the concept of heteronormativity precedes the heterosexuality it seems already to prioritize is, of course, in large part the explanatory context for what I am arguing for here—a female homosexuality that is, in the first place, derivative of sexual organizations that do not precede it.

21. Foucault's argument about the invention of the homosexual and Faderman's argument about romantic friendships characterize two influential and persistent themes in lesbian historiography that their names have come to represent if not actually inaugurate.

22. While I am arguing that the theoretical paradigms of Faderman and Foucault inadvertently reinforce a sense of the historic invisibility of sex between women, Ros Ballaster in " 'The Vices of Old Rome Revived': Representations of Female Same-Sex Desire in Seventeenth and Eighteenth Century England" (in *Volcanoes and Pearl Divers: Essays in Lesbian Feminist Studies*, ed. Suzanne Raitt [New York: Harrington Park Press, 1995]) describes this double bind differently but across the same proper names:

> The central premise of this article is that lesbian history is currently caught in an impasse between two theoretical models: first, a feminocentric account, developed largely from the writings of Adrienne Rich and Lillian Faderman, of women's oppression by a monolithic "compulsory heterosexuality" that inhibits

the expression of a concealed and pre-given "lesbian" identity and second, a homoerotic account, built on the writings of Michel Foucault, of a distinction between pre-modern sex as a variety of "acts" and the modern construction of a discourse of sexuality as constitutive of identity. (16)

23. Castle, *The Apparitional Lesbian*, 241n10, 8.
24. Ibid., 10.
25. Lisa Moore, *Dangerous Intimacies: Toward a Sapphic History of the British Novel* (Durham, N.C.: Duke University Press, 1997), 8.
26. Ibid., 11.
27. See, for example, Valerie Traub's argument in "The (In)Significance of 'Lesbian' Desire in Early Modern England" (in *Queering the Renaissance*, ed. Jonathan Goldberg [Durham, N.C.: Duke University Press, 1994]) that, however much the critical investments in earlier forms of sexual activity between women are underwritten by that "recent discursive invention, the lesbian" (62), the two are, crucially, not the same.
28. See, for example, Lynn Hunt, who argues in "Foucault's Subject in *The History of Sexuality*" (in *Discourses of Sexuality*) that Foucault's inattentiveness to gender across the three volumes of *The History of Sexuality* skews his genealogical account of technologies of the self to the degree that "the genderless functional operation of power is juxtaposed, uncomfortably and even inexplicably, with a profoundly gendered concept of the individual as adult male subject" (84).
29. Michel Foucault, *The History of Sexuality*, vol. 1, *An Introduction*, trans. Robert Hurley (London: Penguin, 1990), 43.
30. Given this, it is important to note that David Halperin in "Forgetting Foucault: Acts, Identities, and the History of Sexuality" (*Representations* 63 [Summer 1999]) has demonstrated that the frequent citation of this passage has licensed a misreading or, in his terms, a forgetting of the work it is doing in Foucault's larger argument. Commonly taken to license an acts versus an identities understanding of premodern and modern conceptions of sexual deviance and consequently to rule against the existence of premodern sexual identities, Halperin argues instead that Foucault is here using the discursively delimited example of the sodomite and the homosexual to demonstrate a larger and crucial shift in "the different modalities of power at work in premodern and modern codifications of sexual prohibition"—the former working through legislation and prescription, the latter through strategies of normalization. He writes,

> [Foucault's] schematic opposition between sodomy and homosexuality is first and foremost a discursive analysis, not a social history, let alone an exhaustive one. *It is not an empirical claim about the historical existence or nonexistence of sexually deviant individuals.* It is a claim about the internal logic and systematic functioning of two different discursive styles of sexual disqualification—and, ultimately, it is a heuristic device for foregrounding what is distinctive about modern techniques of social and sexual regulation. (98 and 99; italics in original)

31. Although sodomy is frequently understood as a definitively male category, in "Presumptive Sodomy and Its Exclusions" (*Textual Practice* 13, no. 2 [1999]), Karma Lochrie critiques this assumption:

> Presumptive sodomy designates the privileging of certain assumptions about what sodomy means without saying it—that it refers to anal sex between men, that it is primarily a masculine form of desire, and that gender exerts a negligible influence on the category. Like presumptive heterosexuality, presumptive

sodomy has the effect of privileging a version of medieval sodomy that excludes women and gender and replicates the very misogyny of the medieval category. (296)

32. Emma Donoghue, *Passions between Women: British Lesbian Culture, 1668–1801* (London: Scarlet Press, 1993; rpt., New York: HarperCollins, 1995), 9.

33. Elizabeth Susan Wahl, *Invisible Relations: Representations of Female Intimacy in the Age of Enlightenment* (Stanford, Calif.: Stanford University Press, 1999), 8.

34. Valerie Traub, "The Perversion of 'Lesbian' Desire," *History Workshop Journal* 41 [1996]: 24.

35. Traub, "The (In)Significance of 'Lesbian' Desire in Early Modern England," 79. Braunschneider's recent argument about the changing significance of the tribade nicely amplifies Traub's observation and, by corollary, my point here that the *visibility* of categories of sexual identity, no less than the categories themselves, is historically specific: "A figure of intense medical interest in the seventeenth century, the tribade wanes as a focus of attention in medical discourse during the eighteenth century—in fact it ceases almost altogether to be an object of medical attention" (Braunschneider, "The Macroclitoride, the Tribade, and the Woman," 513).

36. Traub, "The Perversion of 'Lesbian' Desire," 25 and 41–43.

37. Nevertheless, I am not persuaded by Judith M. Bennett's suggestion in "'Lesbian-Like' and the Social History of Lesbians" (*Journal of the History of Sexuality* 9, nos. 1–2 [January–April 2000]) that the introduction of the term *lesbian-like* will enable the productive articulation of contemporary and historical models of women's sexual and gendered behaviors and identities or, as she writes, "speak to our modern need for a useable past" (14). Although Bennett emphasizes the destabilizing function of her term, it seems to me that its more primary rhetorical effect is to underwrite the historical ambitions of the term *lesbian* itself—a suspicion borne out in the slippages of Bennett's own argument. Having carefully acknowledged many of the risks in formalizing historical affinities with modern identity categories, Bennett admits one further inadequacy of her favored term: "Obviously, 'lesbian-like' will overlook some lesbians in past times" (16). For me, the significance of this admission is not that *lesbian-like* is unable to scoop up every lesbian, past and present, in its signifying grasp but that it consolidates even those historical subjects it is unable to capture not as lesbian-like but simply as lesbians.

38. This desire to think about history in terms that are neither transhistoricist nor alteritist takes as its inspiration Louise Fradenburg and Carla Freccero's account (in the Introduction to *Premodern Sexualities*, ed. Fradenburg and Freccero [New York: Routledge, 1996]) of a queer historiography that would not disavow the productive pleasure in its identifications with the past:

> The opposition between transhistoricist perspectives which seek, in the past, the allure of the mirror image, and historicist perspectives that "accept" the difference of past from present, is itself highly ideological. What has to be asked is whether the observation of similarities or even continuities between past and present inevitably produces an ahistoricist or universalizing effect.... If the practice of queer theory has taught us that neither alterity nor similarity is an inevitable conceptual guarantor of oppositional political force, that the construction of desirous identifications can be potentially destabilizing as well as totalizing, then we must see that positing the power of the past to disrupt and remake the present is not necessarily to adopt a naïve continuism. Is it not indeed pos-

sible that alteritism at times functions precisely to stabilize the identity of "the modern"? (xix)

Offering a further account of a queer history that refuses to discipline itself in relation to the alleged oppositions of "mimetic identification with the past or blanket alteritism," Carolyn Dinshaw in *Getting Medieval: Sexualities and Communities, Pre- and Postmodern* (Durham, N.C.: Duke University Press, 1999) figures history as tactility: "[My queer history] is a history of things touching: contingent <L. *com-* + *tangere*, to touch" (34 and 39).

39. Anne Lister, *I Know My Own Heart: The Diaries of Anne Lister, 1791–1840*, ed. Helena Whitbread (London: Virago Press, 1988); Anne Lister, *No Priest but Love: Excerpts from the Diaries of Anne Lister, 1824–26*, ed. Helena Whitbread (Otley: Smith Settle, 1992); and Anne Lister, *Female Fortune: Land, Gender, and Authority. The Anne Lister Diaries and Other Writings, 1833–36*, ed. Jill Liddington (London: Rivers Oram Press, 1998).

40. Several commentators draw attention to the similarities between Lister's diaries and the Austen novelscape. Castle in *The Apparitional Lesbian* notes that "Lister's world seems at first glance so familiar: very much the cozy domestic universe of a Jane Austen novel," until references to her masculine demeanor and sexual interest in women effect "a kind of surreal slippage" (96). Lisa Moore's reading of *Emma* in *Dangerous Intimacies* draws a comparison between Austen's eponymous heroine and Lister, while arguing more broadly that Austen's representation of female friendship as chaste and succeeded by heterosexual marriage is undone by the fact that by 1816, the year of *Emma*'s publication, "for a heroine-centered novel to represent female friendship at all is to invoke the possibility of sapphism," a prominent contemporary example of which is "the self-conscious sapphic practice and identity of Anne Lister" (111).

41. Lister, *I Know My Own Heart*, 8.
42. Ibid., 102.
43. Ibid., 48.
44. Ibid., 268.
45. Ibid., x.
46. For example, Anna Clark in "Anne Lister's Construction of Lesbian Identity" (*Journal of the History of Sexuality* 7, no. 1 [1996]) argues that "although she did not use the word lesbian, at age thirty, she wrote, " 'I love and only love the fairer sex and thus, beloved by them in turn, my heart revolts from any other love than theirs' " (23). Rictor Norton in *The Myth of the Modern Homosexual: Queer History and the Search for Cultural Unity* (London: Cassell, 1997) quotes the same passage as a demonstration that "Anne Lister [is] a self-conscious lesbian in the psychological sense" (196). Castle (*The Apparitional Lesbian*, 101) and Moore (*Dangerous Intimacies*, 86–87) also cite this sentence.

47. George Chauncey in "From Sexual Inversion to Homosexuality: Medicine and the Changing Conceptualization of Female Deviance" (*Salmagundi* 58–59 [1982]) demonstrates the crucial significance of this distinction when he traces the evolution of female perversion from sexual inversion to homosexuality in late-nineteenth-/early-twentieth-century medical literature: "Sexual inversion, the term used in most of the nineteenth century literature, . . . had a much broader meaning than our present term, homosexuality, which denotes solely the sex of the person one sexually desires. Sexual inversion, rather, connoted a total reversal of one's sex role" (119). Drawing on Chauncey's work, David Halperin in *One Hundred Years of Homosexuality and Other Essays on Greek Love* (New York: Routledge, 1990) argues that this distinction between gender role and sexual role is crucial to the emergence of sexuality as a discrete phenomenon: "Sexual identity . . . is not to be confused with gender identity or gender role: indeed,

one of the chief conceptual functions of sexuality is to distinguish, once and for all, sexual identity from matters of gender—to decouple, as it were, *kinds* of sexual predilection from *degrees* of masculinity and femininity" (25). Ten years later, Halperin in "How to Do the History of Male Homosexuality" (*GLQ: A Journal of Gay and Lesbian Studies* 6, no. 1 [2000]) argues that "homosexuality is more than same-sex sexual object choice, more even than conscious erotic same-sex preference. Homosexuality is the specification of same-sex sexual object choice in and of itself as an overriding principle of sexual and social difference" (112).

48. For an engaging reading that critiques "the unproblematic categorization of Lister and her desire as a lesbian" and interprets her sexual practices as "signs of an active and functional but preidentitarian female masculinity," see Judith Halberstam, *Female Masculinity* (Durham, N.C.: Duke University Press, 1998), 66 and 72.

49. This explains the ease with which a number of critics read Lister's masculinity as not so much a reinforcement but *evidence* of her "lesbianism." Recuperating Lister's sexual style for a mid-twentieth-century sexual taxonomy, Rictor Norton describes Lister and Marianna as "a butch/femme couple" (*The Myth of the Modern Homosexual*, 199), and Sally R. Munt includes Lister on her transhistorical list of "key contemporary icons of butchness" (*Heroic Desire: Lesbian Identity and Cultural Space* [London: Cassell, 1998], 55).

50. Castle, *The Apparitional Lesbian*, 105.

51. Ibid., 105–106.

52. Arguing that Lister lived more or less openly "as a lesbian," Rictor Norton notes as evidence that she "discussed her affairs with [her aunt and uncle] quite openly, barring the explicit sex, comparing the different merits of her potential female partners; they looked forward to the time when she would fix upon a suitable female companion to live with her and settle down" (*The Myth of the Modern Homosexual*, 201). Yet given that "barring the explicit sex"—and even, it has to be said, the inexplicit—Lister's fondest hope is able to circulate within the legitimized discourse of the romantic friendship, her frequent expressions of her desire for a lifelong female companion cannot be mistaken even for a disclosure of her sexual preference, let alone the articulation of that preference as always already "lesbian." More persuasively, Jill Liddington argues that Lister's aunt and uncle's acceptance of her stated desire to set up house with a woman rested on dynastic rather than sexual knowledges (*Female Fortune*, 18–19).

53. Lister, *I Know My Own Heart*, 287. Clearly, Lister imagines her aunt's understanding of the circulation of sexually transmissible diseases enjoys some currency, for previously she has offered a very similar account to her own doctor in seeking treatment: "Consulted the doctor about my complaint and the consequent discharge. Said I had caught it from a married friend whose husband was a dissipated character. I had gone to the water-closet just after her" (230).

54. Lister, *No Priest but Love*, 31–32.

55. In her groundbreaking work on the British novel of the eighteenth and nineteenth century, Lisa Moore demonstrates the ambiguous twining of the discourses of romantic friendship and sapphism, "the lively specter of a freakishly sexualized connection between women haunt[ing] representations of female friendship," which here electrifies Lister's claims to propriety (*Dangerous Intimacies*, 75–76).

56. Lister, *No Priest but Love*, 33.

57. It is not of course necessary that we read Lister's aunt or Mrs. Barlow as hoodwinked by Lister in this regard (after all, Lister herself refers to Mrs. Barlow as "a deepish hand"). Rather, Lister's double bluff suggests that we consider early nineteenth-century relations between women as significantly structured by the strategic mobilization of knowledge or ignorance of sex between women.

58. Lister, *No Priest but Love*, 155.

59. For example, Lister assures Marianna that she has persuaded Anne that "there was nothing more than friendship between Marianna and [herself],"although she withholds from Marianna the fact that her own involvement with Anne has exceeded flirtation (*No Priest but Love*, 127). Lister shows Marianna a letter from Lou in which Lou refers to her understanding that Lister wishes her to take Marianna's position should Lister and Marianna be unable to live together, but, although taken aback, Marianna "was quite convinced Lou had no idea beyond friendship" (*No Priest but Love*, 125).

60. Lister, *I Know My Own Heart*, 139 and 140–41.

61. Lister, *No Priest but Love*, 149–50.

62. Ibid., 151. This possibility doesn't seem extraordinary to Lou. Lister records their subsequent exchange: " 'Why should you not?' [asked Lou]. I said 'What! Engaged to one sister and in love with another?' 'Yes,' said Lou, 'with two of her sisters'—alluding to Mrs Milne [Henrietta]."

63. Clark, "Anne Lister's Construction of Lesbian Identity," 50.

64. Martha Vicinus in " 'They Wonder to Which Sex I Belong': The Historical Roots of the Modern Lesbian Identity" (in *The Lesbian and Gay Studies Reader*) identifies as significant the different sexual stylings of Lister and Marianna—"Within a self-consciously sexual couple two conflicting justifications for their behaviour coexisted uneasily"—but rather than consider this as working against the homogeneity of "lesbianism," she describes Lister at least as "a self-consciously mannish lesbian" (441). Here my position is closer to that of David Halperin, who argues that "the hallmark of 'homosexuality,' in fact, is the refusal to distinguish between same-sex sexual partners or to rank them by treating one of them as more (or less) homosexual than the other" ("How to Do the History of Male Homosexuality," 110).

65. David Halperin, "Historicizing the Sexual Body: Sexual Preferences and Erotic Identities in the Pseudo-Lucianic Erôtes," in *Discourses of Sexuality*, 261.

66. Clark, "Anne Lister's Construction of Lesbian Identity," 23.

67. Agency is a strong theme in much of the discussions of Lister's diaries. Lisa Moore's repeated references to Lister's "sapphic self-construction," her "self-conscious sapphic practice and identity," and "the Byronic self-construction of Anne Lister's sapphic identity" emphasizes the extent to which Lister actively constructs her sexual role (*Dangerous Intimacies*, 89, 111, and 127). Several of the commentators who emphasize the agency at work in Lister's construction of her sexual role follow Clark in characterizing that agency as evidence of a presexological homosexual identity. For example, in a critique of Lillian Faderman's and Esther Newton's theorization of presexological romantic friendships between women as asexual, Martha Vicinus argues that this "den[ies] homosexual agency to pre-twentieth century women," citing Lister's diaries as a much-needed corrective (Introduction to *Lesbian Subjects: A Feminist Studies Reader*, ed. Vicinus [Bloomington: Indiana University Press, 1996], 8–9).

68. Judith Butler, *The Psychic Life of Power: Theories in Subjection* (Stanford, Calif.: Stanford University Press, 1997, 2).

69. For an account of John Lister's treatment of the diaries and the speculative dating of his transcription, see Jill Liddington, Preface to Anne Lister, *Female Fortune: Land, Gender, and Authority*, xv and 254n7. For an account of Phyllis Ramsden's ludicrous self-justifications for not reproducing any of the decoded crypt passages and her attempts to deter future scholars from bending in that direction—"it can be taken for granted that the longer the passage the less it is worth the tedium of decoding"—see Castle, *The Apparitional Lesbian*, 243n13.

70. Angus Gordon, *Plastic Identities: Adolescence, Homosexuality, and Contemporary Culture* (Chicago: University of Chicago Press, forthcoming).

71. For a more detailed account of the compensatory ways in which the figure of the lesbian has been required to function as the utopic outside of the disciplinary structures that more properly constitute her, see my *Lesbian Utopics* (New York: Routledge, 1994).

72. Hart, *Fatal Women*, 9.

73. Castle cites as her evidence a reading list that contains "Juvenal's *Satires*, Martial's *Epigrams*, Ovid's *Metamorphoses*, Ariosto's *Orlando Furioso*, Aretino's *Dialogues*, Sir Philip Sidney's *Arcadia*, Shakespeare's *As You Like It* or *Twelfth Night*, Ben Jonson's *Volpone*, John Donne's *Satires, Epigrams, and Verse Letters*, John Cleland's *Memoirs of A Woman of Pleasure*, Samuel Richardson's *Pamela*, Diderot's *La Religieuse*, Laclos's *Les Liaisons dangereuses*, Coleridge's *Christabel*, Christina Rossetti's *Goblin Market*, Balzac's *La Fille aux yeux d'or*, Swinburne's *Poems and Ballads* or *Lesbia Brandon*, [and] Zola's *Nana*" (*The Apparitional Lesbian*, 9). The textual field referenced here by Castle was certainly read by sexologists as a significant cultural archive. For example, in his chapter "Sexual Inversion in Women," Havelock Ellis in *Sexual Inversion* (London: Wilson and Macmillan, 1897; rpt., New York: Arno Press, 1975) cites many of the same titles—Diderot's *La Religieuse*, Balzac's *La Fille aux Yeux d'Or*, Zola's *Nana*, Swinburne's *Poems and Ballads*—adding Gautier's *Mademoiselle de Maupin*, Belot's *Mademoiselle Giraud, ma Femme*, and Verlaine's *Parallèlement* (78n1). Yet it is worth remembering that the literary and the sexological function as two very different economies of knowledge. It is not that literature possesses a knowledge that sexology can only latterly claim but that sexology bends various literary knowledges to its own project, the taxonomic consolidation of distinctly modern forms of sexual subjectivity.

74. Marylynne Diggs, "Romantic Friends or a 'Different Race of Creatures'? The Representation of Lesbian Pathology in Nineteenth-Century America," *Feminist Studies* 21, no. 2 (Summer 1995): 323. For the positing of the modern lesbian as a subject already in limited circulation in England in the 1840s and 1850s, see also Martha Vicinus, "Lesbian Perversity and Victorian Marriage: The 1864 Codrington Divorce Trial," *Journal of British Studies* 36 (January 1997): 71.

75. Laura Doan, " 'Acts of Female Indecency': Sexology's Intervention in Legislating Lesbianism," in *Sexology in Culture*, 200 and 211.

76. Bland, "Trial by Sexology?" 193.

77. Ellis, *Sexual Inversion*, xi. From the start, Ellis's *Sexual Inversion* raised tangled questions of priority and propriety. The first edition of the work appeared in German translation as *Das konträre Geschlechtsgefühl*, a year before the 1897 publication of the English edition. Anxious about the book's British reception, Ellis thought its previous publication in Europe might assist its critical acceptance at home. See Phyllis Grosskurth, *Havelock Ellis: A Biography* (New York: Alfred Knopf, 1980), 179.

78. Havelock Ellis, *Studies in the Psychology of Sex* (London: William Heinemann, 1948), xxi.

79. Ibid., xxi.

80. Ellis, *Sexual Inversion*, 80, 81, and 82.

81. Ibid., 78. Widely considered to have brokered European sexology to the United States, Ellis's first piece of work to be published in America was the 1895 article "Sexual Inversion in Women." The following year, in the same journal, he published the companion piece, "Sexual Inversion in Men." My sources for these details are Joseph Bristow, "Symond's History, Ellis's Heredity," in *Sexology in Culture*, 96n9, and Siobhan B. Somerville, *Queering the Color Line: Race and the Invention of Homosexuality in American Culture* (Durham, N.C.: Duke University Press, 2000), 19.

82. Ellis, *Sexual Inversion*, 42.

83. Ellis strongly believed that inversion was a congenital condition, arguing that even in those cases that seemed traceable to some formative moment of initiation there must be some underlying predisposition to inversion: "If it is to act on a fairly normal nature the perverted suggestion must be very powerful or iterated, and even then its influence will probably only be temporary, disappearing in the presence of the normal stimulus" (*Sexual Inversion*, 110). He was also keen to dissociate male inversion from any definitive relation to anal sex, stressing its absence in many case studies and in those few case studies in which it featured describing it as "the preferred form of sexual gratification or as a matter of indifference" (*Sexual Inversion*, 54). Reviewing the sexual practices of the twenty-four men of whom he had definite knowledge, Ellis works against his finding that anal sex figured in more than half of the case histories. Again, he distinguishes between what might be called a preference and what might be downgraded simply to a practice, in order to argue that anal sex figures significantly in only one-quarter of the cases, and he insinuates that further research might yet lower this incidence rate:

> In thirteen cases, *i.e.*, more than half, actual *paedicatio*—usually active, not passive—has been exercised. In all these cases, however, *paedicatio* is by no means the habitual or even the preferred method of gratification. It seems to be the preferred method in about six cases. The proportion of paederasts in this group of sexual inverts is larger than I should have been inclined to expect; whether a wider induction of cases would modify the results I cannot say. (*Sexual Inversion*, 118)

84. Ellis, *Sexual Inversion*, 64 and 65.

85. Ibid., 51 and 57.

86. Ibid., 52 and 47.

87. Ibid., 118. Ellis's position on the gendered presentation of male inverts is not consistent, and these contradictions occasionally occur in close argumentative proximity to each other. For example, immediately following his above-cited assertion that gender inversion "is very frequently not the case" in male inverts, Ellis asserts on the next page that "although the invert himself may stoutly affirm his masculinity, and although this femininity may not be very obvious, its wide prevalence may be asserted with considerable assurance, and by no means only among the small minority of inverts who take an exclusively passive *rôle*, though in these, it is usually most marked" (*Sexual Inversion*, 119).

88. Ellis, *Sexual Inversion*, 94. A number of commentators have noted Ellis's differential treatment of the gendered trope of inversion in relation to male and female inverts. Vern L. Bullough writes, "Interestingly, in his discussion of male homosexuality, he did not assert that congenital homosexuals were always effeminate, but he did note that female homosexuals had more virile temperaments than other women." (*Science in the Bedroom: A History of Sex Research* [New York: Basic Books, 1994], 82). Jennifer Terry points out that "[Ellis] dispelled many of the negative stereotypes surrounding male homosexuality, such as the notion that homosexual men were . . . effeminate. But [he] did not extend the same charitable understanding to lesbians. To the contrary, he emphasized their mannishness" (*An American Obsession: Science, Medicine, and Homosexuality in Modern Society* [Chicago: University of Chicago Press, 1999], 51). Rita Felski similarly argues that "while Ellis challenged the stereotype of the effeminate homosexual, he concurred with other sexologists in portraying the lesbian as a gruff, often grotesque, mannish figure" (Introduction to *Sexology in Culture*, 5). See also Lucy Bland, *Banishing*

the Beast: English Feminism and Sexual Morality, 1885–1914 (Harmondsworth: Penguin Books, 1995), 263.

89. Ellis, *Sexual Inversion*, 87.

90. Ibid., 96.

91. Sigmund Freud, "The Psychogenesis of a Case of Homosexuality in a Woman" (1920), in *The Standard Edition of the Complete Psychological Works of Sigmund Freud*, vol. 18, trans. and ed. James Strachey (London: Hogarth Press, 1955), 171.

92. Ibid., 167.

93. Ibid.

94. Ibid., 158.

95. Ibid.

96. The notion of gender's syntax and its relentless sentencing of the subject to heterosexuality is, of course, Judith Butler's: "The heterosexualisation of desire requires and institutes the production of discrete and asymmetrical oppositions between 'feminine' and 'masculine' " (*Gender Trouble*, 17).

97. Freud, "The Psychogenesis of a Case of Homosexuality in a Woman," 170.

98. Christopher Craft argues similarly that "sexual inversion explains homosexual desire as a physiologically misplaced heterosexuality" (*Another Kind of Love: Male Homosexual Desire in English Discourse, 1850–1920* [Berkeley: University of California Press, 1994], 77).

99. Offering 1870 as the date for the invention of the modern category of homosexuality, Michel Foucault identifies gender inversion as the switch point between sexual acts and sexual identities: "Homosexuality appeared as one of the forms of sexuality when it was transposed from the practice of sodomy onto a kind of interior androgyny, a hermaphroditism of the soul" (*The History of Sexuality*, 43).

100. Sigmund Freud, *Three Essays on the Theory of Sexuality* (1905), in *The Standard Edition of the Complete Psychological Works of Sigmund Freud*, vol. 7, trans. James Strachey (London: Hogarth Press, 1960), 147–48. The importance of this passage for lesbian and gay studies is evident in its frequent citation: see for example, Craft, *Another Kind of Love*, 36–37; Teresa de Lauretis, *The Practice of Love*, 17; and Guy Hocquenghem, *Homosexual Desire* (Durham, N.C.: Duke University Press, 1993), 115.

101. In an article that intervenes authoritatively in the debates about Freud's originality, the extent to which psychoanalysis functions as a continuation of or a break from earlier psychiatric or sexological models, Arnold Davidson in "How to Do the History of Psychoanalysis: A Reading of Freud's *Three Essays on the Theory of Sexuality*" (*Critical Inquiry* 13 [Winter, 1987]) analyzes Freud's tendency to contradict himself. He argues that while Freud's splitting of the instinct from its object "was a conceptual innovation worthy of the name of genius," he nevertheless "continued to use the idea of perversion, as if he failed to grasp the real import of his own work" (267 and 275).

102. For critical discussions of this in relation to Freud's theorization of female homosexuality, see Craft, *Another Kind of Love*, 38–42; Diana Fuss, *Identification Papers* (New York: Routledge, 1995), 57–82; Roof, *A Lure of Knowledge*, 174–215.

103. In her reading of Freud's "The Psychogenesis of a Case of Homosexuality in a Woman," Diana Fuss writes, "For Freud, desire for one sex is always secured through identification with the other sex; to desire and identify with the same person at the same time is, in his model, a theoretical impossibility" (*Identification Papers*, 11).

104. Freud, "The Psychogenesis of a Case of Homosexuality in a Woman," 158.

105. Ibid.

106. Mary Jacobus points out the incoherence of this definition of female homosexuality, which draws at once on identification and object choice without specifying the relation between them: "Has the girl *identified* with her father in choosing her ma-

ternal love object, or has she never really yielded up that prior maternal object in the first place?" ("Russian Tactics: Freud's 'Case of Homosexuality in a Woman,' " *GLQ: A Journal of Lesbian and Gay Studies* 2, nos. 1–2 [1995]: 69).

107. Freud, "The Psychogenesis of a Case of Homosexuality in a Woman," 156.

108. Judith Roof reads this and several other details of Freud's analysis as demonstrating his figuration of lesbian sexuality "as an enactment of male homosexuality, as a normative response to an entirely male-defined and male-centred desire" (*Lure of Knowledge*, 204).

109. Freud, "The Psychogenesis of a Case of Homosexuality in a Woman," 147. In this passage, Freud recalls Havelock Ellis's representation of female homosexuality as just as common as, although less visible than, male homosexuality, echoing in part Ellis's actual formulation: "Homosexuality is not less common in women than in men.... Like other anomalies, indeed, in its more pronounced form it may be less frequently met with in women; in its less pronounced forms, almost certainly, it is more frequently found" (*Studies in the Psychology of Sex*, 195).

110. The ambivalent violence of this conversion and the fantasy that it might be secured through surgical intervention at the level of the lesbian body has been noted by Jacobus, who argues that Freud's avowal that psychoanalysis cannot solve the problem of homosexuality is undermined by his closing references to "the drastic intervention of surgical sexchange," which indicate his "undisclosed engagement with the experimental field of endocrinology" ("Russian Tactics," 76 and 77).

Chapter 2: Remembering Miss Wade

1. By one of those happy coincidences in which Dickens specializes, I was employed by the University of Melbourne in the state of Victoria and so found myself surrounded by what I may as well call—following Steven Marcus—"the other Victorians."

2. This kind of interpretative uncertainty may well be proper to Dickens's narrative. An 1857 reviewer, claiming *Little Dorrit* as an "imperishable addition to the literature of [Dickens's] country," nevertheless notes, "We must confess to some disappointment at the explanation, towards the close of the book, of the mystery connected with Mrs Clennam and the old house with its strange noises. It is deficient in clearness, and does not fulfil the expectations of the reader, which have been wound up to a high pitch. Indeed, the woof of the entire story does not hold together with sufficient closeness" (Anonymous, "From a Review of *Little Dorrit*," in *Charles Dickens: Critical Assessments*, vol. 1, ed. Michael Hollington [East Sussex: Helm, 1995], 388). In his 1991 introduction to the novel, Peter Ackroyd makes a similar point when he represents *Little Dorrit* as "more confused" than Dickens's other work, admitting that "it is often hard, even after repeated reading, to understand the full burden of the intrigue" (Introduction to *Little Dorrit* [London: Mandarin, 1991], xvi–xvii).

3. Ackroyd, Introduction, xvii.

4. Charles Dickens, *Little Dorrit* (London: Bradbury & Evans, 1857; rpt., Mandarin, 1991), 26; hereafter cited in the text.

5. The kind of historical research I have in mind here might be represented by Emma Donoghue's *Passions between Women: British Lesbian Culture, 1668–1801* (New York: HarperCollins, 1993). While a thorough and engaging account of textual representations of sexual passion between women, sensitive to the differences between the "long eighteenth" and the twentieth centuries, *Passions between Women* nevertheless characterizes its project as extending the historical reach of the term *lesbian*: "our foresisters who loved women probably differed in many crucial respects from those of us

who love women in the 1990s, but it seems fair to use 'lesbian culture' as an umbrella term for both groups" (7).

6. Recent work has tended to complicate near-axiomatic understandings of Victorian femininity. So Mary Poovey titles her book *Uneven Developments: The Ideological Work of Gender in Mid-Victorian England* (Chicago: University of Chicago Press, 1988), explicitly drawing attention to the contested nature of Victorian models of gender that were "always open to revision, dispute and the emergence of oppositional formulations" (3). Judith Walkowitz in *Prostitution and Victorian Society: Women, Class, and the State* (Cambridge: Cambridge University Press, 1980) corrects what she perceives as a homogenizing tendency in Victorian studies: "Most studies of Victorian sexuality have focused on one single code of sexuality.... In so doing, they have assumed the existence of a unitary Victorian culture. In fact, several Victorian subcultures existed at the same time, each with distinct prescriptions about sex" (5). Jill L. Matus in *Unstable Bodies: Victorian Representations of Sexuality and Maternity* (Manchester: Manchester University Press, 1995) emphasizes the instabilities in Victorian understandings of sexual differentiation, "unsettl[ing] the notion that Victorian medical texts and the narratives of reproductive biology present a unified or coherent representation of female sexuality or sexual difference" (49).

7. As any number of critics have noted, the naturalized twinning of masculine and feminine, public and private, industrious and virtuous, supports a specifically bourgeois fantasy of family, enlisting gender—and, specifically, an idealized femininity—in the rise and reproduction of the middle-class family: "Thus it was the new domestic woman rather than her counterpart, the new economic man, who first encroached upon aristocratic culture and seized authority from it" (Nancy Armstrong, *Desire and Domestic Fiction: A Political History of the Novel* [New York: Oxford University Press, 1987], 59). In turn, the bourgeois family, with its divided take on gender and its dynastic investment in reproduction, is drawn into the service of industrialized capital and its circulation of commodities. Poovey argues that the wife's "self-regulation was a particularly valuable and valued form of labor, for it domesticated man's (sexual) desire in the private sphere without curtailing his ambition in the economy" (*Uneven Developments*, 115). Jeff Nunokawa extends the implications of this analysis, arguing that while the domestic sphere acts as an enabling buffer against the vicissitudes of the marketplace, it is not the home—itself vulnerable to cycles of acquisition and ownership, as the Victorian novel's fascination with bankruptcy and debt tells—but literally the virtuous wife who offers her husband the prospect of protection from capital's ceaseless cycles of gain and loss: "the woman conscripted at home is assigned the duties of propriety that capital can no longer be relied upon to discharge. The angel of the house is the still point in an age of capital whose perpetual crises show no sign of waning" (*The Afterlife of Property: Domestic Security and the Victorian Novel* [Princeton, N.J.: Princeton University Press, 1994], 124). If the analysis of the ideological suturing of gender to class has been the signature of much of contemporary Victorian studies, recent work has begun examining the relationships between the ideological formations of femininity and race or nationality mobilized under the rubric of empire. Thus Elsie B. Michie argues that "the mid-Victorian fantasy of upward mobility that linked questions of class difference to questions of colonial dominance was also explicitly gendered" (*Outside the Pale: Cultural Exclusion, Gender Difference, and the Victorian Woman Writer* [Ithaca, N.Y.: Cornell University Press, 1993], 47).

8. Lynda Nead, *Myths of Sexuality: Representations of Women in Victorian Britain* (Oxford: Basil Blackwell, 1988), 34.

9. Judith Walowitz, *City of Dreadful Delight: Narratives of Sexual Danger in Late-Victorian London* (London: Virago, 1992), 21; and Deborah Epstein Nord, *Walking the Victo-*

rian Streets: Women, Representation, and the City (Ithaca, N.Y.: Cornell University Press, 1995), 9. If prostitution was read as hollowing out the institution of heterosexuality that guaranteed civilized society, as "a negation of the respectable system of marriage and procreation," then it was equally recognizable as an indictment of that order, first-wave feminists finding it "the polluting fact of social existence that tainted all intercourse between the sexes" (Nead, *Myths of Sexuality*, 99; Walkowitz, *City of Dreadful Delight*, 160).

10. Nead, *Myths of Sexuality*, 106.

11. Accordingly, William Acton, the much-cited Victorian venereal disease specialist, glosses an interventionist interest in prostitution as an interest in safeguarding the nation's future: "If the race of the people is of no concern to the State, then has the State no interest in arresting its vitiation. But if this concern and this interest be admitted, then arises the necessity for depriving prostitution not only of its moral, but of its physical venom also" (*Prostitution Considered in its Moral, Social, and Sanitary Aspects in London and Other Large Cities and Garrison Towns with Proposals for the Control and Prevention of its Attendant Evils* [London, 1857; rpt., Frank Cass & Co., 1972], 49).

12. Drawing on the ambivalent location of the prostitute within the commercial exchange that increasingly defined the hegemonic status of the middle-class family, Nead observes that "she stands as worker, commodity and capitalist and blurs the categories of bourgeois economics in the same way that she tests the boundaries of bourgeois morality" (*Myths of Sexuality*, 99).

The extent to which prostitution might be reckoned an economic impropriety is suggested by William Acton, who identifies women's straying from the domestic sphere into the workplace as one of the principal causes of prostitution. Sketching out a downward spiral that follows no economic law save what he offers himself—"Free-trade in female honour follows hard upon that in female labour"—Acton represents prostitution as a disorder of both marital and market relations. Claiming that the advent of women in the workforce lowers men's wages to disastrous effect—"the wages of working men, wherever they compete with female labour, are lowered by the flood of cheap and agile hands, until marriage and a family are an almost impossible luxury or a misery"—and moreover that women are unable to withstand industrialization's further diminution of their wages, Acton offers as a commonplace scenario the prospect of "the famished worker, wearied of [her] useless struggle against capital, . . . tak[ing] virtue itself to market" (*Prostitution*, 296).

13. Walkowitz, *City of Dreadful Delight*, 21. Walter Benjamin's influential work on the city has popularized the nineteenth-century flaneur's recognition of the prostitute as his—albeit desubjectified—double. See Walter Benjamin, *Charles Baudelaire: A Lyric Poet in the Era of High Capitalism*, trans. Harry Zohn (London: New Left Books, 1973; rpt., Verso, 1992). Recent feminist work on modernity has tended to complicate this association, although the connection between the male flaneur and the female prostitute is frequently reiterated. See Susan Buck-Morss, "The Flaneur, the Sandwichman, and the Whore," in *The Problems of Modernity: Adorno and Benjamin*, ed. Andrew Benjamin (London: Routledge, 1989), 141–56.

14. For an excellent account of the cultural operation of "fallenness" in Victorian culture that is attentive to normative configurations of both femininity and masculinity, see Amanda Anderson, *Tainted Souls and Painted Faces: The Rhetoric of Fallenness in Victorian Culture* (Ithaca, N.Y.: Cornell University Press, 1993).

15. Nord, *Walking the Victorian Streets*, 11.

16. Walkowitz, *City of Dreadful Delight*, 50.

17. If I gag over Little Dorrit and her tireless deference to those who only serve to magnify her wholesomeness through their inability to lay claim to so much as a quarter

of her virtue, other critics strenuously suppress any such reaction: "And we do not reject, despite our inevitable first impulse to do so, the character of Little Dorrit herself. Her untinctured goodness does not appall us or make us misdoubt her, as we expect it to do" (Lionel Trilling, "*Little Dorrit,*" *Kenyon Review* 15 [1953]: 590).

More recently, the unmatchable superiority of the sentimental heroine has been identified as enabling an articulation of female homoerotic desire:

> We can clarify the link between nineteenth-century sentimental heroines and the erotic if we recognize how the ideological flawlessness of female sentimentality renders that heroine supremely available for the (highly melodramatic) psychological, sexual, and social dramas of other women who labor under, but do not meet, the same standards of perfection.

Mary Armstrong, "Pursuing Perfection: *Dombey and Son*, Female Homoerotic Desire, and the Sentimental Heroine," *Studies in the Novel* 28 (Fall 1996): 282. A character such as Miss Wade—who, far from laboring under the standards of feminine perfection, defects from them entirely—puts the skids under this feminist reclamation of sentimentality's female-female erotics. After all, an emphatically unsentimentalized homoeroticism between women is facilitated by Miss Wade's perversity, the very knowledge of which is disavowed by the novel's diegetic and extradiegetic economies, while Little Dorrit's epitomizing of femininity articulates a normative gender positionality that will not congeal as a sexuality, the heterosexuality that it underwrites having instead an institutional heft. Finding Little Dorrit irrevocably central to the novel's heterosexualized project of redemption, I read Armstrong's argument about the connection between female homoerotic desire and the sentimental heroine in the nineteenth-century novel as less universalizing than she implies when she writes, "It is time to consider that the nineteenth-century sentimental [novel]—as it does the work of both reflecting female culture and modeling feminine ideological perfection—carries female-female erotics as part of that female experience and model" (Armstrong, "Pursuing Perfection," 302). Compared to the violently disruptive passions Miss Wade excites, the pale and imitative forms of feminine sociality that are enabled by Little Dorrit's flawlessness can barely qualify as erotic.

18. Patricia Ingham, *The Language of Gender and Class: Transformation in the Victorian Novel* (London: Routledge, 1996), 112. Despite having mentioned the importance of "recognizing the measure of justice in the traditional charges against Dickens's novels (that they are melodramatic, falsely pathetic, didactic, repetitive, and so on)," J. Hillis Miller finds this juxtaposition of "innocence" and "impurity" so compelling that he claims it as "one of the most poignant scenes in *Little Dorrit*—perhaps in all Dickens" (*Charles Dickens*, vii and 242).

19. Although Susan David Bernstein in *Confessional Subjects: Revelations of Gender and Power in Victorian Literature and Culture* (Chapel Hill, N.C.: University of North Carolina Press, 1997) makes a case for the Victorian prostitute's elasticity as a trope, arguing for "the steadfastness of the trope of prostitution for degenerate femininity" (80), my reading of Miss Wade suggests that she falls outside that capacious category, articulating an altogether different disorder in the discourses of Victorian femininity.

20. Jonathan Goldberg, *Sodometries: Renaissance Texts, Modern Sexualities* (Stanford, Calif.: Stanford University Press, 1992), 22.

21. Indeed, Miss Wade's status as a minor character may be precisely why she deserves critical attention. Insofar as she is narratively marginalized, subordinated to the demands of heterosexual closure, the character function of Miss Wade may be seen to parallel that of Hollywood's supporting character, whom Patricia White theorizes in

terms of her eccentric relationship to the overwhelmingly heterosexual narrative of classic cinema: "A film may be dismissive of a minor player, portray her fate as gratuitous, but it may take less time and care to assimilate her to its ideological project than it would in the case of the female protagonist" ("Supporting Character: The Queer Career of Agnes Moorhead," in *Out in Culture: Gay, Lesbian, and Queer Essays on Popular Culture,* ed. Corey K. Creekmur and Alexander Doty [Durham, N.C.: Duke University Press, 1995], 94).

22. Valerie Traub, "The Psychomorphology of the Clitoris," *GLQ: A Journal of Lesbian and Gay Studies* 2, nos. 1–2 (1995): 99.

23. Eve Kosofsky Sedgwick in *Epistemology of the Closet* (Berkeley: University of California Press, 1990) critiques these dismissals of homosexuality as an improper historical subject by observing the ways in which they frequently "reflect, as we have already seen, some real questions of sexual definition and historicity. But they only reflect them and don't reflect *on* them" (53).

24. D. A. Miller, "Anal *Rope*," in *Inside/Out: Lesbian Theories, Gay Theories,* ed. Diana Fuss (New York: Routledge, 1991), 124. Elsewhere, Miller notes that the raising of the suspicion of homosexuality is effectively managed through the refusal to countenance it: "What is still most familiarly solicited from the devotees of this proverbially innominate love, or solicited from others *for* them, is not a name, but the continual elision of one. (Consider:—Funny guy, that Al. He's fifty years old and never been married.—Maybe he's gay, Dad.—I didn't say *that.*)" (*Bringing Out Roland Barthes* [Berkeley: University of California Press, 1992], 24).

25. Lest it seem that I am only taking historical liberties with Dickens, let me point out that it is J. Hillis Miller who first argues for Miss Wade as an enviably self-sufficient practitioner of sadomasochism, referring to "the narrow circle of her sadism toward others and her masochism toward herself" (*Charles Dickens,* 230).

26. J. C. Reid, *Charles Dickens: Little Dorrit* (London: Edward Arnold Ltd., 1967), 19. These two lines—that Tattycoram is forced from the house by the Meagles family or lured by Miss Wade—are the most commonly (although not always, as here, simultaneously) held critical explanations for Tattycoram's departure. See, for example, Joan Winslow, where it is argued that "Meagles's treatment of Tattycoram results, although unintentionally, in delivering her to the evil Miss Wade" (190), and Edward Heatley, where great store is put by "Miss Wade's hypnotic power" ("The Redeemed Feminine of *Little Dorrit,*" *Dickens Studies Annual* 4 [1975]: 158).

27. Sarah Winter argues that in this scene Mr. Meagles tries to defend himself against the threat Miss Wade offers "the patriarchal family by her attempt to reproduce herself and her desires through Tattycoram" ("Domestic Fictions: Feminine Deference and Maternal Shadow Labor in Dickens' *Little Dorrit,*" *Dickens Studies Annual* 18 [1989]: 248).

28. Lionel Trilling, for example, uses the vocabulary of homosexuality when he describes Miss Wade in terms of "perversion," observing that she "becomes the more interesting if we think of her as the exact *inversion* of Esther Summerson of *Bleak House*" (*Little Dorrit,* 585; my emphasis).

29. Randolph Splitter, "Guilt and the Trappings of Melodrama in *Little Dorrit,*" *Dickens Studies Annual* 6 (1977): 125. For the missing term that triangulates the dyadic "paranoid jealousy," see Freud's "Some Neurotic Mechanisms in Jealousy, Paranoia, and Homosexuality" (1922), in *Standard Edition of the Complete Psychological Works,* 18: 221–32.

30. Splitter, "Guilt and the Trappings of Melodrama in *Little Dorrit,*" 125.

31. Luce Irigaray, *Speculum of the Other Woman,* trans. Gillian C. Gill (Ithaca, N.Y.: Cornell University Press, 1985), 41; Sigmund Freud, *Standard Edition of the Complete Psy-*

chological Works, 17: 119. If anyone doubts that being a lesbian is as calisthenic as not being one, see Julia Kristeva's account of the post-Oedipal lesbian's convoluted negotiations of desire: " 'I am looking, as a man would, for a woman': or else, 'I submit myself, as if I were a man who thought he was a woman, to a woman who thinks she is a man.' Such are the double or triple twists of what we commonly call female homosexuality" (Julia Kristeva, *About Chinese Women*, trans. Anita Barrows [New York: Urizen, 1977], 29).

32. Patricia Ann Ellen Cahill, "Beginning the World: Women and Society in the Novels of Dickens," Ph.D. diss., University of Massachusetts, 1978 (Ann Arbor, Mich., University Microfilms, 1979), 127.

33. Cahill, "Beginning the World," 131 and 128.

34. Mary Janice Murphy, "Dickens' 'Other Women': The Mature Women in His Novels," Ph.D. diss., University of Louisville, 1975 (Ann Arbor, Mich., University Microfilms, 1976), 122 and 123.

35. Ibid., 123.

36. Ibid., 124.

37. Ibid., 124, 125, 126, 131, and 132.

38. Heatley, "The Redeemed Feminine," 158.

39. Ibid., 158. Heatley's as-if-worldly passing reference to lesbianism reminds me of D. A. Miller's caution that "where homosexuality is concerned, the sophistication that has learned how to drop the subject in passing must be just as suspect as the balder mode of panic that would simply drop the subject, period" ("Anal *Rope*," 122).

40. Heatley, "The Redeemed Feminine," 158.

41. For the connections between the figurings of homosexuality and vampirism, see Christopher Craft, *Another Kind of Love: Male Homosexual Desire in English Discourse, 1850–1920* (Berkeley: University of California Press, 1994), 216–42; and Richard Dyer, "Children of the Night: Vampirism as Homosexuality, Homosexuality as Vampirism," in *Sweet Dreams: Sexuality, Gender, and Popular Fiction*, ed. Susannah Radstone (London: Lawrence & Wishart, 1988), 47–72. For the more specific connections between lesbianism and vampirism, see Sue-Ellen Case, "Tracking the Vampire." *Differences* 3, no. 2 (Summer 1991): 1–20.

42. J. Hillis Miller, *Charles Dickens: The World of His Novels* (Cambridge, Mass.: Harvard University Press, 1958), 235.

43. D. A. Miller, *The Novel and the Police* (Berkeley: University of California Press, 1988), 20.

44. Ibid., 23–24.

45. Dianne F. Sadoff writes of Miss Wade's handing over of her story to Clennam that "no narrative reason can be given for her act; it appears to be motiveless" ("Storytelling and the Figure of the Father in *Little Dorrit*," *PMLA*, no. 95 [March 1980]: 239).

46. John Forster, *The Life of Charles Dickens*, vol. 3 (London: Chapman & Hall, 1874), 138–39.

47. Ibid., 139.

48. Harvey Peter Sucksmith, Introduction to *Little Dorrit* (Oxford: Clarendon Press, 1979), 822.

49. Sucksmith, Introduction, 822.

50. Janet Larson, "Designed to Tell: The Shape of Language in Dickens' *Little Dorrit*," Ph.D. diss., Northwestern University, 1975 (Ann Arbor, Mich., University Microfilms, 1977), 15.

51. Wayne Koestenbaum, *The Queen's Throat: Opera, Homosexuality, and the Mystery of Desire* (London: GMP Publishers, 1993), 55.

52. Consider, for example, just one of this list—Miss Wade's figuring of her love for

Charlotte, her boarding school companion: "I would hold her in my arms till morning: loving her as much as ever, and often feeling as if, rather than suffer so, I could so hold her in my arms and plunge to the bottom of a river—where I would still hold her, after we were both dead" (749). Her fantasy of a fatal but eternally binding embrace recalls Bradley Headstone's identical watery clasp of Rogue Riderhood in *Our Mutual Friend*: "When the two were found, lying under the ooze and scum behind one of the rotting gates, . . . [Riderhood] was girdled still with Bradley's iron ring, and the rivets of the iron ring held tight." This scene—and a similar clinch between Magwitch and Compeyson in *Great Expectations*—has been read by Eve Kosofsky Sedgwick in terms of a homoerotic "sphincter domination" (*Between Men: English Literature and Male Homosocial Desire* [New York: Columbia University Press, 1985; rpt., 1992], 169). Miss Wade's fatalistic, erotic projection places her within a Dickensian troping of same-sex desire.

53. Audrey Jaffe, *Vanishing Points: Dickens, Narrative, and the Subject of Omniscience* (Berkeley: University of California Press, 1991), 5 and 4.

54. Jaffe, *Vanishing Points*, 168. In making this connection between the operations of ignorance and knowledge, I am following Eve Kosofsky Sedgwick: "That a particular ignorance is a product of, implies, and itself structures and enforces a particular knowledge is easy to show, perhaps easiest of all, today, in the realm of sexuality" ("Privilege of Unknowing," *Genders*, no. 1. [Spring 1988]: 104).

55. Jaffe, *Vanishing Points*, 12; my emphasis.

56. Sedgwick, *Epistemology of the Closet*, 84.

Chapter 3: Unmarriageable

1. Henry James, *The Bostonians* (London: Penguin Books, 1986), 187; hereafter cited in the text.

2. Mark Seltzer, *Henry James and the Art of Power* (Ithaca, N.Y.: Cornell University Press, 1984), 18.

3. Ibid., 62.

4. Twenty years on, Judith Fetterley's account of the way in which a naturalized homophobia has shaped twentieth-century criticism of *The Bostonians* remains telling (*The Resisting Reader: A Feminist Approach to Fiction* [Bloomington: Indiana University Press, 1978], 101–15).

5. Despite the fact that at least two critical commentaries on *The Bostonians* take place under the explicit rubric of resistant readings—I am thinking of Fetterley's chapter on the novel in *The Resisting Reader* and Judith Wilt's essay "Desperately Seeking Verena: A Resistant Reading of *The Bostonians*" (*Feminist Studies* 13, no. 2 [Summer 1987]: 293–316)—the reading most resistant to the fine grain of the novel must surely be Manfred Mackenzie's in *Communities of Love and Honor in Henry James* (Cambridge, Mass.: Harvard University Press, 1976), in which not simply the trajectory of the narrative but Olive herself is breathtakingly recuperated for heterosexuality:

> The fact that Olive is originally a sexual reactionary leads one to ask whether she is not . . . in love with the hero, in love in a perverse way that is, tragically, the only way open to one whom "no one could help." . . . Olive's subsequently attaching herself to Verena Tarrant, the heroine who *will* eventually marry the hero, amounts to a tragically perverse consummation of her own susceptibility to the hero. (39–40)

6. Recognizing the persistence of this narrative patterning across James's work,

Hugh Stevens describes these triangulated narratives of desire as "queer rivalry plots," discussing *The Bostonians* as a major example (*Henry James and Sexuality* [Cambridge: Cambridge University Press, 1998], 90).

7. The frequency with which the narrative of heterosexuality is misrecognized as narrative itself is demonstrated by Millicent Bell's cavalier assessment of the novel: "The first half of *The Bostonians* . . . seems static; the narrator's essayistic style and set descriptions of character seem to hold back the unfolding of narrative. Yet in the second half, the action takes on motion as the heroine is subdued to the true marriage-plot even as she struggles to resist Ransom; before he attracted her, there was no plot at all" (*Meaning in Henry James* [Cambridge, Mass.: Harvard University Press, 1991], 148).

8. A number of critical essays give themselves over entirely to this question. See Kristin Boudreau, "Narrative Sympathy in *The Bostonians*," *Henry James Review* 14 (1993): 17–33; Janet A. Gabler, "The Narrator's Script: James's Complex Narration in *The Bostonians*," *Journal of Narrative Technique* 14, no. 2 (Spring 1984): 94–109; Michael Kearns, "Narrative Discourse and the Imperative of Sympathy in *The Bostonians*," *Henry James Review* 17, no. 2 (1996): 162–81; Joan Maxwell, "Delighting in a Bite: James's Seduction of His Readers in *The Bostonians*," *Journal of Narrative Technique* 18, no. 1 (Winter 1988): 18–33 and Philip Page, "The Curious Narration of *The Bostonians*," *American Literature* 46 (1974): 374–83.

9. Those critics who consider Basil more secure in authorial or narratorial sympathy include M. Guilia Fabi, "The Reluctant Patriarch: A Study of *The Portrait of a Lady*, *The Bostonians*, and *The Awkward Age*," *Henry James Review* 13 (1992); Alfred Habegger, *Henry James and the "Woman Business"* (Cambridge: Cambridge University Press, 1989); Patricia Stubbs, *Women and Fiction: Feminism and the Novel, 1880–1920* (Sussex: Harvester Press, 1979); Lionel Trilling, "The Bostonians," in *The Opposing Self: Nine Essays in Criticism* (London: Secker & Warburg, 1955); Merla Wolk, "Family Plot in *The Bostonians*: Silencing the Artist's Voice," *Henry James Review* 10, no. 1 (Winter 1989); and Walter Wright, *The Madness of Art: A Study of Henry James* (Lincoln: University of Nebraska Press, 1962). Critics who read the novel as inclined more favorably toward Olive are less numerous and more guarded. For example, while Judith Fetterley argues that "for better or worse, *The Bostonians* is finally Olive Chancellor's book," she nevertheless allows that James "treats both feminism and male chauvinism with an equal degree of seriousness and an equal degree of irony" (*The Resisting Reader*, 117 and 118). This bet-hedging reading is the most common take on the novel, with most critics finding the novel even-handed in its ambivalence toward both Basil and Olive. See, for example, Sara DeSaussure Davis, "Feminist Sources in *The Bostonians*," *American Literature* 50 (December 1979); Leon Edel, *Henry James: The Middle Years* (Philadelphia: Lippincott, 1962); Lillian Faderman, *Surpassing the Love of Men: Romantic Friendship and Love between Women from the Renaissance to the Present* (New York: William Morrow, 1981); and Tony Tanner, "*The Bostonians* and the Human Voice," in *Scenes of Nature, Signs of Men* (Cambridge: Cambridge University Press, 1987).

10. On first meeting Olive Chancellor, Basil Ransom has recourse to one of the "two or three" generalizations he has come in his early career to favor: "The simplest division it is possible to make of the human race is into the people who take things hard and the people who take them easy. He perceived very quickly that Miss Chancellor belonged to the former class. . . . He himself, by nature, took things easy" (41).

11. Critics who draw comparisons between Basil and Olive include Michael Anesko, *"Friction with the Market": Henry James and the Profession of Authorship* (New York: Oxford University Press, 1986), 94–95; Allan Burns, "Henry James's Journalists as Synecdoche for the American Scene," *Henry James Review* 16 (1995): 5; Judith Fetterley, *The Resist-*

ing Reader, 137; David Howard, "*The Bostonians*," in *The Air of Reality: New Essays on Henry James*, ed. John Goode (London: Methuen & Co. Ltd., 1972), 66–67 and 69; Philip Page, "The Curious Narration of *The Bostonians*," 377–78; and Tony Tanner, "*The Bostonians* and the Human Voice," 156–57.

12. If there is some shiftiness about the source of this voice, then that sense of slipperiness is only increased by the repetition of *morbid*, a word that hints at but falls short of specifying a sexual disorder. For a discussion of the signifying field of *morbid* in the 1880s, see Jeremy Tambling, *Henry James* (New York: St. Martin's Press, 2000), 61–62.

13. Susan Mizruchi, *The Power of Historical Knowledge: Narrating the Past in Hawthorne, James, and Dreiser* (Princeton, N.J.: Princeton University Press, 1988), 136.

14. John Carlos Rowe, *The Other Henry James* (Durham, N.C.: Duke University Press, 1998), xii.

15. In addition to the critics discussed here, see Terry Castle, *The Apparitional Lesbian*, 178; Evelyne Ender, *Sexing the Mind: Nineteenth-Century Fictions of Hysteria* (Ithaca, N.Y.: Cornell University Press, 1995), 107–10 and 119–21; and Alfred Habegger, *Henry James and the "Woman Business,"* 182–229.

16. Claire Kahane, "'Hysteria, Feminism, and the Case of *The Bostonians*," in *Feminism and Psychoanalysis*, ed. Richard Feinstein and Judith Roof (Ithaca, N.Y.: Cornell University Press, 1989), 288 and 289. Kahane reworks this piece in two subsequent publications: "*The Bostonians* and the Figure of the Speaking Woman," in *Psychoanalysis and . . .*, ed. Richard Feldstein and Henry Sussman (New York: Routledge, 1990), 163–74; and "Medusa's Voice: Male Hysteria in *The Bostonians*," in *Passions of the Voice: Hysteria, Narrative, and the Figure of the Speaking Woman, 1850–1915* (Baltimore: Johns Hopkins University Press, 1995), 64–79. The argument I am summarizing above, however, remains unaltered.

17. Kahane, "Hysteria, Feminism," 296.

18. Recent rereadings of James, authorized by a gay theoretical model that has uncoupled the canon from the cultural project of heterosexual transmission, have tended to concentrate on the elaboration of male-male sexual desire.

19. Eve Kosofsky Sedgwick, "Willa Cather and Others," in *Tendencies* (Durham, N.C.: Duke University Press, 1993), 172. Although Sedgwick finds *The Bostonians* ultimately more indentured to the maintenance of hegemonic gender relations than the elaboration of homoeroticism, reading the novel as engaged in "a woman-hating and feminist-baiting violence of panic" rather than "a male-erotic *écriture*," this outcome is nevertheless an effect of the narrative's irresolute wavering between those oppositional models of desire and identification marked by the proper names of Olive Chancellor and Basil Ransom (173).

20. Like Kahane and Sedgwick, Wendy Graham suggests that James's representation of female homosexuality might be partly impelled by his own stake in male homosexuality. Arguing that the class and age differences between Olive and Verena were not typical in the classically egalitarian Boston marriage (although a more recognizable feature of male homosexual relationships), Graham concludes that "in *The Bostonians*, James conflates male and female homosexuality, up to a point, as a means of disguising and representing his own sexual orientation" (*Henry James's Thwarted Love* [Stanford, Calif.: Stanford University Press, 1999], 152).

21. Whereas elsewhere in this chapter, I am using the notion of sexual sequence to delineate the claims to priority and precedence that structure the relationships between heterosexuality and homosexuality, here I use it to suggest again, as I did in my first chapter, the apparent cultural inconsequence of female homosexuality as compared with the more prominent profile of male homosexuality.

22. Arguing that James's novel depicts the relationship between Olive and Verena

as entirely natural and potentially fulfilling, Lillian Faderman attributes contrary twentieth-century readings to "our label-prone post-Freudian world": "In 1885, before the popularization of the sexologists, [James] would have had no reason for viewing love between women as a 'mental malady' and an abnormality" (*Surpassing the Love of Men*, 195). For Faderman, it is twenty years later before the dissemination of sexological understandings of same-sex relationships renders love between women suspect. Yet at least one contemporary critic found the relationship between Olive and Verena unpalatable for exactly those reasons Faderman discounts as inappropriately retrospective: "It is when this interest [in his characters] leads Mr James to push his characters too near the brink of nature that we decline to follow. For instance, the details of the first interview between Olive and Verena in Olive's house carry these young women to dangerous lengths, and we hesitate about accepting the relation between them as either natural or reasonable" (Horace Elisha Scudder, "*The Bostonians*, by Henry James," *Atlantic Monthly* [June 1886]; reprinted in *Henry James: The Contemporary Reviews*, ed. Kevin J. Hayes [Cambridge: Cambridge University Press, 1996], 170).

23. Page, "Curious Narration," 383.

24. I am thinking here of the sexualized outcomes of such diverse, late-nineteenth-century pressures as the development of the mass market, the rise of the mass-circulation newspaper, and the evolution of the seemingly subjective and personalized address of the sensationalist journalism; the production of the charismatic figure of the celebrity, most notably within the public-speaking circuits of the social reform movements; the specific discourses of first-wave feminism, particularly in relation to suffrage, women's economic independence, and domesticity; and the perceived feminization and democratization of culture itself.

The discussion of the novel in terms of public/private distinctions is substantial. See Ian F. A. Bell, "The Personal, the Private, and the Public in *The Bostonians*," *Texas Studies in Literature and Language* 32, no. 2 (Summer 1990): 240–56; Philip Fisher, "Appearing and Disappearing in Public: Social Space in Late-Nineteenth Century Literature and Culture," in *Reconstructing American Literary History*, ed. Sacvan Bercovitch (Cambridge, Mass.: Harvard University Press, 1986), 155–88; Caroline Field Levander, "Bawdy Talk: The Politics of Women's Public Speech in *The Lectress* and *The Bostonians*," *American Literature* 67, no. 3 (September 1995): 467–85; Richard Salmon, "Transformations of the Public Sphere in *The Bostonians*," in *Henry James and the Culture of Publicity* (Cambridge: Cambridge University Press, 1997), 14–45; Brook Thomas, "The Construction of Privacy in and around *The Bostonians*," *American Literature* 64, no. 4 (December 1992): 719–47; Chris Walsh, "Stardom Is Born: The Religion and Economy of Publicity in Henry James's *The Bostonians*," *American Literary Realism* 29, no. 3 (Spring 1997): 15–25; and Lynn Wardley, "Woman's Voice, Democracy's Body, and *The Bostonians*," *ELH* 56, no. 3 (Fall 1989): 639–65.

25. As a number of commentators have noted, the Cayuga community is a fictional name for the Oneida community (1848–79). Founded by the radical perfectionist John Noyes as a utopian alternative to the privatized space of monogamous marriage, the New York State Oneida community was centrally organized around the principles of complex marriage, male continence, and eugenic breeding. For a detailed account of the theological doctrines and the everyday life practices of the Oneida community, see Louis J. Kern, *An Ordered Love: Sex Roles and Sexuality in Victorian Utopias—the Shakers, the Mormons, and the Oneida Community* (Chapel Hill: University of North Carolina Press, 1981), 203–79.

26. This focus also draws attention to the ways in which marriage marked a space of discursive contestation for the closing decades of the nineteenth century, as the conventions that had maintained the Victorian bourgeois family—most prominently, the

gendered logics of separate spheres and the mutually reinforcing license of the patriarchal head of the household and the enfranchised male citizen—increasingly came under question. For an account of the widespread debates about marriage in late-nineteenth-century America, see John D'Emilio and Estelle B. Freeman, *Intimate Matters: A History of Sexuality in America* (New York: Harper & Row, 1988), 139–67.

27. For a discussion of the simultaneously private and public character of late-nineteenth-century marriage, see Nancy F. Cott, "Giving Character to Our Whole Civil Polity: Marriage and the Public Order in the Late Nineteenth Century," in *U.S. Women's History as Women's History: New Feminist Essays*, ed. Linda K. Kerber et al. (Chapel Hill: University of North Carolina Press, 1995), 107–21.

28. *The Bostonians* has been read as actively resisting the generic coincidence of marriage and closure, further evidence of "James's subversive use of the form of the marriage novel." See Robert K. Martin, "Picturesque Misperception in *The Bostonians*," *Henry James Review* 9, no. 2 (Spring 1992): 82.

29. Reading the ending of *The Bostonians* as James's satirizing of his readers' desire for the matrimonially happy ending, Joan Maxwell argues that, propelled by the same desire, criticism has tended to misread the novel's conclusion:

> Nowhere in [*sic*] James's aesthetic concern over the inhibiting effect of the closed marriage ending on the modern novel better vindicated than in the critical history of *The Bostonians* where, despite James's final comment about Verena's tears, and despite entirely persuasive and convincing critical analyses of Ransom's failings, missed in earlier readings, we still feel permitted to read this novel as a vote, however qualified, for marriage and family and established gender roles *simply because it ends with a marriage!* (" 'Delighting in a Bite,' " 21; emphasis in original)

While a major strand of criticism has tended to recuperate *The Bostonians* for the story of heterosexual transcendency, reading roughshod over the many ambivalences of the final pages, it is worth remembering that, contrary to Maxwell's description, the novel *does not end with a marriage!* It is surely not that, in an article that calls for a more careful reading of the novel, Maxwell has the ending wrong, misremembering Basil and Verena's walk along a Boston street outside the Music Hall for one up the aisle. Rather, in a novel in which marriageability, more than marriage, is the measure of cultural attainment, the one scene may as well be the other.

30. As many of us know, it is the alleged simplicity of the request to divulge marital status that makes it so difficult. Flying between New Zealand and Australia more frequently than I'd like, I am asked, coming and going, to identify myself in relation to the following possibilities: never married, married, widowed or divorced. Although nothing could be more truthful than my declaration that I have never been married, the way in which my affective life remains uninterpellated by the structuring discourse of the respective immigration departments means there is always for me in ticking the box a sense of sham, a sense hardly alleviated by the disclaimer "for statistical purposes only," with its implicit reassurance that the brutalities of the questionnaire are merely bureaucratic.

31. For one of the few critical readings of *The Bostonians* to address the novel's reliance on the trope of slavery, see Leland S. Pearson, "In the Closet with Frederick Douglass: Reconstructing Masculinity in *The Bostonians*," *Henry James Review* 16, no. 3 (1995): 292–98.

32. The slaves are not entirely imaginary—after all, Miss Birdseye had once ferried copies of the Bible to them—but they are entirely elsewhere, not simply in the South but, post-Reconstruction, prediegetic.

33. Thad Logan in "Decorating Domestic Space: Middle-Class Women and Victorian Interiors" (in *Keeping the Victorian House: A Collection of Essays*, ed. Vanessa D. Dickerson [New York: Garland Publishing, 1995]) describes the ways in which the assumed connection between femininity and domesticity guaranteed both the heterosexualization of the Victorian home and the fantasy of the separation of private and public life: "The middle-class woman was taught to consider the tasteful decoration of her home as an important part of her duty, a duty whose broader outlines included both the physical and spiritual well-being of her family.... As the home became (ostensibly) set apart from the vicissitudes of public life and the harsh economy of the marketplace, women presided over an interior space that was frequently linked to the 'goodness' in contemporary discourse" (209).

34. Janet Wolf Bowen, "Architectural Envy: 'A Figure Is Nothing without a Setting' in Henry James's *The Bostonians*," *New England Quarterly* 65, no. 1 (March 1992): 9.

35. While Olive's Charles Street home and even her rented cottage at Marmion—their floor plans, their furnishings, their aspects—are described at length in the novel, the narration shies away from any such account of Basil's rooms: "If the opportunity were not denied me here, I should like to give some account of Basil Ransom's interior . . . but we need, in strictness, concern ourselves with it no further than to gather the implication that the young Mississippian . . . had not made his profession very lucrative" (196).

36. Left alone in Olive's parlor shortly after making her acquaintance and taking in the tables and sofas, the books and curtains, the photographs and watercolors, Basil "had never felt himself in the presence of so much organized privacy": "It came over him, while he waited for his hostess to reappear, that she was unmarried as well as rich, that she was sociable . . . as well as single; and he had for a moment a whimsical vision of becoming a partner in so flourishing a firm" (46–47).

37. This fantasized scene is realized some eighty pages later, down to all its imagined details of the tea tray, the lamp, the falling snow, the reading together of books (185–86).

38. Valerie Fulton, "Rewriting the Necessary Woman: Marriage and Professionalism in James, Jewett and Phelps," *Henry James Review* 15 (1995): 245 and 253n5.

39. Janet Wolf Bowen similarly reads Olive as torn between "two major and contradictory ideological movements, domesticity and feminism": "To choose either feminism or home-culture, Olive must mutilate herself" ("Architectural Envy," 15 and 16). Bowen's interpretation runs directly counter to Olive's even as it shares her vocabulary: "Olive of course held that home-culture was perfectly compatible with the widest emancipation" (110).

40. Lauren Berlant and Michael Warner, "Sex in Public," *Critical Inquiry* 24 (Winter 1998): 547. Much of my thinking about *The Bostonians* has taken place under Berlant and Warner's rethinking of the public sphere in relation to the more contemporary emergence of queer culture, particularly their elaboration of the "changed possibilities of identity, intelligibility, publics, culture, and sex that appear when the heterosexual couple is no longer the referent or the privileged example of sexual culture" (548).

Chapter 4: Remembering and Forgetting

1. Virginia Woolf, *The Diary of Virginia Woolf*, vol. 2, ed. Anne Olivier Bell (London: Hogarth Press, 1978), 249.

2. Elizabeth Abel, *Virginia Woolf and the Fictions of Psychoanalysis* (Chicago: University of Chicago Press, 1989), xvi. According to Abel,

> In 1925, the year *Mrs Dalloway* presented Woolf's version of the daughter's Oedipal narrative, Freud turned his attention to the feminine [Oedipal] plot. In "Some Psychical Consequences of the Anatomical Distinction between the Sexes," he articulates for the first time the inverted sequence of this plot: the knowledge of "castration" that propels the boy toward the conclusion of his Oedipal narrative inaugurates the girl's by initiating her turn from her mother, the initial object of all children's attachment, to her father, the object of her Oedipal love.... In realizing that the girl's Oedipus complex is a "secondary formation," built on an earlier layer of exclusive and powerful love for the mother, Freud radically gendered developmental narrative, decisively split between a maternal prehistory and a paternal history. (7 and 8)

Where Abel's account of the simultaneity of Woolf's *Mrs. Dalloway* and Freud's development of the Oedipal narrative takes gender as its organizing frame, in my analysis the emphasis falls somewhat differently on sexuality, particularly the ways in which, for Woolf as for Freud, the distinction between homosexuality and heterosexuality is made sequential in narrative.

3. Notwithstanding Woolf's well-documented hostility toward psychoanalysis, a number of critics have read her work in tandem with Freud's. While Abel's work remains the most sustained example of this intertextual criticism, Joseph Allen Boone describes Woolf's 1920s novels as "revisions of the Freudian family romance" (*Libidinal Currents: Sexuality and the Shaping of Modernism* [Chicago: University of Chicago Press, 1998], 177).

4. Woolf, *The Diary of Virginia Woolf*, 2: 272.

5. Ibid., 2: 263.

6. A number of contemporary reviewers of *Mrs. Dalloway* assessed the novel in relation to the representational strategies of "stream of consciousness." Joseph Wood Krutch ("The Stream of Consciousness," *Nation* 120 [3 June 1925]; reprinted in *Virginia Woolf: Critical Assessments*, vol. 3, ed. Eleanor McNees [London: Helm Information, 1994]) described Woolf as "a sort of decorous James Joyce." "Her method," he wrote, "consists in recording the stream of consciousness as it flows through the minds of her characters" (273). Similarly, E. W. Hawkins in "The Stream of Consciousness Novel" (*Atlantic Monthly*, September 1926; reprinted in *Virginia Woolf: The Critical Heritage*, ed. Robin Majumdar and Allen McLaurin [London: Routledge & Kegan Paul, 1975]) wrote, "*Mrs. Dalloway*, the history of one day in the life of a woman, is a stream of consciousness undiluted, and pure pattern" (187).

Recent critical readings reveal some hesitancy about describing *Mrs. Dalloway* as a stream-of-consciousness novel, partly because of the perceived outmodishness of that descriptor in relation to the late-twentieth-century proliferation of narratological terms that refine and complicate its definitional ambit, partly because of Woolf's innovations, post–James Joyce and Dorothy Richardson, in the technical field. For instance, Edward A. Hungerford points out that in her considerable diary entries "Virginia Woolf did not herself use the term 'stream of consciousness' to describe the characteristic style of her best-known novels" ("'My Tunnelling Process': The Method of *Mrs Dalloway*," *Modern Fiction Studies* 3 [Summer 1957]: 164). Similarly, in discussing *Mrs. Dalloway*, Makiko Minow-Pinkney in *Virginia Woolf and the Problem of the Subject* (Brighton: Harvester Press, 1987) refers to "the so-called 'stream of consciousness' " (54), echoing almost exactly J. Hillis Miller's reference to Woolf's "use of the so-called stream-of-consciousness technique" (*Fiction and Repetition*, 176). Taking a position closer to my own, Joseph Boone finds "stream of consciousness" useful in his discussion of *Mrs. Dalloway*, while admitting its deviation from the standard usage of the term: "Although the phrase 'stream of consciousness' is generally taken to apply to a character's immediate thought processes, in Woolf's case the phrase aptly conveys her vision of the fluidity of all life" (*Libidinal Currents*, 174).

7. Of course, *Mrs. Dalloway* famously expands the character-based bounds of consciousness, a point I take up later in my discussion. For now, I simply note that the novel's temporal incoherencies are, for the most part, stabilized by its coherency of character.

8. Virginia Woolf, "Modern Fiction," in *The Crowded Dance of Modern Life: Selected Essays*, vol. 2, ed. Rachel Bowlby (London: Penguin Books, 1993), 8–9.

9. Sigmund Freud, "Resistance and Repression," in *The Complete Introductory Lectures of Psychoanalysis*, trans. and ed. James Strachey (London: George Allen & Unwin, 1963; rpt., 1971), 287.

10. Freud, "Resistance and Repression," 287, and "Remembering, Repeating, and Working-Through (Further Recommendations on the Technique of Psycho-Analysis II)" (1914), in *The Standard Edition of the Complete Psychological Works*, 12: 150.

11. Freud, "Remembering, Repeating, and Working-Through," 150.

12. In an earlier gloss of this resistant silence, Freud identifies this homosexual refusal to remember as masculine rather than feminine, differentiating along gendered lines the types of patients likely to maintain their silence at the onset of treatment: "Women who are prepared by events in their past history to be subjected to sexual aggression and men with over-strong repressed homosexuality are the most apt thus to withhold the ideas that occur to them at the outset of their analysis" ("On Beginning the Treatment: [Further Recommendations on the Technique of Psycho-Analysis I]" [1913]), in *The Standard Edition of the Complete Psychological Works*, 12: 138.

13. Sigmund Freud, "The Psychogenesis of a Case of Homosexuality in a Woman" (1920), in *The Standard Edition of the Complete Psychological Works*, 13: 155.

14. Judith Butler argues persuasively that this psychoanalytic insistence on homosexual originality is in the service of a teleological heterosexuality: "If the incest taboo regulates the production of discrete gender identities, and if that production requires the prohibition and sanction of heterosexuality, then homosexuality emerges as a desire which must be produced in order to remain repressed" (*Gender Trouble: Feminism and the Subversion of Identity* [New York: Routledge, 1990], 77).

15. As Diana Fuss points out, "In the history of psychoanalysis, female homosexuality is theorized almost exclusively in terms of the 'pre': the preoedipal, the presymbolic, the prelaw, the premature, even the presexual" (*Identification Papers* [New York: Routledge, 1995], 58).

16. See, for example, Teresa de Lauretis, who argues that in Freudian psychoanalysis "the 'normal' is conceived only by approximation, is more a projection than an actual state of being, while perversion and neurosis (the repressed form of perversion) are the actual forms and contents of sexuality" (*The Practice of Love: Lesbian Sexuality and Perverse Desire* [Bloomington: Indiana University Press, 1994], xii). Judith Roof similarly claims that "throughout his career, Freud's case histories of lesbian women seem to catalyze his work on theories of general sexuality" (*A Lure of Knowledge: Lesbian Sexuality and Theory* [New York: Columbia University Press, 1991], 176).

17. Sigmund Freud, "Female Sexuality" (1931), in *The Standard Edition of the Complete Psychological Works*, 21: 226.

18. Sigmund Freud, "Five Lectures on Psychoanalysis" (1910), in *The Standard Edition of the Complete Psychological Works*, 11: 16.

19. Richard Terdiman uses this phrase to describe how memory provides the overarching rubric for the various diverse concepts with which psychoanalysis sought to account for the psychic constitution of the subject: "With Freud, preoccupation with

memory proliferates and pervades psychological and cultural theory until the individual almost seems to have been reconceived as a cluster of mnemonic operations and transformations. Desire, instinct, dream, association, neurosis, repression, repetition, the unconscious—all the central notions of psychoanalysis—then appear to have been rewritten as memory functions or disfunctions" (*Present Past: Modernity and the Memory Crisis* [Ithaca, N.Y.: Cornell University Press, 1993], 241).

20. Virginia Woolf, *Mrs. Dalloway* (London: Hogarth Press, 1925; rpt., 1963), 5; hereafter cited in the text.

21. For a more detailed discussion of the temporal ambiguities of this opening passage—particularly the ways in which the vividness of recollected memory "displaces the present of the novel and becomes the virtual present of the reader's experience"—see J. Hillis Miller, *Fiction and Repetition: Seven English Novels* (Oxford: Basil Blackwell, 1982), 184–88. For a more general technical consideration of the sentence structure of the opening paragraphs, see Richard Pearce, *The Politics of Narration: James Joyce, William Faulkner, and Virginia Woolf* (New Brunswick, N.J.: Rutgers University Press, 1991), 146–48.

22. If Clarissa turns fifty-one in 1923—"She had just broken into her fifty-second year" (41)—then she was born in 1872. Because Clarissa's birthday is mid-year—Harvena Richter goes so far as to identify her as "born under the sign of Gemini" ("The *Ulysses* Connection: Clarissa Dalloway's Bloomsday," in *Virginia Woolf: Critical Assessments*, 3: 463)—and the Bourton episodes take place in summer when Clarissa was "a girl of eighteen" (5), they can be dated to 1890—a fact substantiated by Peter's recollection of "Bourton that summer, early in the 'nineties" (65). Jeremy Tambling errs when he locates Clarissa's affair with Sally "as taking place before 1889" ("Repression in *Mrs Dalloway*'s London," in *Virginia Woolf: Critical Assessments*, 3: 445).

23. Miller, *Fiction and Repetition*, 184.

24. Sigmund Freud, *Psychopathology of Everyday Life*, vol. 5, The Pelican Freud Library, ed. James Strachey, trans. Alan Tyson (London: Pelican Books, 1978), 339–40.

25. Emily Jensen identifies Clarissa's "fear of interruption [as] the most important feature of her personality" ("Clarissa Dalloway's Respectable Suicide," in *Virginia Woolf: A Feminist Slant*, ed. Jane Marcus [Lincoln: University of Nebraska Press, 1983], 162). Joseph Boone also suggests that "Clarissa's identity or being hinges on the paradox of a momentary suspension or 'pause' in the midst of motion" (*Libidinal Currents*, 182).

26. Other connecting devices are the dignitary's motorcar, the sky-writing airplane, the old woman who sings outside Regent's Park station, the double-decker bus that Elizabeth catches, the ambulance that comes for Septimus's body.

27. William James, *The Principles of Psychology*, vol. 1 (London: Macmillan, 1890; rpt., New York: Dover Publications, 1950), 239.

28. Ibid., 238–39.

29. Ibid., 226.

30. The understanding between Clarissa and Peter, for instance, is characterized as a merging of consciousnesses: "They had always this queer power of communicating without words" (67). In his one moment of rationality, Septimus can intercept his wife's thoughts: "He could feel her mind, like a bird, falling from branch to branch, and always alighting, quite rightly; he could follow her mind" (161). Lady Bruton imagines her attenuated connection with her departed lunch guests: "And they went further and further from her, being attached to her by a thin thread (since they had lunched with her) which would stretch and stretch, get thinner and thinner as they walked across London; as if one's friends were attached to one's body, after lunching with them, by a thin thread" (124). This expansiveness of consciousness is the counterpart to Woolf's earlier claustrophobic dissatisfaction with the character-based re-

strictiveness of James Joyce's use of stream of consciousness in *Ulysses* when she asks, "Is it due to the method that we feel neither jovial nor magnanimous, but centred in a self which, in spite of its tremor of susceptibility, never embraces or creates what is outside itself and beyond?" ("Modern Fiction," 10).

31. Virginia Woolf, "Introduction to the Modern Library Edition of *Mrs. Dalloway* (1928)," in *Mrs. Dalloway*, ed. Morris Beja (Oxford: Blackwell, 1996), 198. During the period in which she was retyping the manuscript of *Mrs. Dalloway*, Woolf wrote in her diary, "The reviewers will say that it is disjointed because of the mad scenes not connecting with the Dalloway scenes" (*The Diary of Virginia Woolf*, 2: 323).

32. David Dowling, *Mrs Dalloway: Mapping Streams of Consciousness* (Boston: Twayne Publishers, 1991), 92.

33. Mitchell A. Leaska, *The Novels of Virginia Woolf from Beginning to End* (London: Weidenfeld & Nicolson, 1977), 114.

34. In maintaining equivalent emphasis on Septimus's homosexuality and his war experience, I follow the lead of a number of other critics. Patricia Juliana Smith, for example, notes that Septimus's crisis about his sexuality "aris[es] from experiences acquired and traumas sustained primarily in the military, perhaps the most deeply demarcated site of male homosocial sexual politics" (*Lesbian Panic: Homoeroticism in Modern British Women's Fiction* [New York: Columbia University Press, 1997], 194n33). Julie Abraham identifies the war as "the location of [Septimus's] homosexuality" (*Are Girls Necessary? Lesbian Writing and Modern Histories* [New York: Routledge, 1996], 149).

35. A number of critics stress the importance of the class differences separating Clarissa and Septimus—a fact registered most poignantly in their realization that even had Clarissa known Septimus, he would not have been able to attend her party. See, for example, Elaine Showalter, Introduction to *Mrs. Dalloway*, in *Virginia Woolf: Introductions to the Major Works*, ed. Julia Briggs (London: Virago, 1994), 152; Tambling, "Repression in *Mrs. Dalloway*'s London," 458; and Alex Zwerdling, *Virginia Woolf and the Real World* (Berkeley: University of California Press, 1986), 151.

36. Elaine Showalter notes that "shell-shock cannot account for all of Septimus's symptoms. He is far more acutely disturbed than shell-shock patients" (Introduction to *Mrs. Dalloway*, 149). See also Martin Stone, "Shellshock and the Psychologists," in *The Anatomy of Madness: Essays in the History of Psychiatry*, ed. W. F. Bynum et al., vol. 2 (London: Tavistock Publications, 1985), 251.

37. Although, as I argued earlier, the exclusion of any detailed consideration of his war experience marks Septimus as the only major character in *Mrs. Dalloway* to have the most significant aspect of his past occluded from the narration, this oblique representation of war is consistent with Woolf's novelistic representations elsewhere, which take the measure of the horror of war in its indirect effects. Mark Hussey foregrounds the strategic effects of this indirectness in his reading of Woolf as "a war novelist": "Perhaps what is most valuable in Woolf's work for us now is her insistence that we turn away from the battlefront to the home front, to the home, in thinking about war" ("Living in a War Zone: An Introduction to Virginia Woolf as a War Novelist," in *Virginia Woolf and War: Fiction, Reality, and Myth*, ed. Mark Hussey [New York: Syracuse University Press, 1991], 13).

38. Miller, *Fiction and Repetition*, 190.

39. For Freudian psychoanalysis, identification is a spectral affair: "To be open to an identification is to be open to a death encounter, open to the very possibility of communing with the dead" (Fuss, *Identification Papers*, 1).

40. Given my argument about the distorted connection in *Mrs. Dalloway* between

homosexuality and temporality, it is provocative to note that Septimus's initial near-orgasmic surrender to time—the word itself splitting its husk and pouring its riches over him—recalls one of the novel's most cited passages, in which Clarissa gives an opaque account of her feelings for women:

> She did undoubtedly then feel what men felt. Only for a moment; but it was enough. It was a sudden revelation, a tinge like a blush which one tried to check and then, as it spread, one yielded to its expansion, and rushed to the furtherest verge and there quivered and felt the world come closer, swollen with some astonishing significance, some pressure of rapture, which split its thin skin and gushed and poured with an extraordinary alleviation over the cracks and sores. Then, for that moment, she had seen an illumination; a match burning in a crocus; an inner meaning almost expressed. (36)

41. Freud, *Psychopathology of Everyday Life*, 44.

42. Freud, *The Complete Introductory Lectures of Psychoanalysis*, 24. *Mrs. Dalloway*, as its very title suggests, is fascinated by the patronymic production of women's married names, in large part because it marks, while naturalizing, heterosexuality's transformative claim on a past frequently enough figured homoerotically. So Clarissa can feel alienated rather than interpellated by her own name—"this being Mrs Dalloway; not even Clarissa anymore; this being Mrs Richard Dalloway" (13)—and fail to recognize her former love's name when announced at her party: "*What* name? Lady Rosseter? But who on earth was Lady Rosseter? . . . It was Sally Seton! Sally Seton!" (188).

43. Miller, *Fiction and Repetition*, 185.

44. The near ubiquity of this reading of Septimus's death is registered in its almost formulaic rendering, with Susan M. Squier's "Septimus dies so that Clarissa may live on" (*Virginia Woolf and London: The Sexual Politics of the City* [Chapel Hill: University of North Carolina Press, 1985], 116) a close echo of Suzette A. Henke's "Septimus dies so that Clarissa may live" ("*Mrs. Dalloway*: The Communion of Saints," in *New Feminist Essays on Virginia Woolf*, ed. Jane Marcus [Lincoln: University of Nebraska Press, 1981], 126). This reading no doubt takes shape under the sway of Woolf's own declaration, cited earlier, that "in the first version Septimus, who later is intended to be her double, had no existence; and that Mrs Dalloway was originally to kill herself, or perhaps merely to die at the end of the party."

45. The homosexualized connections between Clarissa's account of Septimus's death and her earlier accounts of her passion for women are numerous and much discussed by critics. The difficulty of human connection that Clarissa mentions in relation to Septimus's suicide—"closeness drew apart; rapture faded; one was alone"—is described in similar terms as Clarissa's opaque account of the fading of an intensity between women: "the close withdrew; the hard softened. It was over—the moment." Similarly, the figure of Septimus's "treasure" recalls Sally's kiss, which Clarissa experiences as "a present . . . a diamond, something infinitely precious" (40). See, for example, Abel, *Virginia Woolf and the Fictions of Psychoanalysis*, 39; Jensen, "Clarissa Dalloway's Respectable Suicide," 167–68.

46. Alex Zwerdling writes, "Clarissa allows herself to think about Septimus's suicide with full imaginative sympathy, understanding his feelings and situation instinctively" (*Virginia Woolf and the Real World*, 141). Deborah Guth is an exception to those critics who read Septimus's suicide in the wake of Clarissa's rendering. Arguing that Clarissa's take on Septimus's death reveals her self-delusion rather than their psychic sympathy, Guth writes,

Septimus expresses none of the exalted self-affirmation that Clarissa sees in his death. There is no treasure, no mystical embrace, no joyous communication or lyrical prose-musing. Instead, there is the terror of the hunted beast, the short spasmodic thoughts of panic that focus almost exclusively on the menial trappings of daily life—the breadknife, the gas fire, and the razor—which must now help him to escape. What is more significant in Clarissa's reconstruction is that he does not want to die at all. (" 'What a Lark! What a Plunge!': Fiction as Self-Evasion in *Mrs. Dalloway*," in *Virginia Woolf: Critical Assessments*, 3: 437)

47. E. M. Forster, "The Novels of Virginia Woolf," in *Virginia Woolf: The Critical Heritage*, 175.

48. Jensen, "Clarissa Dalloway's Respectable Suicide," 162; Abel, *Virginia Woolf and the Fictions of Psychoanalysis*, 39.

49. Jensen, "Clarissa Dalloway's Respectable Suicide," 178.

50. Abel, *Virginia Woolf and the Fictions of Psychoanalysis*, 39 and 40. Abel is not herself endorsing the final prioritization of heterosexuality over homosexuality; rather, she argues that "in retreating from her most radical position [the valorization of homosexuality over compulsory heterosexuality], Woolf produces a less than perfectly convincing resolution" (*Virginia Woolf and the Fictions of Psychoanalysis*, 41). This is worth noting, as Abel's critique of the terms of Woolf's closure have been misread as their advocacy: "If Abel can establish the past as female and the present as male . . . then the passage of time itself requires and naturalizes Clarissa's 'development' towards a heterosexuality identified with adulthood" (Julie Abraham, *Are Girls Necessary?* 147).

51. Patricia Smith argues similarly that "Septimus's suicide thus forces Clarissa to examine her heretofore unexamined life and judge whether or not it is, or has been, worth living. . . . [Woolf] allows her protagonist a reconciliation with the past through a moment of psychological healing, tempered by an acknowledgment of that which she has lost" (*Lesbian Panic*, 61–62).

52. In another context, Woolf acknowledges the way in which recollection does not distinguish between past and present but draws them together in what is experienced as an intensification of the present: "The past only comes [b]ack when the present runs so smoothly that it is like the sliding surface of a deep river. Then one sees through the surface to the depths. In those moments I find one of my greatest satisfactions, not that I am thinking of the past; but that it is then that I am living most fully in the present. For the present when backed by the past is a thousand times deeper than the present when it presses so close that you can feel nothing else" ("A Sketch of the Past," in *Moments of Being*, 109).

53. Noting that the dramatic structures of *Mrs. Dalloway* that endorse Clarissa's perspective disenfranchise Miss Kilman's, John Batchelor argues that even when the narration is focalized through the character of Miss Kilman, she remains outside the novel's comprehensive circuits of sympathy: "Miss Kilman's anguish is fully realised from within—and it commands no sympathy at all" (*Virginia Woolf: The Major Novels* [Cambridge: Cambridge University Press, 1991], 87). Even lesbian readings of the novel are strapped to find Miss Kilman a sympathetic character: "any sympathy she elicits is adulterated by her alienating demeanor" (Smith, *Lesbian Panic*, 58).

54. Woolf's representation of Miss Kilman has caused at least one critic to remember, after a fashion, that other self-tormentor discussed in my second chapter, *Little Dorrit*'s Miss Wade: "Doris Kilman . . . has relatively few antecedents save the sinister governess Miss Lane [*sic*] in Charles Dickens's *Little Dorrit*" (Smith, *Lesbian Panic*, 58). Misremembering Miss Wade's name (no less her occupation), Smith nevertheless rec-

ognizes her peculiar brand of aggressive marginality—the articulation of her same-sex desires from a position of social disenfranchisement—in Miss Kilman.

55. Kevin Kopelson, *Love's Litany: The Writing of Modern Homoerotics* (Stanford, Calif.: Stanford University Press, 1994), 84.

56. This reading of Miss Kilman as Clarissa's double is a critical commonplace. See Abraham, *Are Girls Necessary?* 153; Boone, *Libidinal Currents*, 193–98; and Smith, *Lesbian Panic*, 53.

57. This unpredictable shuttling between hate and love was only identified by Woolf as ambivalence on first reading Freud, some fifteen years after the publication of *Mrs. Dalloway*: "It was only the other day when I read Freud for the first time, that I discovered that this violently disturbing conflict of love and hate is a common feeling; and is called ambivalence" ("A Sketch of the Past," in *Moments of Being*, 120).

Chapter 5: First Wife, Second Wife

1. One such regulatory narrative is the psychoanalytic rendering of the incest taboo. In arguing, after Foucault, that the regulatory law produces rather than represses that which it legislates against, Judith Butler persuasively demonstrates that the sequentiality of the incest taboo—or what she calls "the founding temporality of the account" (*Gender Trouble: Feminism and the Subversion of Identity* [New York: Routledge, 1990], 78)—does not rule against homosexuality so much as yield it up, in relation to heterosexuality, as secondary and unauthorized: "The incest taboo, then, would repress no primary dispositions, but effectively create the distinction between 'primary' and 'secondary' dispositions to describe and reproduce the distinction between a legitimate heterosexuality and an illegitimate homosexuality" (73).

2. The logics of sexual sequence can be seen to have a defensive operation insofar as their reliance on the temporal ordering of categories of sexual identification is recognizable as an attempt to safeguard the priority of heterosexuality and justify the devaluation of homosexuality. Lee Edelman unpacks precisely this defensive investment in sexual sequence when he argues that the representation of male homosexuality within sodomitical relations, with its "troubling resistance to the binary logic of before and behind" (*Homographesis: Essays in Gay Literary and Cultural Theory* [New York: Routledge, 1994], 184), destabilizes the temporal assumptions that secure hegemonic psychoanalytic accounts of the instantiation of sexual difference through the primal scene and the law of castration: "Playing out the possibility of multiple, non-exclusive erotic identifications and positionings, the spectacle of sodomy would seem to confirm precisely those infantile sexual speculations that the male, coerced by the bogy of castration, is expected to have put behind him.... Indeed, the sodomitical spectacle... cannot fail to implicate the heterosexual male who is situated to observe it since it constitutes an affront to the primary narrative that orients his sexuality" (185). Although he is primarily describing the unsettling effects of the male-male sodomitical spectacle, Edelman suggests that homosexual identities in general, including lesbianism, are frequently figured as temporal and spatial aberrations that maintain heterosexuality as the proper culmination of sexual sequence:

> Modern masculinist heterosexual culture conceptualizes lesbian and gay male sexuality in terms of a phallocentric positional logic, insistently (and dismissively) articulating lesbianism as a form of extended non-productive foreplay and gay male sexual relations as a form of extended non-productive behind-

play. The scene of sodomy comes to figure, therefore, both a spatial disturbance in the logic of positions and a temporal disturbance in the logic essential to narrative development. (183)

3. Throughout this chapter, I want to keep a critical pressure on the widespread refusal to figure sexuality as unpatterned by sequence or chronology, as inexplicable in terms of narrative causality. The cultural sway of sexual sequence and its attendant solidification of sexual categories means that such a critical project might be misheard as arguing for a utopic sexuality outside the confining limits of current sexual identifications. Let me say, then, that my interest in the ways in which sexual sequence refuses the possibility of a sexual field that is untrussed by a temporally ordered narrative of development is not animated by the fantasy that some chaos-theory version of sexuality might deliver us from those more recognizable categories of sexuality in which we see ourselves but, in no small part, by the realization that the stakes of this refusal have significant representational and experiential effects for the relations between—among others—those very categories of heterosexuality and homosexuality.

4. Quoted in Margaret Forster, *Daphne du Maurier* (London: Chatto & Windus, 1993), 136 and 140. Joanna Russ argues that these two novels are definitive of the generic constitution of modern gothic itself, describing twentieth-century gothics as "a crossbreed of *Jane Eyre* and Daphne du Maurier's *Rebecca*" (" 'Someone's Trying to Kill Me and I Think It's My Husband': The Modern Gothic," *Journal of Popular Culture* 6, no. 4 [1973]: 666). The comparisons between *Rebecca* (both the novel and its cinematic adaptation) and *Jane Eyre* have been persistent. See, for example, Mary Ann Doane, *The Desire to Desire: The Woman's Film of the 1940s* (London: Macmillan, 1988), 125; John Fletcher, "Primal Scenes and the Female Gothic: *Rebecca* and *Gaslight*," *Screen* 36, no. 4 (1995): 345–46 and 354; Michelle A. Massé, "This Hurts Me More Than It Does You: The Beater and *Rebecca*," in *In the Name of Love: Masochism and the Gothic* (Ithaca, N.Y.: Cornell University Press, 1992), 150, 156, and 188; Patsy Stoneman, *Brontë Transformations: The Cultural Dissemination of "Jane Eyre" and "Wuthering Heights"* (London: Prentice Hall, 1996), 99–108 and 143–50; and Robin Wood, *Hitchcock's Films Revisited* (New York: Columbia University Press, 1989), 347.

5. Coming to *Jane Eyre* backwards through my reading of *Rebecca* criticism—and not insensitive to that reversal in relation to a novel that, I will argue, is fascinated by precedence but even more fascinated by the horrific prospect of its overturn—I experienced firsthand a kind of complacency surrounding the dissemination of canonic plot details that everyone is presumed already to know. The night before she intends to marry Mr. Rochester and the chapter before the existence of his wife—the insane Bertha Rochester secretly incarcerated in his attic—is revealed, Jane Eyre is woken by a terrifying figure of a woman, "tall and large" with a "discoloured face" and a "fiery eye" examining her wedding clothes laid out for the next day. Although Mr. Rochester soothes Jane, telling her that this apparition is nothing but "the creature of an overstimulated brain" (298), Margaret Smith, the editor of the Oxford University Press edition of *Jane Eyre*, steals Brontë's thunder, in a gloss that sacrifices narrative pacing to a note on fashion—"the bridal veil did not cover the face until the 1860s; Charlotte Brontë intended us to imagine Bertha Rochester's face clearly reflected in the glass" (490)—as if there is no possibility of anyone reading the novel for the first time.

6. Daphne du Maurier, *Rebecca* (London: Random Century, 1992), 5; hereafter cited in the text.

7. Peter Brooks, *Reading for the Plot: Design and Intention in Narrative* (Cambridge, Mass.: Harvard University Press, 1984), 23; emphasis in original.

8. It is worth noting that this constant plunging from now to then—as if narration

were nothing more than a series of unstable trapdoors over a more memorable past, a more magnetic future—is in radical counterpoint to the narrator's frequent expression of an impossible and almost pathological desire to remain arrested in the present. Preferring the banal comforts of the present to time's inexorable forward movement, the narrator often and vainly attempts to hold herself apart from temporality, to exist in a frozen moment beyond the blandishments of past and future:

> I wanted to go on sitting there, not talking, not listening to the others, keeping the moment precious for all time, because we were peaceful, all of us, we were content and drowsy even as the bee who droned above our heads. In a little while it would be different, there would come tomorrow, and the next day, and another year. And we would be changed perhaps, never sitting quite like this again. Some of us would go away, or suffer, or die; the future stretched away in front of us, unknown, unseen, not perhaps what we wanted, not what we planned. This moment was safe enough, this could not be touched. Here we sat together, Maxim and I, hand-in-hand, and the past and the future mattered not at all.(109)

9. Given the ways in which my argument represents *Rebecca*'s narration as crucially unable to distinguish between past and present, first and second, perversion and normativity and consequently unable to secure the sequence of its own story, it is provocative that Judith Halberstam has defined the gothic in terms of "the crisis occasioned by the inability to 'tell,' meaning both the inability to narrate and the inability to categorize" (*Skin Shows: Gothic Horror and the Technology of Monsters* [Durham, N.C.: Duke University Press, 1995], 23).

10. Discussing *Rebecca* in terms of the psychoanalytic beating fantasy, Michelle A. Massé's "This Hurts Me More Than It Does You" similarly emphasizes the narrator's "fragile ego boundaries" (148). Massé's argument is limited, however, by her maintenance of heterosexuality as her primary frame of reference.

11. To differentiate these triangles from each other in this fashion is simply another way of recognizing the peculiarly trigonometric reorientations and reversals at play in any erotic triangle where rivalry and love are configured not only in each other's backwash but in each other's form. For a consideration of the homoerotic potential of the heterosexual erotic triangle, see Eve Kosofsky Sedgwick, *Between Men*, 21–27.

12. Tania Modleski, *Loving with a Vengeance: Mass-Produced Fantasies for Women* (New York: Methuen, 1984): "Romantic literature performs a crucial function in assuring us that although some men may actually enjoy inflicting pain on women, there are also 'bullies' whose meanness is nothing more than the overflow of their love or the measure of their resistance to our extraordinary charms" (43).

13. Unusually for the romance narrative—which tends to represent the heroine's social ascension as something she has neither desired nor much considered—*Rebecca* has its narrator explicitly instructing herself about how heterosexuality secures and domesticates for her what had previously been a remote, public architecture:

> I leant back in my chair, glancing about the room, trying to instil into myself some measure of confidence, some genuine realization that I was here, at Manderley, the house of the picture post-card, the Manderley that was famous. I had to teach myself that all this was mine now, mine as much as his, the deep chair I was sitting in, that mass of books stretching to the ceiling, the pictures on the walls, the gardens, the woods, the Manderley I had read about, all this was mine now because I was married to Maxim. (74)

14. Reading the correspondence between Joseph Breen, head of the Production Code Administration, and David Selznick, Hitchcock's producer, in relation to the preliminary script of *Rebecca*, Rhona Berenstein argues for "a compelling suggestion in Breen's correspondence that the primary form of perversion exhibited by Rebecca is decidedly nonheterosexual" ("Adaptation, Censorship, and Audiences of Questionable Type: Lesbian Sightings in *Rebecca* [1940] and *The Uninvited* [1944]," *Cinema Journal* 37, no. 3 [1998]: 17).

15. In his capacity as administrator of the Production Code, Joseph Breen wrote in a letter to Selznick, "There must be no suggestion whatever of a perverted relationship between Mrs. Danvers and Rebecca. If any possible hint of this creeps into this scene, we will of course not be able to approve the picture" (quoted in Leonard Jeff, *Hitchcock and Selznick*, 70).

16. And so Vito Russo supplements his filmography with a less conventional "necrology"—a table that summarizes the deaths of homosexual characters in film. This column, with its bludgeonings, shootings, and poisonings, its castration and cannibalism, its institutionalized electric chair, and its vigilante stake through the heart, demonstrates the near synonymy—for the cinema, at least—of homosexuality and death. See Vito Russo, *The Celluloid Closet: Homosexuality in the Movies* (New York: Harper & Row, 1981), 261–62.

17. As Tania Modleski argues, "What is interesting about *Rebecca* . . . is that it makes the tendency of women to merge with other women, the tendency taken for granted by Selznick, its chief 'problem,' the solution to which it shows to be extremely difficult" (*The Women Who Knew Too Much* [New York: Methuen, 1988], 44).

18. It is worth saying here that my objection is not to psychoanalysis but to the tendency of a certain sort of film theory to assess the efficacy of psychoanalytic paradigms in terms of gender while occluding its implications for sexuality, privileging what turns out to be in effect an unacknowledged heterosexual femininity. For a corrective use of psychoanalysis that is attuned to the fact that the positive Oedipal complex instantiates not only sexual difference but heterosexuality, see Kaja Silverman, *Male Subjectivity at the Margins* (New York: Routledge, 1992). In particular, Silverman's attention to the ideological dimension of psychoanalytic narratives is helpful here: "It is . . . difficult to sustain the distinction between the dominant fiction and the positive Oedipus complex, but it is nevertheless crucial that we grasp the latter as the psychic consequence of a conventional interpellation into the former" (41).

19. Fletcher, "Primal Scenes and the Female Gothic," 348.

20. Ibid., 351.

21. Ibid., 353.

22. Like Fletcher, I understand the fantastic dimension of the primal scene, the etymological weight of "scenario," its "*putting into scenic form* of a temporal narrative drive, its condensation into a layout that tells a tale of before and after, that hints at an absent or unrepresentable drama; but one that leaves its traces and clues within the manifest scenario that comes to assume a vivid even fixating power, like a Freudian screen memory" ("Primal Scenes and the Female Gothic", 342; emphasis in original).

23. Maxim's photograph was introduced at the suggestion of Selznick himself, who called for "a handsomely framed photo of Maxim on dressing table . . . the only photograph in the room" (Jeff, *Hitchcock and Selznick*, 69). Selznick's installation of Maxim's portrait is pointed given his desire to be directed elsewhere by the descriptions in the novel: "Pursuing authenticity, he asked the art director to heed 'the descriptions given in the novel in dressing the sets, the props, atmosphere, etc.' " (Jeff, *Hitchcock and Selznick*, 59).

24. For a similarly evenhanded reading of this same scene, see Rhona J. Berenstein,

" 'I'm Not the Sort of Person Men Marry': Monsters, Queers, and Hitchcock's *Rebecca*," in *Out in Culture: Gay, Lesbian, and Queer Essays on Popular Culture*, ed. Corey Creekmuir and Alexander Doty (Durham, N.C.: Duke University Press, 1995), 252–54, where she concludes that "neither heterosexual nor queer romance finds smooth representation in this sequence" (254).

25. Fletcher, "Primal Scenes and the Female Gothic," 351.
26. Ibid., 354.
27. Ibid., 350–51.
28. Ibid., 369.
29. To this small library of feminist film theory that graphically references its reliance on Hitchcock's *Rebecca* must now be added Patricia White's *Uninvited: Classical Hollywood Cinema and Lesbian Representability* (Bloomington: Indiana University Press, 1999), the cover of which has a wide-eyed Fontaine rearing back from Judith Anderson's Mrs. Danvers at the closed doorway to Rebecca's former bedroom.
30. The larger significance of these two essays on *Rebecca* for feminist film theory has been widely acknowledged. See, for example, Judith Mayne, "Feminist Film Theory and Criticism," in *Multiple Voices in Feminist Film Criticism*, ed. Diane Carson et al. (Minneapolis: University of Minnesota Press, 1994), where she writes, "Tania Modleski challenges the view of Hitchcock's cinema as a monument to male desire by reading Hitchcock's *Rebecca* as a female oedipal drama" (54), and Janet Walker, "Psychoanalysis and Feminist Film Theory: The Problem of Sexual Difference and Identity," in *Multiple Voices in Feminist Film Criticism*, in which it is argued that "Mary Ann Doane's analysis of . . . *Rebecca* points to cinematic passages that operate to resist the objectification of the woman as spectacle for the male gaze" (90).
31. Mary Ann Doane, *The Desire to Desire*, 174.
32. Ibid., 169.
33. Ibid., 157.
34. In a reading of the same passage in Doane's essay, Patricia White comes to a differently weighted, although no less critical, conclusion: "In what seems to me a profoundly disempowering proposition, the very possibility of female desire as well as spectatorship is relinquished in the retreat from the ghost of lesbian desire" ("Female Spectator, Lesbian Specter: *The Haunting*," in *Inside/Out: Lesbian Theories, Gay Theories*, ed. Diana Fuss [New York: Routledge, 1991], 148).
35. Modleski, *The Women Who Knew Too Much*, 50 and 51.
36. Ibid., 54.
37. Ibid., 51. A similar miscalculation structures Teresa de Lauretis's account of *Rebecca*: "If the heroine of *Rebecca* is made to kill off the mother, it is not only because the rules of the drama and Lotman's 'mythical mechanism' demand narrative closure; it is also because, like them, cinema works for Oedipus" (*Alice Doesn't: Feminism, Semiotics, Cinema* [London: Macmillan, 1984], 153). Oedipus's payroll seems larger than even de Lauretis might have hazarded. Berenstein critiques this conflation in Modleski's reading of *Rebecca*: "Her reading is, however, limited by her conflation of Rebecca's roles as a maternal figure with her position as an object of female sexual desire" (" 'I'm Not the Sort of Person Men Marry,'" 249).
38. I am emboldened in what I had previously and privately held as my idiosyncratic assessment of Judith Anderson by Harry Benshoff's listing of her as one of those classic Hollywood actors who "regardless of their off-screen lives, bring an unmistakable homosexual 'air' to the characters they create," who "suggest queerness in their characterizations by virtue of their gender-bending personas [sic]" (*Monsters in the Closet: Homosexuality and the Horror Film* [Manchester: Manchester University Press, 1997], 14 and 87). The fact that, alongside Judith Anderson in this regard, Benshoff also twice

lists George Sanders, the actor who plays Jack Favell, only reinforces my argument here that Hitchcock's film goes to some length to give sexual perversion a nonheterosexual spin.

39. *Rebecca*'s refusal to license the operations of sexual sequence—perhaps most evident in its generic ambivalence, the way it shies clear of the conventional romance closure—might be held responsible for the widespread desire to sequelize the novel, mentioned by du Maurier's biographer, Margaret Forster: "Never a month went by without someone informing [du Maurier] they were writing a sequel to *Rebecca*" (*Daphne du Maurier*, 391).

Sally Beauman's *Rebecca's Tale* (New York: William Morrow & Co., 2001) is the most recent sequel, this time sanctioned by the du Maurier estate. Although not published by the time my book went to proof, advance publicity suggests that Beauman's novel, like Hill's, is impelled by *Rebecca*'s refusal of the logics of sexual sequence, its fetishistic first line—"Last night I dreamt I went to Manderley again"—implying that it would like to tell the same story, differently.

The urge to imagine *Rebecca* otherwise is demonstrably strong. See Oriel Malet, *Daphne du Maurier: Letters from Menabilly, Portrait of a Friendship* (London: Weidenfeld & Nicolson, 1993), 283–84, where there is an account of an Antonia Fraser short story, "Rebecca's Story," published in 1976 in *Harper's & Queen*, that rescripted the narrative with Rebecca as the innocent victim of Maxim's cruelty. See also Mary Wings, "Rebecca Redux: Tears on a Lesbian Pillow," in *Daring to Dissent: Lesbian Culture from Margin to Mainstream*, ed. Liz Gibbs (London: Cassell, 1994), 11–33, for a fairly plodding account of how the author wrote her lesbian gothic, *Divine Victim*, as an update of *Rebecca*. Even the Hitchcock adaptation of *Rebecca*, itself a rewriting of the original, generates the urge for further remakes. See Teresa de Lauretis, where, dissatisfied with the masculinist trajectory of the Oedipal narrative that structures *Rebecca*, she imagines it being made over differently: "As for *Rebecca*, it too could be remade in several ways, some of which may actually already be available as films: *Les Rendez-vous d'Anna* or *Jeanne Dielman* (Chantal Akerman), *Thriller* (Sally Potter), probably many others" (*Alice Doesn't*, 157).

40. Susan Hill, *Mrs. de Winter* (London: Sinclair-Stevenson, 1993); hereafter cited in the text.

41. Although the blurb of *Mrs. de Winter* goes to some lengths to represent the end of *Rebecca* as teasingly open-ended, its description of Manderley seen burning at a distance seems to me heavily weighted with the cadences of closure: "There was no moon. The sky above our heads was inky black. But the sky on the horizon was not dark at all. It was shot with crimson, like a splash of blood. And the ashes blew towards us with the salt wind from the sea" (397). As the contextualizing explanation for the de Winters' exile and the narrator's earlier lament that "Manderley was ours no longer. Manderley was no more" (8), these lines, their heavy-handed metaphoric recall of Rebecca's murder— "shot with crimson, like a splash of blood"—framing the loss of the ancestral home as her spectral revenge, overturn the conventions of the romance plot with their refusal to cede narrative closure to the happy futurity of the heterosexual couple. While *Mrs. de Winter* frames du Maurier's novel as tantalizingly withholding the outcome of crucial narrative lines, I argue that, on the contrary, it is precisely the emphatic terms of *Rebecca*'s closure that the sequel contests.

42. Lest I seem as deterministic as Hill herself in suturing an essential indifference to those readers she represents as enduringly curious, I note that writing here of *Rebecca*'s readers, I have in mind the implied reader, the notion of the reader constituted and projected by the text itself.

43. D. A. Miller, *Narrative and Its Discontents: Problems of Closure in the Traditional*

Novel (Princeton, N.J.: Princeton University Press, 1981), 5. Miller defines the nonnarratable when he writes, "The nonnarratable elements of a text are precisely those that . . . serve to supply the specified narrative lack, or to answer the specified narrative question. It is not the case that such elements cannot be designated by the text's language, or that they cannot literally be mentioned. The nonnarratable is not the unspeakable. What defines a nonnarratable element is its incapacity to generate a story" (5).

44. I mean this sentence to resonate with Rachel Blau du Plessis's phrase "writing beyond the ending," as Hill's sequel can be read as effecting an exact reversal of the terms prioritized in du Plessis's argument about subverting the conventions of romance and particularly the ideological work undertaken by the romance closure. Du Plessis argues that "as a narrative pattern, the romance plot muffles the main female character, represses quest, valorises heterosexual as opposed to homosexual ties, incorporates individuals within couples as a sign of their personal and narrative success. . . . Writing beyond the ending means the transgressive invention of narrative strategies, strategies that express critical dissent from dominant narrative" (*Writing beyond the Ending: Narrative Strategies of Twentieth-Century Women Writers* [Bloomington: Indiana University Press, 1985], 5). While *Rebecca* subverts the romantic conventions specified by du Plessis, the writing beyond the ending effected by Hill's sequel is a conservative attempt to rehouse the gothic inside the romance, to prioritize heterosexuality—particularly the heterosexual couple—over other sexual formations.

45. These narrative economies are so well and widely understood that when Joseph Breen, on behalf of the Motion Picture Association Board, vetoed—among other things—any hint of "sex perversion" in the film adaptation of du Maurier's novel, a reporter asked Hitchcock "whether it would be necessary to kill him (meaning de Winter) at the end of *Rebecca*." Hitchcock's apocryphal reply was " 'You mean Breen? I don't think so.' " Quoted in Jeff, *Hitchcock and Selznick*, 71.

46. This effect is only heightened when *Mrs. de Winter* closes with the narrator sprinkling her husband's ashes on the cove beneath the ruins of Manderley, citing the last sentence of *Rebecca* that earlier had been cast as intriguingly open-ended: "I went to the side and waited a moment, and then I opened the small box, and overturned it gently, tipping its fine pale powder out, and as I did so, the ashes lifted, and blew away from me, carried towards Manderley with the salt wind from the sea" (374).

47. Peter Kemp, "Imitation Gothic," *Times Literary Supplement*, 15 October 1993, 19.

48. These cultural discourses make themselves perhaps most tryingly felt in the narrativizations of everyday life, where the attempts to refuse their structurings of sexual precedence are met with, if not hostility then incomprehension. Because I had no satisfaction at the time, let me use as an example my recent exchange on my front doorstep with an interviewer from the Australian Bureau of Statistics, collecting data on employment patterns. On learning that I was not married, the interviewer categorized me as "single," a misattribution I was prepared to let stand in this context. She then asked who else lived in the house, what was this person's birth date, occupation, and relation to me. Writing down my partner's details, she categorized her also as "single," which seemed to me objectionable as, even within the limited scope of the interview, to be both someone's partner and single seemed an insulting contradiction in terms. I pointed this out; she pointed out in turn that the computer would not recognize the nomination of "de facto" for a same-sex relationship. Sensing that our interview had taken a turn for the worse and much more committed to securing my employment than my sexual history, the interviewer moved to reassure me by saying, "I use the word *partner* to describe my own relationship," and then, as she packed away

her papers, added, as if inconsequentially, "Well, I did before we were married. He's my husband now."

Chapter 6: Wild Life Photography

1. Frank Caprio, *Female Homosexuality: A Psychodynamic Study of Lesbianism* (New York: Citadel, 1954; rpt., Melbourne: Gold Star Publications, 1971); hereafter cited in the text. The influence of Caprio's text can be measured by its frequent citation in later pulp sexology texts. See, for example, Matt Bradley, *Lesbian Lane* (Hollywood, Calif.: Jade Books, 1963); Foster Craddock, *Sex without Men: An Authentic Report on Lesbianism* (North Hollywood, Calif.: Challenge Publications, 1966), 26; R. Leighton Hasselrodt, *Lesbianism around the World* (New York: Tower Publication, 1963), 20 and 54; and Carlson Wade, *The Troubled Sex* (n.p.: Beacon Envoy, 1961), 38–39 and 46.

2. Although outside the scope of this study, the postwar boom in pulp sexology that focused on homosexuality is enabled by various cultural conditions and forces, including the rise of the mass-market paperback and its widespread distribution networks; the popular influence of Kinsey's *Sexual Behavior in the Human Male* and *Sexual Behavior in the Human Female*, which demonstrated the widespread occurrence of sexual variation, disputing any clear-cut distinction between homosexual and heterosexual populations; the second-wave emergence of homophile movements; and the cold war's homosexualization of the internal threat to American national security.

3. Benjamin Morse, *The Lesbian: A Frank, Revealing Study of Women Who Turn to Their Own Sex for Love* (Derby, Conn.: Monarch Books, 1961). This title was published in the Monarch Human Behavior series alongside such studies as William E. Miles's *The College Female* and Don James's *Girls and Gangs*. Other titles in the series by Morse include *Sexual Surrender in Women*, *The Homosexual*, *The Sexual Revolution*, *The Sexually Promiscuous Male*, and *The Sexually Promiscuous Female*.

4. Morse, *The Lesbian*, 5.

5. The cover copy of Donald Webster Cory's *The Lesbian in America* reads, "Why does she desire other females? What are her sexual needs and habits? Is she a moral degenerate? *Here is the frank and documented truth about the homosexual woman and her world*" (*The Lesbian in America* [New York: Citadel Press, 1964; rpt., MacFadden Books, 1965], emphasis in original). In his foreword to Maurice Chideckel's *Female Sex Perversion*, Dr. S. Wolman figures knowledge as illumination: "Many sincere students believe that truth is liberating, and that out of light is engendered safety and guidance. The following book is an outcome of the belief that for the enlightened mind, knowledge is power" (Foreword to Maurice Chideckel, *Female Sex Perversion: The Sexually Aberrated Woman* [North Hollywood, Calif.: Brandon House, 1967], 5).

6. This sweeping comprehensiveness is evident in Morse's chapter headings: "The College Girl," "The Working Girl," "The Tomboy," "The Career Girl," "The Bored Matron," "The Prostitute," "The Eternal Female," "The Man Hater," "The Bohemian," "The Bisexual Woman," "The Unsuccessful Heterosexual," and "The Frigid Abstainer." W. D. Sprague organizes his chapters along similar lines—"The Office Lesbian," "The Homosexual Housewife," "The Lesbian Call-Girl"—and includes an equally elasticized historical survey: "The Greeks Had a Word for It," "The Ribald Renaissance," "From Voltaire to Victoria" (*The Lesbian in Our Society* [New York: Tower Publications, 1962]). R Leighton Hasselrodt's equally comprehensive survey (*Lesbianism around the World*) takes the form of comparative anthropology, each chapter—"Canadian Capers," "Down Mexico Way," and "The Torrid Tropics"—associating lesbianism with a differ-

ent national or geographic region, the combined effect of which, as his title suggests, is a fairly undifferentiated globalization.

7. Morse, *The Lesbian*, 20; emphasis in original.

8. For a discussion of the rhetorical function of the young person in relation to the framing of American obscenity laws, see Walter Kendrick, *The Secret Museum: Pornography in Modern Culture* (Berkeley: University of California Press, 1987; rpt., 1996), 122–23 and 138–43.

9. The camp sensibility of Jaye Zimet's recent *Strange Sisters: The Art of Lesbian Pulp Fiction, 1949–1969* (New York: Viking Studio, 1999) manages at once to dismiss and reclaim the genre. Taking as its own the title of a 1962 pulp novel and reproducing as its cover art the image from the 1963 pulp novel *I Prefer Girls*, Zimet's book recuperates the tawdry eroticism of lesbian pulp for a 1990s readership for whom the once-erotic now registers as comic. Considering pulp sexology in the chapter "Psycho-Babble," Zimet emphasizes the bogus nature of its claims to scientific knowledge: "A book could not be censored if it was, or could pretend to be, a serious scientific study. Thus, all sorts of 'scientific' studies of sexuality and deviant sexuality were printed. Couched in medical terminology, with introductions and testimonials by alleged psychiatrists and M.D.s, these books were doused in legitimacy, and often offered more risqué reading material than the novels" (83). Thomas Waugh similarly describes the 1950s as "a time when science was the favorite alibi of taboo sexual discourses, and many of the commodities of the imminent Sexual Revolution had a distinct pseudoscientific flavor. It was a time when *Playboy* aspired to sexological authority . . . and when pseudojournalistic exposés of perversion, decorated with pictures and dubious Ph.D.'s, were standard fare in men's entertainment media" (*Hard to Imagine: Gay Male Eroticism in Photography and Film from Their Beginnings to Stonewall* [New York: Columbia University Press, 1996], 396). David Bergman also foregrounds the way in which the sexological enabled the erotic: "By casting erotic descriptions as either medical or sociological studies, which construed homosexuality as either social deviance or mental disease, pulp publishers were able to circumvent the law" ("The Cultural Work of Sixties Gay Pulp Fiction," in *The Queer Sixties*, ed. Patricia Juliana Smith [New York: Routledge, 1999], 29).

10. Justice William J. Brennan, quoted in Kendrick, *The Secret Museum*, 201. Kendrick argues that while Brennan's opinion eliminated the possibility of First Amendment protection for obscenity, his definition of obscenity "as utterly without redeeming social importance" meant that the smallest claim to social importance could redeem what had formerly been considered obscene, "that if the tiniest nugget of 'social importance' could be dug out of a book, it would neutralize a mountain of prurience" (*The Secret Museum*, 201–202).

11. The histories of lesbian pulp sexology's production and reception are outside the brief of this chapter and, to a significant extent, remain to be written. It seems worth mentioning, however, that, whatever its other functions, lesbian pulp sexology, like lesbian pulp fiction, has played an important part in the self-fashioning of twentieth-century lesbian identities. For an account of the role of lesbian pulp fiction in the articulation of 1950s and 1960s lesbian identity, see Angela Weir and Elizabeth Wilson, "The Greyhound Bus Station in the Evolution of Lesbian Popular Culture," in *New Lesbian Criticism: Literary and Cultural Readings*, ed. Sally Munt (Hertfordshire: Harvester Wheatsheaf, 1992), 95–113.

Something of the interaction between pulp sexology and lesbian identity can be seen in the writings of Marijane Meaker and her reader response. Writing as Ann Aldrich—she also wrote as Vin Packer—Meaker self-identifies as lesbian in her pulp sexological writings—a disclosure that revitalizes rather than short-circuits pulp sexology's generic commitment to an authoritative brokering of sexual ethnography: "I have seen them often, known them, watched them, listened to them, talked with them and been a part of their life. I have seen them, and I am one of them" (Ann Aldrich, *We Walk Alone* [New York: Gold Medal Books, 1955], 13). Moreover, three years later, Aldrich published *We, Too, Must Love* (New York: Gold Medal Books, 1958; rpt., New South Wales: Eclipse Paperbacks, n.d.), an account of lesbian life in New York City, in which she publishes several of the 600 letters she received from readers of her earlier book, many of whom found in her descriptions of lesbian subculture a reinforcing narrative for their own established or proto-lesbian identities (170–79). In this connection, it is interesting to see that Monica Bachmann has recently analyzed readers' correspondence with Jo Sinclair, the author of the 1946 lesbian-themed *Wasteland*, arguing from that archive that lesbian fiction, through its "networks of reading and writing," has functioned historically as an important "site of sexual identity formation" (" 'Someone like Debby': (De)Constructing a Lesbian Community of Readers," *GLQ: A Journal of Lesbian and Gay Studies*. 6, no. 3 [2000]: 378).

12. See, for example, David Bergman's reference to the "generally homophobic genres of gay pulp novels as the medical study or the sociological tract" of the 1960s ("The Cultural Work of Sixties Gay Pulp Fiction," 29).

13. While anxiety is most commonly the affect that deconstructive readings attribute to such futile attempts to fix the unstable fields of sexual identity and desire, it is equally plausible to think about these endeavors, like their failures, as the occasion for the not entirely distinct affect of ecstasy, the sexual satisfaction of the intended reader—frequently the heterosexual male despite the apostrophized address to the vulnerable young heterosexual woman—sutured to the notorious unreliability of homosexual difference. This account is not intended to overlook the possibility of a lesbian—or, indeed, any other—reader. (After all, the model of a reading subject in the satiating grip of an erotic anxiety derives from my own adolescent reading of sexology, a reading position whose anxieties and erotic satisfactions came retrospectively to be described as "lesbian.") Rather, it is meant to suggest, in contradistinction to the dominant characterization of the pornographic vision in terms of exploitation, objectification, and male-inflected spectatorial mastery, the range of different identificatory positions and different embodied effects that constitute the reception of pulp sexology.

14. Even the abstention from lesbian sex practices is evidence for Caprio of the desire to participate in them: "In those instances where prostitutes do not engage in lesbian activities, it is not because, unconsciously, they do not want to. The explanation lies in the fact that they have never been able to break through their homosexual repressions" (112).

15. Dr. La Forrest Potter, quoted in *Female Homosexuality*, 153.

16. For a discussion of the function of language—particularly "the ever-present caption"—in suturing the viewer's relationship to the visual field of the photograph, see Victor Burgin, "Photography, Phantasy, Function," in *Thinking Photography*, ed. Victor Burgin (London: Macmillan, 1982), 191–92.

17. Roland Barthes, *Camera Lucida: Reflections on Photography*, trans. Richard Howard (New York: Hill & Wang, 1981), 89. My understanding of the mutually reinforcing discourses of ethnography and pornography is taken from Christian Hansen, Catherine Needham, and Bill Nichols's "Skin Flicks: Pornography, Ethnography, and the Discourses of Power" (*Discourse: Journal for Theoretical Studies in Media and Culture* 11, no. 2 [Spring–Summer 1989]). Although my reading of the photo-essay under discussion rejects many of the conflations "Skin Flicks" makes between structures of power and structures of vision, I am interested in their project of linking knowledge and desire—those discourses that I characterized earlier as respectively scientific and obscene:

"[Pornography and ethnography] represent impulses born of desire: the desire to know and possess, to 'know' by possessing and possess by knowing. . . . Both rely on a documentary impulse, a guarantee that we will behold 'the thing itself,' caught in the indexical grain of the cinematographic image" (67–68).

18. Barthes, *Camera Lucida*, 89.

19. Roland Barthes, *Image/Music/Text*, trans. Stephen Heath (London: Fontana Press, 1977), 19. As W. J. T. Mitchell glosses Barthes's argument: "One connotation always present in the photograph is that it is a pure denotation; that is simply what it means to recognize it as a photograph rather than some other sort of image" (*Picture Theory: Essays on Verbal and Visual Representation* [Chicago: University of Chicago Press, 1994], 284).

20. Mandy Merck notes the way in which the photographic project confirms the sexological insofar as sexology's insistence on the corporeal inscription of sexual deviance is reinforced by "one function of the newly invented medium [of photography], the visualization of socio-sexual deviance as an image of the body, whose every feature—from carriage to clothing—is biologically ordained and medically legible" (*Perversions: Deviant Readings* [London: Virago Press, 1993], 90–91). For a further discussion of the reinforcing legitimizations of sexology and photography, see Jennifer Terry, *An American Obsession*, 196–98.

21. In her historic account of the development of hard-core pornography in twentieth-century America, Linda Williams describes pornography as "a 'drive for knowledge' that takes place through a voyeurism structured as a cognitive urge" (*Hard Core: Power, Pleasure, and the "Frenzy of the Visible"* [London: Pandora Press, 1990], 48). While the photo-essay under discussion is decidedly soft-core and—perhaps even more crucially—noncinematic, Williams's argument enables a consideration of the mutual concerns of its scientific and pornographic framing.

22. Burgin, "Photography, Phantasy, Function," 190. Régis Durand further complicates this characterization of the photograph. He argues that the frozen temporality of the photograph ever only registers a lag or delay in relation to present time: "a film sequence, although it is entirely fabricated, can give us a sense of an authentic duration, whereas the sharpest, crudest photograph will always be somewhat off the mark (dreamlike, unreal, pensive, depending on the value we give to this discrepancy, this lagging), in a state of temporal unbalance" ("How to See [Photographically]," in *Fugitive Images: From Photography to Video*, ed. Patrice Petro [Bloomington: Indiana University Press, 1995], 147). However, whether the photograph is regarded as an arrested coordinate of time and space or a moment whose registration of time is always belated, as marked by the fixing or the failure to fix time, my interest in the photo-essay depends on the way in which its sequencing makes recognizable its desire to narrate, to register meaning across a passage of time.

23. The photograph's lack of narrative capacity is a commonplace. Susan Sontag writes, "Strictly speaking, one never understands anything from a photograph. . . . Only that which narrates can make us understand" (*On Photography* [New York: Farrar, Strauss & Giroux, 1977], 20–21). John Berger similarly asserts that "photographs in themselves do not narrate" (*About Looking* [New York: Pantheon Books, 1980], 58).

24. Durand, "How to See (Photographically)," 144.

25. My argument here is indebted to Lee Edelman's productive insistence (in *Homographesis: Essays in Gay Literary and Cultural Theory* [New York, Routledge, 1994]) that the cultural stake in representing homosexuality as a visible difference testifies to an anxiety that an unmarked difference internal to gender categories works against the naturalization of heterosexuality:

For the recurrent tropology of the inscribed gay body indicates, by its defensive assertion of a visible marker of sexual otherness, a fear that the categorical institutionalization of "homosexual difference" might challenge the integrity and reliability of anatomical sameness as the guarantor of sexual identity: that the elaboration of difference among and within the proliferating categories of sex, gender and sexuality might vitiate the certainty by which one's own self-identity could be known. (12)

26. The idea that sexual identities are made self-evident in certain sexual acts is a dubious one, complicated in any number of post-Foucauldian denaturalizations of the seemingly causal relationship between acts and identities. Nevertheless, the idea of two women together, in the sexual relationship that the phrase "in bed" functions to guarantee, is often understood to fix the otherwise ambiguous status of lesbian representation. For example, de Lauretis argues that lesbian visibility is secured through relationality, lesbianism somehow acquiring the status of representation *between* two women: "It takes two women, not one, to make a lesbian" (*The Practice of Love*, 92).

Bibliography

Abel, Elizabeth. *Virginia Woolf and the Fictions of Psychoanalysis.* Chicago: University of Chicago Press, 1989.
Abraham, Julie. *Are Girls Necessary? Lesbian Writing and Modern Histories.* New York: Routledge, 1996.
Ackroyd, Peter. Introduction to *Little Dorrit.* London: Mandarin, 1991.
Acton, William. *Prostitution Considered in Its Moral, Social, and Sanitary Aspects in London and Other Large Cities and Garrison Towns with Proposals for the Control and Prevention of Its Attendant Evils.* London, 1857; rpt., Frank Cass & Co., 1972.
Aldrich, Ann. *We, Too, Must Love.* New York: Gold Medal Books, 1958; rpt., New South Wales: Eclipse Paperbacks, n.d.
———. *We Walk Alone.* New York: Gold Medal Books, 1955.
Anderson, Amanda. *Tainted Souls and Painted Faces: The Rhetoric of Fallenness in Victorian Culture.* Ithaca, N.Y.: Cornell University Press, 1993.
Anesko, Michael. *"Friction with the Market": Henry James and the Profession of Authorship.* New York: Oxford University Press, 1986.
Anonymous. "From a Review of *Little Dorrit.*" In *Charles Dickens: Critical Assessments.* Vol. 1. Edited by Michael Hollington, pp. 386–88. East Sussex: Helm, 1995.
Armstrong, Nancy. *Desire and Domestic Fiction: A Political History of the Novel.* New York: Oxford University Press, 1987.
Bachmann, Monica. " 'Someone like Debby': (De)Constructing a Lesbian Community of Readers." *GLQ: A Journal of Lesbian and Gay Studies* 6, no. 3 (2000): 377–88.
Ballaster, Ros. " 'The Vices of Old Rome Revived': Representations of Female Same-sex Desire in Seventeenth and Eighteenth Century England." In *Volcanoes and Pearl Divers: Essays in Lesbian Feminist Studies,* edited by Suzanne Raitt, pp. 13–36. New York: Harrington Park Press, 1995.
Banta, Martha. "The Excluded Seven: Practice of Omission, Aesthetics of Refusal."

In *Henry James's New York Edition: The Construction of Authorship*, edited by David McWhirter, pp. 240–60. Stanford, Calif.: Stanford University Press, 1995.

Barthes, Roland. *Camera Lucida: Reflections on Photography*. Translated by Richard Howard. New York: Hill & Wang, 1981.

———. *Image/Music/Text*. Translated by Stephen Heath. London: Fontana Press, 1977.

Batchelor, John. *Virginia Woolf: The Major Novels*. Cambridge: Cambridge University Press, 1991.

Bell, Ian F. A. "The Personal, the Private, and the Public in *The Bostonians*." *Texas Studies in Literature and Language* 32, no. 2 (Summer 1990): 240–56.

Bell, Millicent. *Meaning in Henry James*. Cambridge, Mass.: Harvard University Press, 1991.

Benjamin, Walter. *Charles Baudelaire: A Lyric Poet in the Era of High Capitalism*. Translated by Harry Zohn. London: New Left Books, 1973; rpt., Verso, 1992.

Bennett, Judith M. " 'Lesbian-Like' and the Social History of Lesbians." *Journal of the History of Sexuality* 9, nos. 1–2 (January–April 2000): 1–24.

Benshoff, Harry. *Monsters in the Closet: Homosexuality and the Horror Film*. Manchester: Manchester University Press, 1997.

Berenstein, Rhona. "Adaptation, Censorship, and Audiences of Questionable Type: Lesbian Sightings in *Rebecca* (1940) and *The Uninvited* (1944)." *Cinema Journal* 37, no. 3 (1998): 16–37.

———. " 'I'm Not the Sort of Person Men Marry': Monsters, Queers, and Hitchcock's *Rebecca*." In *Out in Culture: Gay, Lesbian, and Queer Essays on Popular Culture*, edited by Corey Creekmuir and Alexander Doty, pp. 240–58. Durham, N.C.: Duke University Press, 1995.

Berger, John. *About Looking*. New York: Pantheon Books, 1980.

Bergman, David. "The Cultural Work of Sixties Gay Pulp Fiction." In *The Queer Sixties*, edited by Patricia Juliana Smith, pp. 26–41. New York: Routledge, 1999.

Berlant, Lauren, and Michael Warner. "Sex in Public." *Critical Inquiry* 24 (Winter 1998): 547–66.

Bernstein, Susan David. *Confessional Subjects: Revelations of Gender and Power in Victorian Literature and Culture*. Chapel Hill: University of North Carolina Press, 1997.

Bland, Lucy. *Banishing the Beast: English Feminism and Sexual Morality, 1885–1914*. Harmondsworth: Penguin Books, 1995.

———. "Trial by Sexology? Maud Allan, *Salome*, and the 'Cult of the Clitoris' Case." In *Sexology in Culture: Labelling Bodies and Desires*, edited by Lucy Bland and Laura Doan. Chicago: University of Chicago Press, 1998.

Boone, Joseph Allen. *Libidinal Currents: Sexuality and the Shaping of Modernism*. Chicago: University of Chicago Press, 1998.

Boudreau, Kristin. "Narrative Sympathy in *The Bostonians*." *Henry James Review* 14 (1993): 17–33.

Bowen, Janet Wolf. "Architectural Envy: 'A Figure Is Nothing without a Setting' in Henry James's *The Bostonians*." *New England Quarterly* 65, no. 1 (March 1992): 3–23.

Bradley, Matt. *Lesbian Lane*. Hollywood, Calif.: Jade Books, 1963.

Braidotti, Rosi. *Patterns of Dissonance: A Study of Women in Contemporary Philosophy.* Translated by Elizabeth Guild. Cambridge: Polity Press, 1991.

———. "Revisiting Male Thanatica." *Differences: A Journal of Feminist Cultural Studies* 6, nos. 2–3 (1994): 199–207.

Braunschneider, Theresa. "The Macroclitoride, the Tribade, and the Woman: Configuring Gender and Sexuality in English Anatomical Discourse." *Textual Practice* 13, no. 3 (1999): 509–32.

Bristow, Joseph. "Symonds's History, Ellis's Heredity." In *Sexology in Culture: Labelling Bodies and Desires,* edited by Lucy Bland and Laura Doan, pp. 79–99. Chicago: University of Chicago Press, 1998.

Brooks, Peter. *Reading for the Plot: Design and Intention in Narrative.* Cambridge, Mass.: Harvard University Press, 1984.

Buck-Morss, Susan. "The Flaneur, the Sandwichman, and the Whore." In *The Problems of Modernity: Adorno and Benjamin,* edited by Andrew Benjamin, pp. 141–56. London: Routledge, 1989.

Burgin, Victor. "Photography, Phantasy, Function." In *Thinking Photography,* edited by Victor Burgin, pp. 177–216. London: Macmillan, 1982.

Burns, Allan. "Henry James's Journalists as Synecdoche for the American Scene." *Henry James Review* 16 (1995): 1–17.

Burns, Bonnie. "*Dracula's Daughter*: Cinema, Hypnosis, and the Erotics of Lesbianism." In *Lesbian Erotics,* edited by Karla Jay. New York: New York University Press, 1995.

Butler, Judith. *Gender Trouble: Feminism and the Subversion of Identity.* New York: Routledge, 1990.

———. "Imitation and Gender Insubordination." In *Inside/Out: Lesbian Theories, Gay Theories,* edited by Diana Fuss, pp. 13–31. New York: Routledge, 1991.

———. *The Psychic Life of Power: Theories in Subjection.* Stanford, Calif.: Stanford University Press, 1997.

———. "Sexual Inversions." In *Discourses of Sexuality: From Aristotle to AIDS,* edited by Domna C. Stanton, pp. 344–61. Ann Arbor: University of Michigan Press, 1992.

Cahill, Patricia Ann Ellen. "Beginning the World: Women and Society in the Novels of Dickens." Ph.D. dissertation, University of Massachusetts, 1978. Ann Arbor, Mich.: University Microfilms, 1979.

Caprio, Frank. *Female Homosexuality: A Psychodynamic Study of Lesbianism.* New York: Citadel, 1954; rpt., Melbourne: Gold Star Publications, 1971.

Case, Sue-Ellen. "Tracking the Vampire." *Differences: A Journal of Feminist Cultural Studies* 3, no. 2 (Summer 1991): 1–20.

Castle, Terry. *The Apparitional Lesbian: Female Homosexuality and Modern Culture.* New York: Columbia University Press, 1993.

Chauncey, George, Jr. "From Sexual Inversion to Homosexuality: Medicine and the Changing Conceptualisation of Female Deviance." *Salmagundi* 58–59 (1982): 114–46.

Chideckel, Maurice. *Female Sex Perversion: The Sexually Aberrated Woman.* North Hollywood, Calif.: Brandon House, 1967.

Clark, Anna. "Anne Lister's Construction of Lesbian Identity." *Journal of the History of Sexuality* 7, no. 1 (1996): 23–50.

Cohen, Ed. *Talk on the Wilde Side: Toward a Genealogy of a Discourse on Male Sexualities.* New York: Routledge, 1993.
Cory, Donald Webster. *The Lesbian in America.* New York: Citadel Press, 1964.
Cott, Nancy F. "Giving Character to Our Whole Civil Polity: Marriage and the Public Order in the Late Nineteenth Century." In *U.S. Women's History as Women's History: New Feminist Essays,* edited by Linda K. Kerber et al., pp. 107–21. Chapel Hill: University of North Carolina Press, 1995.
Craddock, Foster. *Sex without Men: An Authentic Report on Lesbianism.* North Hollywood, Calif.: Challenge Publications, 1966.
Craft, Christopher. *Another Kind of Love: Male Homosexual Desire in English Discourse, 1850–1920.* Berkeley: University of California Press, 1994.
Davidson, Arnold I. "How to Do the History of Psychoanalysis: A Reading of Freud's *Three Essays on the Theory of Sexuality.*" *Critical Inquiry* 13 (Winter 1987): 252–77.
Davis, Sara DeSaussure. "Feminist Sources in *The Bostonians.*" *American Literature* 50 (December 1979): 570–603.
De Lauretis, Teresa. *Alice Doesn't: Feminism, Semiotics, Cinema.* London: Macmillan, 1984.
———. *The Practice of Love: Lesbian Sexuality and Perverse Desire.* Bloomington: Indiana University Press, 1994.
———. "Sexual Indifference and Lesbian Representation." In *The Lesbian and Gay Studies Reader,* edited by Henry Abelove et al., pp. 141–58. New York, Routledge, 1993.
D'Emilio, John, and Estelle B. Freeman. *Intimate Matters: A History of Sexuality in America.* New York: Harper & Row, 1988.
Dickens, Charles. *Little Dorrit.* 1857; rpt., London: Mandarin, 1991.
Diggs, Marylynne. "Romantic Friends or a 'Different Race of Creatures'? The Representation of Lesbian Pathology in Nineteenth-Century America." *Feminist Studies* 21, no. 2 (Summer 1995): 317–40.
Dinshaw, Carolyn. *Getting Medieval: Sexualities and Communities, Pre- and Postmodern.* Durham, N.C.: Duke University Press, 1999.
Doan, Laura. "'Acts of Female Indecency': Sexology's Intervention in Legislating Lesbianism." In *Sexology in Culture: Labelling Bodies and Desires,* edited by Lucy Bland and Laura Doan, pp. 199–213. Chicago: University of Chicago Press, 1998.
———. *Fashioning Sapphism: The Origin of a Modern English Lesbian Culture.* New York: Columbia University Press, 2001.
Doane, Mary Ann. *The Desire to Desire: The Woman's Film of the 1940s.* London: Macmillan, 1988.
Donoghue, Emma. *Passions between Women: British Lesbian Culture, 1668–1801.* London: Scarlet Press, 1993; rpt., New York: HarperCollins, 1995.
Dowling, David. *Mrs. Dalloway: Mapping Streams of Consciousness.* Boston: Twayne Publishers, 1991.
Du Maurier, Daphne. *Rebecca.* London: Victor Gollancz, 1938; rpt., Random Century, 1992.
Du Plessis, Rachel Blau. *Writing beyond the Ending: Narrative Strategies of Twentieth-Century Women Writers.* Bloomington: Indiana University Press, 1985.

Durand, Régis. "How to See (Photographically)." In *Fugitive Images: From Photography to Video*, edited by Patrice Petro, pp. 141–51. Bloomington: Indiana University Press, 1995.

Dyer, Richard. "Children of the Night: Vampirism as Homosexuality, Homosexuality as Vampirism." In *Sweet Dreams: Sexuality, Gender, and Popular Fiction*, edited by Susannah Radstone, pp. 47–72. London: Lawrence & Wishart, 1988.

Edel, Leon. *Henry James: The Middle Years*. Philadelphia: Lippincott, 1962.

Edelman, Lee. *Homographesis: Essays in Gay Literary and Cultural Theory*. New York: Routledge, 1994.

Ellis, Havelock. *Sexual Inversion*. London: Wilson & Macmillan, 1897; rpt., New York: Arno Press, 1975.

Ender, Evelyne. *Sexing the Mind: Nineteenth-Century Fictions of Hysteria*. Ithaca, N.Y.: Cornell University Press, 1995.

Fabi, M. Guilia. "The Reluctant Patriarch: A Study of *The Portrait of a Lady*, *The Bostonians*, and *The Awkward Age*." *Henry James Review* 13 (1992): 1–18.

Faderman, Lillian. *Surpassing the Love of Men: Romantic Friendship and Love between Women from the Renaissance to the Present*. New York: William Morrow, 1981.

Felski, Rita. Introduction to *Sexology in Culture: Labelling Bodies and Desires*, edited by Lucy Bland and Laura Doan, pp. 1–8. Chicago: University of Chicago Press, 1998.

Fetterley, Judith. *The Resisting Reader: A Feminist Approach to Fiction*. Bloomington: University of Indiana Press, 1978.

Fisher, Philip. "Appearing and Disappearing in Public: Social Space in Late-Nineteenth Century Literature and Culture." In *Reconstructing American Literary History*, edited by Sacvan Bercovitch, pp. 155–88. Cambridge, Mass.: Harvard University Press, 1986.

Fletcher, John. "Primal Scenes and the Female Gothic: *Rebecca* and *Gaslight*." *Screen* 36, no. 4 (1995): 341–70.

Forster, E. M. "The Novels of Virginia Woolf." *New Criterion* (April 1926): 277–86. Reprinted in *Virginia Woolf: The Critical Heritage*, edited by Robin Majumdar and Allen McLaurin, pp. 171–78. London: Routledge & Kegan Paul, 1975.

Forster, John. *The Life of Charles Dickens*. Vol. 3. London: Chapman & Hall, 1874.

Forster, Margaret. *Daphne du Maurier*. London: Chatto & Windus, 1993.

Foucault, Michel. *The History of Sexuality*. Vol. 1, *An Introduction*. Translated by Robert Hurley. London: Penguin, 1990.

Fradenburg, Louise, and Carla Freccero. "Introduction: Caxton, Foucault, and the Pleasures of History." In *Premodern Sexualities*, edited by Louise Fradenburg and Carla Freccero, pp. xiii–xxiv. New York: Routledge, 1996.

Freud, Sigmund. *The Complete Introductory Lectures of Psychoanalysis*. Translated and edited by James Strachey. London: George Allen & Unwin, 1963; rpt., 1971.

———. "Female Sexuality" (1931). In *The Standard Edition of the Complete Psychological Works of Sigmund Freud*. Vol. 21. Translated and edited by James Strachey, pp. 221–43. London: Hogarth Press, 1961.

———. "Five Lectures on Psychoanalysis" (1910). In *The Standard Edition of the Complete Psychological Works of Sigmund Freud*. Vol. 11. Translated and edited by James Strachey, pp. 1–55. London: Hogarth Press, 1957.

———. "Introduction to *Psycho-analysis and the War Neuroses*" (1919). In *The Standard Edition of the Complete Psychological Works of Sigmund Freud.* Vol. 17. Translated and edited by James Strachey, pp. 205–10. London: Hogarth Press, 1955.
———. "On Beginning the Treatment: (Further Recommendations on the Technique of Psycho-Analysis I)" (1913). In *The Standard Edition of the Complete Psychological Works of Sigmund Freud.* Vol. 12. Translated and edited by James Strachey, pp. 121–44. London: Hogarth Press, 1958.
———. "The Psychogenesis of a Case of Homosexuality in a Woman" (1920). In *The Standard Edition of the Complete Psychological Works of Sigmund Freud.* Vol. 18. Translated and edited by James Strachey, pp. 145–72. London: Hogarth Press, 1955.
———. *The Psychopathology of Everyday Life* (1901). In *The Standard Edition of the Complete Psychological Works of Sigmund Freud.* Vol. 6. Translated and edited by James Strachey. London: Hogarth Press, 1960.
———. "Remembering, Repeating and Working-Through (Further Recommendations on the Technique of Psycho-Analysis II)" (1914). In *The Standard Edition of the Complete Psychological Works of Sigmund Freud.* Vol. 12. Translated and edited by James Strachey, pp. 145–56. London: Hogarth Press, 1958.
———. "Some Neurotic Mechanisms in Jealousy, Paranoia, and Homosexuality" (1922). In *The Standard Edition of the Complete Psychological Works of Sigmund Freud.* Vol. 18. Translated and edited by James Strachey. London: Hogarth Press, 1955.
———. *Three Essays on the Theory of Sexuality* (1905). In *The Standard Edition of the Complete Psychological Works of Sigmund Freud.* Vol. 7. Translated and edited by James Strachey. London: Hogarth Press, 1953.
Frye, Marilyn. *The Politics of Reality: Essays in Feminist Theory.* New York: Crossing Press, 1983.
Fulton, Valerie. "Rewriting the Necessary Woman: Marriage and Professionalism in James, Jewett, and Phelps." *Henry James Review* 15 (1995): 242–56.
Fuss, Diana. *Essentially Speaking: Feminism, Nature, and Difference.* New York: Routledge, 1989.
———. *Identification Papers.* New York: Routledge, 1995.
Gabler, Janet A. "The Narrator's Script: James's Complex Narration in *The Bostonians.*" *Journal of Narrative Technique* 14, no. 2 (Spring 1984): 94–109.
Goldberg, Jonathan. *Sodometries: Renaissance Texts, Modern Sexualities.* Stanford, Calif.: Stanford University Press, 1992.
Graham, Wendy. *Henry James's Thwarted Love.* Stanford, Calif.: Stanford University Press, 1999.
Grosskurth, Phyllis. *Havelock Ellis: A Biography.* New York: Alfred Knopf, 1980.
Grosz, Elizabeth. *Space, Time, and Perversion.* Sydney: Allen & Unwin, 1995.
Guth, Deborah. " 'What a Lark! What a Plunge!' Fiction as Self-Evasion." In *Virginia Woolf: Critical Assessments.* Vol. 3. Edited by Eleanor McNees, pp. 435–44. London: Helm Information, 1994.
Habegger, Alfred. *Henry James and the "Woman Business".* Cambridge: Cambridge University Press, 1989.
Habermas, Jürgen. *The Structural Transformation of the Public Sphere: An Inquiry into*

a Category of Bourgeois Society. Translated by Thomas Burger. Cambridge, Mass.: MIT Press, 1991; rpt., 1993.

Haggerty, George E. "Heteromachia." *GLQ: A Journal of Lesbian and Gay Studies* 6, no. 3 (2000): 435–50.

Halberstam, Judith. *Female Masculinity.* Durham, N.C.: Duke University Press, 1998.

———. *Skin Shows: Gothic Horror and the Technology of Monsters,* Durham, N.C.: Duke University Press, 1995.

Halperin, David. "Forgetting Foucault: Acts, Identities, and the History of Sexuality." *Representations* 63 (Summer 1999): 93–120.

———. "Historicizing the Sexual Body: Sexual Preferences and Erotic Identities in the Pseudo-Lucianic Erôtes." In *Discourses of Sexuality: From Aristotle to AIDS,* edited by Domna C. Stanton, pp. 236–61. Ann Arbor: University of Michigan Press, 1992.

———. "How to Do the History of Male Homosexuality." *GLQ: A Journal of Gay and Lesbian Studies* 6, no. 1 (2000): 87–123.

———. "Is There a History of Sexuality?" In *The Lesbian and Gay Studies Reader,* edited by Henry Abelove et al., pp. 416–31. New York: Routledge, 1993.

———. *One Hundred Years of Homosexuality and Other Essays on Greek Love.* New York: Routledge, 1990.

Hansen, Christian, Catherine Needham, and Bill Nichols. "Skin Flicks: Pornography, Ethnography, and the Discourses of Power." *Discourse: Journal for Theoretical Studies in Media and Culture* 11, no. 2 (Spring–Summer 1989): 65–79.

Hart, Lynda. *Fatal Women: Lesbian Sexuality and the Mark of Aggression.* London: Routledge, 1994.

Hasselrodt, R. Leighton. *Lesbianism around the World.* New York: Tower Publications, 1963.

Hawkins, E. W. "The Stream of Consciousness Novel." *Atlantic Monthly* (September 1926). Reprinted in *Virginia Woolf: The Critical Heritage,* edited by Robin Majumdar and Allen McLaurin, pp. 187–88. London: Routledge & Kegan Paul, 1975.

Hayes, Kevin J., ed. *Henry James: The Contemporary Reviews.* Cambridge: Cambridge University Press, 1996.

Heatley, Edward. "The Redeemed Feminine of *Little Dorrit.*" *Dickens Studies Annual* 4 (1975): 153–64.

Henke, Suzette A. "*Mrs. Dalloway*: The Communion of Saints." In *New Feminist Essays on Virginia Woolf,* edited by Jane Marcus, pp. 125–47. Lincoln: University of Nebraska Press, 1981.

Hill, Susan. *Mrs. de Winter.* London: Sinclair-Stevenson, 1993.

Hocquenghem, Guy. *Homosexual Desire.* Durham, N.C.: Duke University Press, 1993.

———. "On Homo-Sex, or Is Homosexuality a Curable Vice?" *New Formations* 39 (Winter 1999–2000): 70–74.

Hoogland, Renée C. *Lesbian Configurations.* New York: Columbia University Press, 1997.

Hope, Trevor. "Melancholic Modernity: The Hom(m)osexual Symptom and the

Homosocial Corpse." *Differences: A Journal of Feminist Cultural Studies* 6, nos. 2–3 (1994): 174–98.

———. "The 'Returns' of Cartography: Mapping Identity-In(-)Difference." *Differences: A Journal of Feminist Cultural Studies* 6, nos. 2–3 (1994): 208–11.

Howard, David. "*The Bostonians.*" In *The Air of Reality: New Essays on Henry James*, edited by John Goode, pp. 60–80. London: Methuen & Co. Ltd., 1972.

Hungerford, Edward A. " 'My Tunnelling Process': The Method of *Mrs. Dalloway.*" In *Virginia Woolf: Critical Assessments*. Vol. 3. Edited by Eleanor McNees, pp. 287–90. London: Helm Information, 1994.

Hunt, Lynn. "Foucault's Subject in *The History of Sexuality.*" In *Discourses of Sexuality: From Aristotle to AIDS*, edited by Domna C. Stanton, pp. 78–93. Ann Arbor: University of Michigan Press, 1992.

Hussey, Mark. "Living in a War Zone: An Introduction to Virginia Woolf as a War Novelist." In *Virginia Woolf and War: Fiction, Reality, and Myth*, edited by Mark Hussey, pp. 1–13. Syracuse, N.Y.: Syracuse University Press, 1991.

Ingham, Patricia. *The Language of Gender and Class: Transformation in the Victorian Novel*. London: Routledge, 1996.

———. "Nobody's Fault: The Scope of the Negative in *Little Dorrit.*" In *Dickens Refigured: Bodies, Desires and Other Histories*, edited by John Schad, pp. 98–116. Manchester: Manchester University Press, 1996.

Irigaray, Luce. *Speculum of the Other Woman*. Translated by Gillian C. Gill. Ithaca, N.Y.: Cornell University Press, 1985.

Jacobus, Mary. "Russian Tactics: Freud's 'Case of Homosexuality in a Woman.' " *GLQ: A Journal of Lesbian and Gay Studies* 2, nos. 1–2 (1995): 65–79.

Jaffe, Audrey. *Vanishing Points: Dickens, Narrative, and the Subject of Omniscience*. Berkeley: University of California Press, 1991.

Jagose, Annamarie. *Lesbian Utopics*. New York: Routledge, 1994.

James, Henry. *The Bostonians*. London: Penguin Books, 1986.

James, William. *The Principles of Psychology*. Vol. 1. London: Macmillan, 1890; rpt., New York: Dover Publications, 1950.

Jeff, Leonard. *Hitchcock and Selznick*. Berkeley: University of California Press, 1999.

Jensen, Emily. "Clarissa Dalloway's Respectable Suicide." In *Virginia Woolf: A Feminist Slant*, edited by Jane Marcus, pp. 162–79. Lincoln: University of Nebraska Press, 1983.

Johansen, Lenie, ed. *The Penguin Book of Australian Slang: A Dinkum Guide to Oz English*. Ringwood: Penguin, 1988; rpt., 1996.

Kahane, Claire. "*The Bostonians* and the Figure of the Speaking Woman." In *Psychoanalysis and...*, edited by Richard Feldstein and Henry Sussman, pp. 163–74. New York: Routledge, 1990.

———. " 'Hysteria, Feminism, and the Case of *The Bostonians.*" In *Feminism and Psychoanalysis*, edited by Richard Feinstein and Judith Roof, pp. 280–97. Ithaca, N.Y.: Cornell University Press, 1989.

———. *Passions of the Voice: Hysteria, Narrative, and the Figure of the Speaking Woman, 1850–1915*. Baltimore: Johns Hopkins University Press, 1995.

Kearns, Michael. "Narrative Discourse and the Imperative of Sympathy in *The Bostonians.*" *Henry James Review* 17, no. 2 (1996): 162–81.

Kemp, Peter. "Imitation Gothic." *Times Literary Supplement*, 15 October 1993, 19.

Kendrick, Walter. *The Secret Museum: Pornography in Modern Culture.* Berkeley: University of California Press, 1987; rpt., 1996.

Kern, Louis J. *An Ordered Love: Sex Roles and Sexuality in Victorian Utopias—the Shakers, the Mormons, and the Oneida Community.* Chapel Hill: University of North Carolina Press, 1981.

Koestenbaum, Wayne. *The Queen's Throat: Opera, Homosexuality, and the Mystery of Desire.* London: GMP Publishers, 1993.

Kopelson, Kevin. *Love's Litany: The Writing of Modern Homoerotics.* Stanford, Calif.: Stanford University Press, 1994.

Kristeva, Julia. *About Chinese Women.* Translated by Anita Barrows. New York: Urizen, 1977.

Krutch, Joseph Wood. "The Stream of Consciousness." *The Nation* 120 (3 June 1925). Reprinted in *Virginia Woolf: Critical Assessments.* Vol. 3. Edited by Eleanor McNees, pp. 273–75. London: Helm Information, 1994.

Larson, Janet. "Designed to Tell: The Shape of Language in Dickens' *Little Dorrit.*" Ph.D. dissertation, Northwestern University, 1975. Ann Arbor, Mich.: University Microfilms, 1977.

Leaska, Mitchell A. *The Novels of Virginia Woolf from Beginning to End.* London: Weidenfeld & Nicolson, 1977.

Levander, Caroline Field. "Bawdy Talk: The Politics of Women's Public Speech in *The Lectress* and *The Bostonians.*" *American Literature* 67, no. 3. (September 1995): 467–85.

Lister, Anne. *Female Fortune: Land, Gender, and Authority. The Anne Lister Diaries and Other Writings, 1833–1836.* Edited by Jill Liddington. London: Rivers Oram Press, 1998.

———. *I Know My Own Heart: The Diaries of Anne Lister, 1791–1840.* Edited by Helena Whitbread. London: Virago Press, 1988.

———. *No Priest but Love: Excerpts from the Diaries of Anne Lister, 1824–1826.* Edited by Helena Whitbread, Otley: Smith Settle Ltd., 1992.

Lochrie, Karma. "Presumptive Sodomy and Its Exclusions." *Textual Practice* 13, no. 2 (1999): 295–310.

Logan, Thad. "Decorating Domestic Space: Middle-Class Women and Victorian Interiors." In *Keeping the Victorian House: A Collection of Essays*, edited by Vanessa D. Dickerson, pp. 207–34. New York: Garland Publishing, 1995.

Mackenzie, Manfred. *Communities of Love and Honor in Henry James.* Cambridge, Mass.: Harvard University Press, 1976.

Malet, Oriel. *Daphne du Maurier: Letters from Menabilly, Portrait of a Friendship.* London: Weidenfeld & Nicolson, 1993.

Marcus, Steven. *The Other Victorians: A Study of Sexuality and Pornography in Mid-Nineteenth Century England.* London: Weidenfeld & Nicolson, 1967.

Martin, Biddy. *Femininity Played Straight: The Significance of Being Lesbian.* New York: Routledge, 1996.

Martin, Robert K. "Picturesque Misperception in *The Bostonians.*" *Henry James Review* 9, no. 2 (Spring 1992): 77–86.
Massé, Michelle A. *In the Name of Love: Masochism and the Gothic.* Ithaca, N.Y.: Cornell University Press, 1992.
Matus, Jill L. *Unstable Bodies: Victorian Representations of Sexuality and Maternity.* Manchester: Manchester University Press, 1995.
Maxwell, Joan. "Delighting in a Bite: James's Seduction of His Readers in *The Bostonians.*" *Journal of Narrative Technique* 18, no. 1 (Winter 1988): 18–33.
Mayne, Judith. "Feminist Film Theory and Criticism." In *Multiple Voices in Feminist Film Criticism,* edited by Diane Carson et al., pp. 48–64. Minneapolis: University of Minnesota, 1994.
Merck, Mandy. *Perversions: Deviant Readings.* London: Virago Press, 1993.
Michie, Elsie B. *Outside the Pale: Cultural Exclusion, Gender Difference, and the Victorian Woman Writer.* Ithaca, N.Y.: Cornell University Press, 1993.
Miller, D. A. "Anal *Rope.*" In *Inside/Out: Lesbian Theories, Gay Theories,* edited by Diana Fuss, pp. 119–41. New York: Routledge, 1991.
——. *Bringing Out Roland Barthes.* Berkeley: University of California Press, 1992.
——. *Narrative and Its Discontents: Problems of Closure in the Traditional Novel.* Princeton, N.J.: Princeton University Press, 1981.
——. *The Novel and the Police.* Berkeley: University of California Press, 1988.
Miller, J. Hillis. *Charles Dickens: The World of His Novels.* Cambridge, Mass.: Harvard University Press, 1958.
——. *Fiction and Repetition: Seven English Novels.* Oxford: Basil Blackwell, 1982.
Minow-Pinkney, Makiko. *Virginia Woolf and the Problem of the Subject.* Brighton: Harvester Press, 1987.
Mizruchi, Susan. *The Power of Historical Knowledge: Narrating the Past in Hawthorne, James, and Dreiser.* Princeton, N.J.: Princeton University Press, 1988.
Modleski, Tania. *Loving with a Vengeance: Mass-Produced Fantasies for Women.* New York: Methuen, 1984.
——. *The Women Who Knew Too Much.* New York: Methuen, 1988.
Moore, Lisa. *Dangerous Intimacies: Toward a Sapphic History of the British Novel.* Durham, N.C.: Duke University Press, 1997.
Morrison, Paul. "End Pleasure." *GLQ: A Journal of Lesbian and Gay Studies* 1, no. 1 (1993): 53–78.
Morse, Benjamin. *The Lesbian: A Frank, Revealing Study of Women Who Turn to Their Own Sex for Love.* Derby, Conn.: Monarch Books, 1961.
Munt, Sally R. *Heroic Desire: Lesbian Identity and Cultural Space.* London: Cassell, 1998.
Murphy, Mary Janice. "Dickens' 'Other Women': The Mature Women in His Novels." Ph.D. dissertation, University of Louisville, 1975. Ann Arbor, Mich.: University Microfilms, 1976.
Nead, Lynda. *Myths of Sexuality: Representations of Women in Victorian Britain.* Oxford: Basil Blackwell, 1988.
Nord, Deborah Epstein. *Walking the Victorian Streets: Women, Representation, and the City.* Ithaca, N.Y.: Cornell University Press, 1995.

Norton, Rictor. *The Myth of the Modern Homosexual: Queer History and the Search for Cultural Unity.* London: Cassell, 1997.
Nunokawa, Jeff. *The Afterlife of Property: Domestic Security and the Victorian Novel.* Princeton, N.J.: Princeton University Press, 1994.
Padgug, Robert A. "Sexual Matters: On Conceptualising Sexuality in History." *Radical History Review* 20 (1979): 3–23.
Page, Philip. "The Curious Narration of *The Bostonians.*" *American Literature* 46 (1974): 374–83.
Pearce, Richard. *The Politics of Narration: James Joyce, William Faulkner, and Virginia Woolf.* New Brunswick, N.J.: Rutgers University Press, 1991.
Pearson, Leland S. "In the Closet with Frederick Douglass: Reconstructing Masculinity in *The Bostonians.*" *Henry James Review* 16, no. 3 (1995): 292–98.
Poovey, Mary. *Uneven Developments: The Ideological Work of Gender in Mid-Victorian England.* Chicago: University of Chicago Press, 1988.
Reid, J. C. *Charles Dickens: Little Dorrit.* London: Edward Arnold Ltd., 1967.
Rich, Adrienne. "Compulsory Heterosexuality and Lesbian Existence." In *The Lesbian and Gay Studies Reader*, edited by Henry Abelove et al., pp. 227–54. New York: Routledge, 1993.
Richter, Harvena. "The *Ulysses* Connection: Clarissa Dalloway's Bloomsday." In *Virginia Woolf: Critical Assessments.* Vol. 3. Edited by Eleanor McNees, pp. 459–72. London: Helm Information, 1994.
Rohy, Valerie. *Impossible Women: Lesbian Figures and American Literature.* Ithaca, N.Y.: Cornell University Press, 2000.
Roof, Judith. *Come as You Are: Sexuality and Narrative.* New York: Columbia University Press, 1996.
——. *A Lure of Knowledge: Lesbian Sexuality and Theory.* New York: Columbia University Press, 1991
Rowe, John Carlos. *The Other Henry James.* Durham, N.C.: Duke University Press, 1998.
Russ, Joanna. " 'Someone's Trying to Kill Me and I Think It's My Husband': The Modern Gothic." *Journal of Popular Culture* 6, no. 4 (1973): 78–92.
Russo, Vito. *The Celluloid Closet: Homosexuality in the Movies.* New York: Harper & Row, 1981.
Sadoff, Dianne F. "Storytelling and the Figure of the Father in *Little Dorrit.*" *PMLA*, no. 95 (March 1980): 234–45.
Salmon, Richard. *Henry James and the Culture of Publicity.* Cambridge: Cambridge University Press, 1997.
Sedgwick, Eve Kosofsky. *Between Men: English Literature and Male Homosocial Desire.* New York: Columbia University Press, 1985; rpt., 1992.
——. *Epistemology of the Closet.* Berkeley: University of California Press, 1990.
——. "Privilege of Unknowing." *Genders*, no. 1 (Spring 1988): 102–24.
——. *Tendencies.* Durham, N.C.: Duke University Press. 1993.
Seltzer, Mark. *Henry James and the Art of Power.* Ithaca, N.Y.: Cornell University Press, 1984.

Showalter, Elaine. *The Female Malady: Women, Madness, and English Culture, 1830–1980.* New York: Pantheon Books, 1985.

———. "Introduction to *Mrs. Dalloway.*" In *Virginia Woolf: Introductions to the Major Works,* edited by Julia Briggs, pp. 125–56. London: Virago, 1994.

Silverman, Kaja. *Male Subjectivity at the Margins,* New York: Routledge, 1992.

Smith, Patricia Juliana. *Lesbian Panic: Homoeroticism in Modern British Women's Fiction.* New York: Columbia University Press, 1997.

Somerville, Siobhan B. *Queering the Color Line: Race and the Invention of Homosexuality in American Culture.* Durham, N.C.: Duke University Press, 2000.

Sontag, Susan. *On Photography.* New York: Farrar, Straus & Giroux, 1977.

Splitter, Randolph. "Guilt and the Trappings of Melodrama in *Little Dorrit.*" *Dickens Studies Annual* 6 (1977): 119–33.

Sprague, W. D. *The Lesbian in Our Society.* New York: Tower Publications, 1962.

Squier, Susan M. *Virginia Woolf and London: The Sexual Politics of the City.* Chapel Hill: University of North Carolina Press, 1985.

Stevens, Hugh. *Henry James and Sexuality.* Cambridge: Cambridge University Press, 1998

———. "Homoeroticism, Identity, and Agency in James's Late Tales." In *Enacting History in Henry James: Narrative, Power, and Ethics,* edited by Gert Buelens, pp. 126–47. Cambridge: Cambridge University Press, 1997.

Stone, Martin. "Shellshock and the Psychologists." In *The Anatomy of Madness: Essays in the History of Psychiatry,* edited by W. F. Bynum et al. Vol. 2, pp. 242–71. London: Tavistock Publications, 1985.

Stoneman, Patsy. *Brontë Transformations: The Cultural Dissemination of "Jane Eyre" and "Wuthering Heights."* London: Prentice Hall, 1996.

Stubbs, Patricia. *Women and Fiction: Feminism and the Novel, 1880–1920.* Sussex: Harvester Press, 1979.

Sucksmith, Harvey Peter. Introduction to *Little Dorrit,* pp. xiiv–lii. Oxford: Clarendon Press, 1979.

Tambling, Jeremy. *Henry James.* New York: St. Martin's Press, 2000.

———. "Repression in *Mrs. Dalloway*'s London." In *Virginia Woolf: Critical Assessments.* Vol. 3. Edited by Eleanor McNees, pp. 445–58. London: Helm Information, 1994.

Tanner, Tony. *Scenes of Nature, Signs of Men.* Cambridge: Cambridge University Press, 1987.

Terdiman, Richard. *Present Past: Modernity and the Memory Crisis.* Ithaca, N.Y.: Cornell University Press, 1993.

Terry, Jennifer. *An American Obsession: Science, Medicine, and Homosexuality in Modern Society.* Chicago: University of Chicago Press, 1999.

Thomas, Brook. "The Construction of Privacy in and around *The Bostonians.*" *American Literature* 64, no. 4 (December 1992): 719–47.

Traub, Valerie. "The (In)Significance of 'Lesbian' Desire in Early Modern England." In *Queering the Renaissance,* edited by Jonathan Goldberg, pp. 62–83. Durham, N.C.: Duke University Press, 1994

———. "The Perversion of 'Lesbian' Desire." *History Workshop Journal* 41 (1996): 23–49.

———. "The Psychomorphology of the Clitoris." *GLQ: A Journal of Lesbian and Gay Studies* 2, nos. 1–2 (1995): 81–113.
———. *The Renaissance of Lesbianism in Early Modern England.* Oxford: Oxford University Press, forthcoming.
Travis, Jennifer. "Clits in Court: *Salome*, Sodomy, and the Lesbian 'Sadist.' " In *Lesbian Erotics*, edited by Karla Jay. New York: New York University Press, 1995.
Trilling, Lionel. "*Little Dorrit.*" *Kenyon Review* 15 (1953): 577–90.
———. *The Opposing Self: Nine Essays in Criticism.* London: Secker & Warburg, 1955.
Vicinus, Martha. Introduction to *Lesbian Subjects: A "Feminist Studies" Reader*, edited by Martha Vicinus, pp. 1–14. Bloomington: Indiana University Press, 1996.
———. "Lesbian Perversity and Victorian Marriage: The 1864 Codrington Divorce Trial." *Journal of British Studies* 36 (January 1997): 70–98.
———. " 'They Wonder to Which Sex I Belong': The Historical Roots of the Modern Lesbian Identity." *Feminist Studies* 18, no. 3 (Fall 1992): 467–97.
Wade, Carlson. *The Troubled Sex.* N.p.: Beacon Envoy, 1961.
Wahl, Elizabeth Susan. *Invisible Relations: Representations of Female Intimacy in the Age of Enlightenment.* Stanford, Calif.: Stanford University Press, 1999.
Walker, Janet. "Psychoanalysis and Feminist Film Theory: The Problem of Sexual Difference and Identity." In *Multiple Voices in Feminist Film Criticism*, edited by Diane Carson et al., pp. 89–92. Minneapolis: University of Minnesota Press, 1994.
Walkowitz, Judith. *City of Dreadful Delight: Narratives of Sexual Danger in Late-Victorian London.* London: Virago, 1992.
———. *Prostitution and Victorian Society: Women, Class, and the State.* Cambridge: Cambridge University Press, 1980.
Walsh, Chris. "Stardom Is Born: The Religion and Economy of Publicity in Henry James's *The Bostonians.*" *American Literary Realism* 29, no. 3 (Spring 1997): 15–25.
Wardley, Lynn. "Woman's Voice, Democracy's Body, and *The Bostonians.*" *ELH* 56, no. 3 (Fall 1989): 639–65.
Waugh, Thomas. *Hard to Imagine: Gay Male Eroticism in Photography and Film from Their Beginnings to Stonewall.* New York: Columbia University Press, 1996.
White, Patricia. "Female Spectator, Lesbian Specter: *The Haunting.*" In *Inside/Out: Lesbian Theories, Gay Theories*, edited by Diana Fuss, pp. 142–72. New York: Routledge, 1991.
———. "Supporting Character: The Queer Career of Agnes Moorhead." In *Out in Culture: Gay, Lesbian, and Queer Essays on Popular Culture*, edited by Corey K. Creekmur and Alexander Doty, pp. 91–114. Durham, N.C.: Duke University Press, 1995.
———. *Uninvited: Classical Hollywood Cinema and Lesbian Representability.* Bloomington: Indiana University Press, 1999.
Williams, Linda. *Hard Core: Power, Pleasure, and the "Frenzy of the Visible."* London: Pandora Press, 1990.
Wilt, Judith. "Desperately Seeking Verena: A Resistant Reading of *The Bostonians.*" *Feminist Studies* 13, no. 2 (Summer 1987): 293–316.
Wings, Mary. "Rebecca Redux: Tears on a Lesbian Pillow." In *Daring to Dissent: Lesbian Culture from Margin to Mainstream*, edited by Liz Gibbs. London: Cassell, 1994.

Winslow, Joan. "Dicken's Sentimental Plot: A Formal Analysis of Three Novels." Ph.D. dissertation, University of California, Berkeley, 1974. Ann Arbor, Mich.: University Microfilms International, 1977.

Winter, Sarah. "Domestic Fictions: Feminine Deference and Maternal Shadow Labor in Dickens' *Little Dorrit.*" *Dickens Studies Annual* 18 (1989): 243–54.

Wittig, Monique. *The Straight Mind and Other Essays.* Boston: Beacon, 1992.

Wolk, Merla. "Family Plot in *The Bostonians*: Silencing the Artist's Voice." *Henry James Review* 10, no. 1 (Winter 1989): 118–32.

Wood, Robin. *Hitchcock's Films Revisited.* New York: Columbia University Press, 1989.

Woolf, Virginia. *The Diary of Virginia Woolf.* Vol. 2. Edited by Anne Olivier Bell. London: Hogarth Press, 1978.

——. "Introduction to the Modern Library Edition of *Mrs. Dalloway* (1928)." Reprinted in *Mrs. Dalloway,* edited by Morris Beja, pp. 197–99. Oxford: Basil Blackwell, 1996.

——. "Modern Fiction." In *The Crowded Dance of Modern Life: Selected Essays.* Vol. 2. Edited by Rachel Bowlby, pp. 5–12. London: Penguin Books, 1993.

——. *Mrs. Dalloway.* London: Hogarth Press, 1925; rpt., 1963.

——. "Old Bloomsbury." In *Moments of Being,* edited by Jeanne Schulkind, pp. 195–218. London: Grafton Books, 1989.

——. "A Sketch of the Past." In *Moments of Being,* edited by Jeanne Schulkind, pp. 72–173. London: Grafton Books, 1989.

Wright, Walter. *The Madness of Art: A Study of Henry James.* Lincoln: University of Nebraska Press, 1962.

Zimet, Jaye. *Strange Sisters: The Art of Lesbian Pulp Fiction, 1949–1969.* New York: Viking Studio, 1999.

Zwerdling, Alex. "*Mrs. Dalloway* and the Social System." In *Virginia Woolf's "Mrs. Dalloway,"* edited by Harold Bloom, pp. 145–64. New York: Chelsea House Publishers, 1988.

Index

Abel, Elizabeth, 78, 96–97
Abraham, Julie, 176 n. 34, 178 n. 50
Ackroyd, Peter, 37–38
Acton, William, 163 nn. 11, 12
Allan, Maud, 149–50 n. 8
Anderson, Amanda, 163 n. 14
Armstrong, Mary, 164 n. 17
Armstrong, Nancy, 162 n. 7

Bachmann, Monica, 188 n. 11
Ballaster, Ros, 152–53 n. 22
Barthes, Roland, 188 n. 17; 189 nn. 18, 19
Batchelor, John, 178 n. 53
Beauman, Sally, 184 n. 39
Bell, Millicent, 168 n. 7
Bennett, Judith, 154 n. 37
Benshoff, Harry, 183–84 n. 38
Berenstein, Rhona, 182 n. 14, 182–83 n. 24
Bergman, David, 187 n. 9, 188 n. 12
Berlant, Lauren, 151 n. 12, 172 n. 40
Bernstein, Susan David, 164 n. 19
Bland, Lucy, 25, 150 n. 8, 159–60 n. 88
Boone, Joseph Allen, 173 n. 3
The Bostonians, 57–76
    marriage and domesticity, 67–76
    and narrative sympathy, 59–67
    and sexual contest, 58–60, 62–63
Boston marriage, 57, 70–72, 169 n. 20

Bowen, Janet Wolf, 172 nn. 34, 39
Braidotti, Rosi, 6–7, 151 n. 13
Braunschneider, Theresa, 152 n. 20, 154 n. 35
Brooks, Peter, 180 n. 7
Buck-Morss, Susan, 163 n. 13
Bullough, Vern, 159 n. 88
Burgin, Victor, 189 n. 22
Burns, Bonnie, 148 n. 1
Butler, Judith, 22, 147 n. 1, 160 n. 96, 174 n. 14, 179 n. 1

Cahill, Patricia, 166 n. 32
Caprio, Frank, 122, 131–39
Castle, Terry, 1, 2, 9, 17, 24, 155 n. 40
Chauncey, George, 155 n. 47
Clark, Anna, 20–22, 155 n. 46
Cohen, Ed, 150 n. 8
Cory, Donald Webster, 186 n. 5
Craft, Christopher, 160 nn. 98, 100, 102

Davidson, Arnold, 160 n. 101
De Lauretis, Teresa, 160 n. 100, 174 n. 16, 183 n. 37, 184 n. 39, 190 n. 26
Diggs, Marylynne, 24–25
Dinshaw, Carolyn, 155 n. 38
Doane, Mary Ann, 115–16
Doan, Laura, 25, 150 n. 8
Donoghue, Emma, 11–12, 161–62 n. 5

Du Plessis, Rachel Blau, 185 n. 44
Durand, Régis, 189 n. 22

Edelman, Lee, 179 n. 2, 189–90 n. 25
Ellis, Havelock, 25–30

Faderman, Lillian, 9–10, 169–70 n. 22
Felski, Rita, 159 n. 88
Female perversion, 18–21, 41–44, 53–54, 102–3, 108–10, 121
Fetterley, Judith, 167 n. 4, 168 n. 9
Fletcher, John, 113–15
Forster, E. M., 96
Forster, Margaret, 184 n. 39
Foucault, Michel, 9–12, 160 n. 99
Fradenburg, Louise, 154–55 n. 38
Freccero, Carla, 154–55 n. 38
Freud, Sigmund, 30–36, 78–82, 84–85
Frye, Marilyn, 151 n. 13
Fulton, Valerie, 172 n. 38
Fuss, Diana, 160 nn. 102, 103; 174 n. 15; 176 n. 39

Goldberg, Jonathan, 164 n. 20
Graham, Wendy, 169 n. 20
Grosz, Elizabeth, 148 n. 1
Guth, Deborah, 177–78 n. 46

Haggarty, George, 152 n. 19
Halberstam, Judith, 149 nn. 5, 7; 156 n. 48; 181 n. 9
Halperin, David, 21, 153 n. 30, 155–56 n. 47, 157 n. 64
Hansen, Catherine, 188–89 n. 17
Hart, Lynda, 6–7, 23, 148 n. 1, 165 n. 23, 166–67 n. 52
Heatley, Edward, 165 n. 26
Henke, Suzette, 177 n. 44
Heteronormativity, 76, 151 n. 11, 152 n. 20, 185–86 n. 48
Heterosexuality, 4–5, 59–60, 77–78, 82, 105, 108–110
  as narrative, 78, 112, 117, 168 n. 7
Hocquenghem, Guy, 148 n. 4, 160 n. 100
Hoogland, Renée, 148 n. 1
Hope, Trevor, 151 n. 17
Hunt, Lyn, 153 n. 28
Hussey, Mark, 176 n. 37

Ingham, Patricia, 164 n. 18
Irigaray, Luce, 151 n. 13

Jacobs, Mary, 160–61 n. 106, 161 n. 110
Jaffe, Audrey, 167 n. 53
James, Henry
  and sexual identity, 63–65
James, William, 87–88
Jensen, Emily, 96–97

Kahane, Claire, 63–64
Kemp, Peter, 185 n. 47
Kendrick, Walter, 187 n. 8
Kinsey, Alfred, 131–32
Kopelson, Kevin, 99
Kristeva, Julia, 116, 166 n. 31

Leaska, Mitchell, 176 n. 33
Lesbian historiography, 8–24, 38–39, 154 n. 37, 161–62 n. 5
Lesbian invisibility, 1–13, 122
  and historiography, 12–13, 22–24
  and photography, 122, 139–44
  and race, 148–49 n. 5
Lesbian representation, 1–2, 8–9, 24
Lesbianism
  and derivation, 7–8, 12, 23–24, 31, 35–36
  and femininity, 6–7, 12–13
  and heterosexuality, 2, 8, 33–36, 57–58, 78, 111–17, 130–33, 151 n. 11
  and male homosexuality, 3–7, 11–12, 34–35, 65, 149–50 n. 8, 150 n. 9
  and masculinity, 3, 6–7, 12, 156 n. 49
Liddington, Jill, 156 n. 52
Lister, Anne, 14–24
Little Dorrit, 37–56
  contemporary readings of, 47–50
  narrative structuring of, 50–55
  and sexual contagion, 43–47
  and sexual suspicion, 42–43, 47, 55
  and Victorian femininity, 39–42
Lochrie, Karma, 153–53 n. 31
Logan, Thad, 172 n. 33

Mackenzie, Manfred, 167 n. 5
Marriage, 12, 14, 37, 68–74, 120, 170 n. 25, 170–71 n. 26, 171 n. 27
  and narrative closure, 60–61; 69; 77; 171 nn. 28, 29
  See also Boston marriage
Martin, Biddy, 149 n. 5
Martin, Robert, 171 n. 28
Massé, Michelle, 181 n. 10

Index

Matus, Jill, 162 n. 6
Maxwell, Joan, 171 n. 29
Mayne, Judith, 183 n. 30
Memory, 80–87, 97–100
Merck, Mandy, 189 n. 20
Michie, Elsie, 162 n. 7
Miller, D. A., 50–51, 165 n. 24, 166 n. 39, 184–85 n. 43
Miller, J. Hillis, 164 n. 18, 165 n. 25, 175 n. 21
Mizruchi, Susan, 169 n. 13
Modleski, Tania, 107–8, 115–17
Moore, Lisa, 9–10, 155 n. 40, 156 n. 55, 157 n. 67
Morrison, Paul, 148 n. 4
Morse, Benjamin, 123–26
Mrs Dalloway, 77–100
  and memory, 82–87, 98–99
  and stream of consciousness, 87–89
Mrs de Winter, 117–20,
  heterosexual closure of, 120
  as sequel, 117–19
Munt, Sally, 156 n. 49
Murphy, Mary Janice, 166 n. 34

Nead, Lynda, 162 n. 8; 163 nn. 9, 12
Needham, Catherine, 188–89 n. 17
Nichols, Bill, 188–89 n. 17
Nord, Deborah Epstein, 162–63 n. 9
Norton, Rictor, 155 n. 46; 156 nn. 49, 52
Nunokawa, Jeff, 162 n. 7

Obscenity, 126–28
Omniscient narration, 50–51, 53–55

Poovey, Mary, 162 nn. 6, 7
Pornography, 14, 126–29
Prostitution, 39–41, 134–37

Rebecca (film), 111–17,
  feminist analysis of, 112–17
  heterosexual closure of, 111–13, 117
Rebecca (novel), 101–11,
  as gothic romance, 103, 105, 108
  and heterosexuality, 108–10
  retrospective narration of, 108–10
Retrospection, 22–23, 30–31, 38, 56, 86, 104
Rich, Adrienne, 151 n. 13
Rohy, Valerie, 147 n. 2
Romance narrative, 59, 77, 103, 107–08

Romantic friendship, 9–10, 18–19, 57–58, 65, 68–69, 72–76
Roof, Judith, 147–48 n. 4; 148 nn. 1, 4; 160 n. 102; 161 n. 108; 174 n. 16
Russ, Joanna, 180 n. 4
Russo, Vito, 182 n. 16

Sadoff, Dianne, 166 n. 45
Sedgwick, Eve Kosofsky, 5, 64, 147 n. 3, 165 n. 23, 166–67 n. 52
Seltzer, Mark, 58
Sex acts, 4–5, 21
  and the law, 25, 149–50 n. 8
  and slang, 150 n. 9
Sex-gender system, 3, 5, 13, 16–18, 64
Sexology, 1, 9, 17, 24–36, 122, 158 n. 73, 169–70 n. 22
Sexual contamination, 43–46, 102, 109–11, 132–33, 137–39
Sexual inversion, 25–30, 155 n. 47
Sexual knowledge, 16–18, 55, 123–29, 137–38, 156 n. 57
Sexuality, 21–22
  and gender, 3, 5–8
  and vision, 2–3, 35
Showalter, Elaine, 176 n. 36
Silverman, Kaja, 182 n. 18
Smith, Patricia Juliane, 176 n. 34, 178 n. 51, 178–79 n. 54
Sontag, Susan, 189 n 23
Splitter, Randolph, 165 n. 29
Squier, Susan, 177 n. 44
Stevens, Hugh, 167–68 n. 6
Stream of consciousness, 79, 82–84, 87–89, 173–74 n. 6

Tambling, Jeremy, 169 n. 12, 175 n. 22
Terdiman, Richard, 174–75 n. 19
Terry, Jennifer, 159 n. 88, 189 n. 20
Traub, Valerie, 12–13, 152 n. 19, 153 n. 27
Travis, Jennifer, 150 n. 8
Tribade, 12–13
Trilling, Lionel, 163–64 n. 17, 165 n. 28
Trumbach, Randolph, 8, 151–52 n. 19

Vicinus, Martha, 157 nn. 64, 67; 158 n. 74

Wahl, Susan, 11–12
Walker, Janet, 183 n. 30
Walkowitz, Judith, 162 n. 6, 162–63 n. 9

Warner, Michael, 151 n. 12, 172 n. 40
Waugh, Thomas, 187 n. 9
Whitbread, Helene, 15
White, Patricia, 164–65 n. 21; 183 nn. 29, 34
Wilde, Oscar, 149–50 n. 8
Williams, Linda, 189 n. 21
Wilt, Judith, 167 n. 5

Winter, Sarah, 165 n. 27
Wittig, Monique, 2, 151 n. 13
Woolf, Virginia:
   and modernism, 79
   and psychoanalysis, 80, 173 n. 3

Zimet, Jaye, 187 n. 9
Zwerdling, Alex, 177 n. 46

OHIO UNIVERSITY LIBRARY
Please return this book as soon as you have finished with it. In order to avoid a fine it must be returned by the latest date stamped below. All books are subject to recall after two weeks or immediately if needed for reserve.